In the Wake of Theory

PAUL A. BOVÉ ❧

❧In the Wake of THEORY

WESLEYAN UNIVERSITY PRESS

Published by University Press of New England

Hanover and London

Wesleyan University Press
Published by University Press of New England, Hanover, NH 03755
© 1992 by Wesleyan University
Printed in the United States of America   5   4   3   2   1
CIP data appear at the end of the book

And may her bridegroom bring her to a house
Where all's accustomed, ceremonious;
For arrogance and hatred are the wares
Peddled in the thoroughfares.
How but in custom and in ceremony
Are innocence and beauty born?
Ceremony's a name for the rich horn,
And custom for the spreading laurel tree.

Contents

Preface

౿∾౷ Several of the chapters in this book appeared in different versions during the 1980s, and some others were written near the end of the decade as occasional pieces, responding to requests by conference organizers and lecture committees to address some aspect of contemporary critical debate. Taken together, they are more than a loose assemblage of materials. Unlike the traditional book, however, which departs from a thesis that winds on to its conclusion, this text is made up of chapters that relate to a similar quandary, to a specific sense of circumstances. They all emerged from the "crisis of criticism" about which United States academics have spoken at least since 1970, and more particularly, they all issued from my ongoing interest in the relationship of literary theory to intellectual practice and of critical intellectual work to some of the institutions of U.S. education and culture.

The 1980s began with a feeling that the "theory movement"—as it had come to be embodied in the works of Derrida, Foucault, Kristeva, and others from France, the United States, and elsewhere—was nearly victorious in its decades-long struggles against well-entrenched New Critical, liberal, and mythic criticisms and that its "victory" was about to have important payoffs in curriculum, pedagogy, the allocation of professional resources, and, most important, the establishment of a critical discourse that would sustain political interrogations of the dominant and often repressive and exploitative, uneven institutions and languages of "postmodern" neocolonial cultures and politics. The decade ended, however, with a different feeling.

The institutional cultural equivalents of Reaganism essentially ended "theory's" run in the academy. Indeed, as became increasingly clear throughout the 1980s and on into the 1990s, the cultural agents of Reaganism were and still are often the same as the "anti-theory" agents within the universities and the media. Alan Bloom's anti-theoretical harangues joined with William Bennett's various screeds against "cultural diversity" and "multicultural" education; together they symptomatically became allied with any number of sometimes "progressive" intellectuals' efforts to degrade theoretical work as "irrational," "anarchic," and—depending on the accuser—either "Fascist" or "Communist." (The ambiguities on this are interesting: by some of the central figures of the very conservative *Partisan Review* I have myself been called, in print, both a Marxist defender of the Kremlin and an anti-Communist Foucauldian. At different times, by Gerald Graff I have been called "hyperpolitical" and Stalinist; I can't tell if there's an oxymoron there or not.) But what matters most, and we can see this when Lynne Cheney criticizes the likes of Stanley Fish and Paul de Man all at once, is that for the Reaganauts and their allies, "theory," or as I prefer to call it, "criticism" is not "American." (I try to argue about some of the implications of this charge in my essay on Sacvan Bercovitch, chapter 3, this volume.) Or as Dinesh D'Souza, the heir of the moment to Alan Bloom might have it: deconstruction—and somehow theory is always equated with deconstruction, which is then misnamed as "deconstructionism"—is relativism, and that way lies fascism; but "theory" is also "French," and that way lies "socialism." In any event, as one of my analytic philosophical colleagues has it, these are all "failed models"—like Marxism—that should not be brought into the United States, its programs, its cultures, its universities.

What is most important, of course, about the utterly vicious assault on "theory," and its corollary assaults on English departments and literary professors, is that it is being carried on so blatantly and crudely in some of the major public journals of record—*The New York Times* (and its *Book Review*) and *Newsweek*, for example—as well as in conventional homes of intellectual terrorism such as *Commentary*. Whether it be George Will writing on "Literary Politics" in the 22 April 1991 issue of *Newsweek* or Camille Paglia battering French theory in *The New York Times Book Review* of 5 May 1991,

readers who can long enough tolerate the exaggerated and insup-
portable caricatures and reductions that dominate prose that calls the
MLA a greater threat to America than Saddam Hussein—who is, as
we know, "worse than Hitler"—these readers are either strong-
stomached professionals obliged to mark the degradation of public
intellectual life in the United States or already committed to the common sense of a right-wing cultural politics that is opposed to "affirmative action," "feminism," and "multiculturalism." Of course, one
can argue that these intellectual terrorists must be opposed on direct
political grounds alone: they encourage retrograde forces interested
in recouping ground for what are still dominant forms of cultural reproduction, and since culture is always and everywhere a struggle, a
struggle of resistance and for the production of identities, they must
be opposed as part of the effort to form a freer and more equal society. It matters greatly, however, in what ways they are opposed. Indeed, it matters if cultural production slides, almost unnoticed, into
a pattern of resistance based on simple binary opposition to these intellectual terrorists. "Hegemony" means, among other things, setting
the terms of debate; "resisting" those who hypocritically speak on
behalf of "free speech" and against "political correctness" in the
terms they have established or appropriated means succumbing to
their efforts to become "hegemonic." "Resistance," we must keep in
mind, requires building alternative structures of culture and imagination, of language and discourse to those so easily taken up by the
Wills and Paglias of the world. It also means, for those of us in "literary criticism," continually reexamining the history, position, value,
effects, and anticipated future of our critical languages, practices, and
institutions. It means, as I have tried to show in some of what follows,
coming to awareness of how difficult it is to be "oppositional" or "alternative"—not impossible, simply difficult and complex. It also
means testing how apparent defeats require reconsiderations of
tactics and histories; and that means, among other things, writing
critical histories that let us understand how the current terms of discourse—"academic" and "public," to sustain an older fictional binary—have come to be: why, for example, the talk about the crisis of
the "subject," "the state," "identity," "multiculturalism," and so
on—all in relation to massive geopolitical economic and social
changes in the orders of power and capital. And along the way, we

should try to understand why certain other seemingly powerful and useful concepts have become vacuous and have lost their critical edge—sometimes as they die down into professional success, leaving unaltered in their deaths, that unique set of relations between power, the state, knowledge, and people that Michel Foucault once called "the regime of truth."

What I mean is simply this: the oppositional possibilities embodied in and made possible by the major critical movements of the period from 1964 to 1984—from the Johns Hopkins conference on the sciences of man to the deaths of Foucault and de Man and the "discovery" of Heidegger's Nazism—have been exhausted. Sometimes they have declined down into success; sometimes they simply have lost their legitimacy or novelty and so have been abandoned by professionals interested in establishing prominence for themselves; and sometimes they have been overwhelmed by the larger changes in a culture that, at least since 1980, has been moving backward at the very same time as its economic decline makes its "military prowess" tragically more important and when a large number of unallied "subcultural" groups struggle to achieve identity and maintain their own humanity in the face of tacit official censorship. (The censorship is not tacit, however, when even the medical profession notes [in *The New England Journal of Medicine,* Spring 1991] that universal medical care does not exist in the United States as a result of racism.) And, of course, censorship became fairly overt and semiofficial in the recent Persian Gulf War when the dominant news media failed to resist the Pentagon's plan to make them into agents of warfare: even when "facts" did get through, they were presented in such distantiated, "Americanized" fashion that the deaths of hundreds of thousands seem to have made little impact on the *Gesellschaft* of critical intellectuals in the United States.

Furthermore, the "oppositional" qualities of the criticism and theory movements have been profoundly damaged from within the profession of criticism, from within the academy, and not simply by the renewed opposition to theoretical and critical variety embodied and articulated by the so-called National Association of Scholars (NAS). Without a doubt, a number of the professors in that association belong to the same traditions as those such as M. H. Abrams and Wayne Booth or indeed, in the 1950s, Henri Picard, who assaulted "theory" as a threat to civilization. Now, of course, the assault's tactics differ, but the point is the same; now the aim is to provoke "opposition" so that the NAS can claim that some abstraction called "free speech" has been violated. This is only a new version of an old position; from the 1960s to the present the "old guard" has always charged that the young guard lacked decorum and were "terrorists." (Indeed, I was shocked to see that even apparently "progressive" colleagues of my own in "cultural studies" accuse theoretically interested colleagues of being "terrorists.") But the point that needs to be made in opposition is not only the old one—that "decorum" can and does mask violence as when, for example, abstract discussions of "free speech" commit NAS types to support racist professors in their "decorous" because "scientific" assaults on nonwhite peoples—but also that, at least in the critical arenas, the new accusers themselves lack decorum. They cannot justify the extreme rhetorics that characterize a Paglia or an Edward Alexander in calling Edward W. Said a "professor of terror" in the pages of *Commentary*. Moreover, they cannot hope to justify the utter and absolute lack of intellectual care and rigor that, at its best, U.S. criticism once expected at the highest levels. In a previously unpublished essay that follows, I call Alan Bloom's *The Closing of the American Mind* unreadable precisely because it lacks the characteristics that alone earn intellectual respect and legitimacy; in this lack it exemplifies the "new right's" utter failure even to recall the decorum of critical intelligence.

Joseph Buttigieg has elegantly observed that Gramsci's attention to the history of Italian intellectuals emerged from a profound conviction that the decline of Italian democracy into fascism was aided and characterized by the decline of Italian intellectual work. Of course, Gramsci's perception itself belongs to a long tradition dating back, in his genealogy, at least to Hegel in *The Philosophy of Right* (1821). It matters less, in this context, which ideological position a given intellectual proposes or defends than does the rigor and care with which it is pursued. Gramsci, for example, attended to Croce not only because of the latter's dominant and so exemplary position among Italian intellectuals but also because Croce's work mattered to Gramsci; it was and is well-argued, historically grounded, careful, and rigorous, worthy of debate and discussion; Gramsci learned from an engagement with it. In the terms of the late Paul de Man—which I invoke antithetically in my own comments on Alan Bloom—Croce's texts are important because they provoke the production of other valuable texts, in this case, some of Gramsci's—and indeed some by Gramsci's ideological opposite, T. S. Eliot.

But what I try to argue about Bloom's book, and this argument extends to his cronies and heirs, is that it lacks scholarly and critical decorum, that it is unreadable, it is unproductive, and it typifies a national intellectual decline. Buttigieg shows that Gramsci took "Lorianism" as a sign of Italian politics' decline into fascism, and I am suggesting that U.S. critics should be deeply troubled and should oppose a similar intellectual decline marked by the "importance" of those busy hurling terrorist accusations of "political correctness" against defenders of affirmative action, minorities, and those "others" normally not heard within predominant political and cultural discourses. (Wlad Godzich, in an as yet unpublished lecture text, "The Thirty-Year Struggle for Theory," eloquently and carefully describes theory's foundation in listening to and echoing the cry of those excluded by the state and its discourses.)

Yet for the most part, troubling and important as the public political debate over "pc" and "theory" might be, the essays in this volume are predominantly concerned with the decline of critical theory, indeed, the decline of criticism, within the professions of critical studies into the (sometimes) unacknowledged service of a repressive "American" state apparatus and its cultural institutions—to borrow loosely an Althusserean notion. Of course, there will be those critics, not all of whom are "reactionary" in their conscious position, who will charge that to formulate an issue in the terms I have just used is to share somehow in a set of "problems" or "positions" themselves not given adequate theoretical—whether social or psychoanalytic— reflection. And of course, it is true that phrases and words such as "state apparatus," "hegemony," "dominant culture," "struggle," "resistance," and so on are indeed common throughout much of the professional discourse of the academy. The terms have been vulgarized, in a literal sense; they are part of a vernacular, albeit a rarefied one. The "vulgarity" itself tempts some critics to turn away from these terms, from their usage, from their past values. I am myself tempted to do so. At a recent conference, for example, when confronted by a paper that spoke endlessly of the "hegemony of the New

Criticism," I could only reply to the speaker with a certain deeply felt disgust that a term, "hegemony," which Gramsci had worked so carefully to give critical and political utility, could be made into a professional mule to carry the burden of a belated and finally nonsensical argument.

The problem, however, lies not with the term "hegemony," nor with the work of Gramsci and those, such as Stuart Hall, who, in adapting Gramsci's notion have added much of value to Gramsci's work; the problem lies, rather, with the facile professionalization of the U.S. academy. There have been innumerable studies of the processes by which the "new class" of intellectuals, as Alvin Gouldner calls us, transforms intellectual values into social and economic capital. The facts of commodification and fetishism within the professions do not need to be established, and I do not attempt to repeat the facts in this volume—although I do touch on them, especially in chapter 6.

What is interesting, however, and what has not yet, I think, been adequately worked out—and these chapters barely begin the process—is an analysis of the discursive and institutional mechanisms by and through which "theory" and "radical" or "oppositional" criticisms substantially begin and remain within the dominant, even if "postmodern," modes of intellectual work. Of course, as we all know, there is no escaping the given regime of truth that defines and enables intellectual practice. But there are different ways of dealing with the given: the essays that follow try to detail various tactics in the game, from Alan Bloom's vulgar defense of neoconservative cultural politics, through the violence of certain vestigial humanists who cannot tolerate the critical engagement of a figure such as Edward W. Said, to the illusory commitment to "opposition" within the "dissensus" model of the leading "Americanist," Sacvan Bercovitch, the most recent instantiation of a long tradition of Harvard scholars involved in shaping the canon of U.S. literature.

In a sense, then, the essays that follow treat examples of conservative antimodernism, such as Bloom; of liberal establishment "opposition," such as Bercovitch; and of professionalized "radical" figures, such as the so-called "against theory," neopragmatist, new historicist Steven Knapp and Walter Benn Michaels. The collection is, as it were, weakest in its specific analysis of this last type of contemporary critical figure but offers a reading of Regis Debray's theory of postmodern intellectuals as a sort of conceptual guide for how to go about the analysis, as well as a reconsideration of Heidegger's *Being and Time* as a way of understanding the neopragmatist misprision of theory. Throughout the essays, however, particularly "The Function of the Literary Critic in the Postmodern World," my emphasis is on the ways in which so-called oppositional critics operate "professionally" with little significant "oppositional" value or function at all. Of course, in trying to describe the ways in which "oppositional" criticism is sometimes devalued by its reinscription within professional practices and dominant U.S. institutions, I am, in one sense, doing no more than elaborating on Edward W. Said's argument of the late 1970s against "radical chic." Or, put another way, I am merely repeating what Buttigieg has shown to be Gramsci's central charge against Loria: the failure of the "left" to understand the nature of its opponent and its own position within the new political forms that opponent exploits. This failure Gramsci calls "Lorianism."

A more detailed look at the issues involved would require a specific and sustained examination of the relations between certain kinds of professional phenomena—cover stories of literary academics in *The New York Times Magazine*—forms of intellectual practice, and the general characteristics of postmodern culture and politics, with their emphasis on the "subject," "consumerism," cultural amnesia, and critical laissez-faire that takes the shape of "pop" intellectual work published in short books on "hot" topics. Theory and criticism have been put too often in the service of such postmodern professionalism. But of course, there is a more serious side to such "postmodern professionalism" as well. It involves critics aligned with groups struggling for social identity—often with the theory and politics of identity itself the issue at hand.

One wants to make some careful distinctions at this point. There are postmodern critics involved in struggles against political and economic repression, on behalf of cultural expressions of emergent difference, who resist the processes of commodification in the name of struggle. The fact of the matter is, of course, that such critics often, by virtue of their project and their functional positions within struggles, do not and often cannot produce "high scholarly treatises." Their struggles are tactical; their writings, political in an immediate sense that does not allow time for the research, theoretical reflection, and linguistic subtleties that those committed either to some sort of higher "theoretical" purity or belated humanist ideal of disinterestedness demand of them. It is only the worst of resentment to find in these critics the worst of postmodern professionalism.

But there are the professionals, and there are the worst among them. One must think about them as a political, cultural, historical phenomenon. Ethical outrage in face of their institutional "success" is itself mere resentment; and in light of what I try to derive from Debray's considerations of French intellectuals, it is increasingly necessary for critics *not* to denigrate progressive intellectuals' access to mainstream media. So rather than generalized ethical outrage in the face of certain "radical" intellectuals' success within dominant institutions, we require of critics detailed descriptions of this professional activity and specific historical analysis of its relations to ideologies, discourses, and institutions that belong to the history of modernity, the state, and Western regimes of truth, especially within an imperial Anglo-American culture. Such analyses would show that despite its efforts at policing critical thought through liberals and neocons alike, the state, even as the agent of the corporate and military interests that substantially fund U.S. universities, has not been able to align all of the practitioners of criticism within a single ideological or pragmatic position. It would, however, be a mistake to find in the proliferation of positions a failure of the state or even a radical pluralism.

It has been primarily Fredric Jameson who has described the effects "late capital" induces in the culture as pastiche, variety, fragmentation, and apparent difference. His analysis suggests that we would not be far wrong if we said that the very "efforts" the state makes to critique and displace the proliferation are themselves belated but importantly coercive neoconservative gestures, often and typically made against the victims by those who resent the efforts to be heard by those who suffer at the hands of the "regime of truth."

By focusing on this notion of the "regime of truth," it becomes possible to sketch some tentative links. The theoretical and critical opponents of the regime invent and use, as weapons, special kinds of language—often aesthetic, often political, often importantly derived from non-Western writers and cultures—that have the power both to draw attention to the victims created by the irreversible relations of power within the colonial regime and to challenge what to most in the United States remains the "natural" integrity of the regime itself. Neither the state nor its neocon nor its liberal allies can tolerate that challenge and so assault its languages and the peoples who produce them as obscure or inferior, and its critiques and struggles as terrorism.

In one sense, however, they need not bother with the assault. The colonial regime is so capable, so adaptable, so inventive that, in its postmodern proliferations, it repeatedly stages "passive revolutions," as Gramsci would have it—perhaps as a feature of modernity, itself. While conceding academic places to many who speak the forbidden words and while hemming them in with tenure and battles against the likes of the NAS, hindering, even where the impulse exists, the critique of the regime itself—the regime obscures its opponents into what Beckett would call *foirades*.

II

One consequence of what I have just been trying to describe is, for me, a discovery of the need to look away from academic criticism as a place for work and indeed as an object of study. There seems so little left worth saying about the relatively sad state of the critical professions in the United States that unless and until—and I am not optimistic about the "until"—fundamental changes occur within the institution and in relations between the institution and the material realities that define it, critical work will have to find a way to get done elsewhere. Writing "about" and "against" the current regime—especially with the horrific combination of "radical chic-ers" and NAS'ies throughout the academy and so much of public discourse about the academy and teaching—seems particularly sterile and, even worse, reproductive of problems one tries to describe.

What is to be done, is an old question put in a different context by a person who felt he had a certain answer. What is to be done? The answer seems less than obvious right now, despite "individuals'" efforts to discover "their own" theoretical and critical concerns; despite a consensus that purely "occasional" work has displaced sustained critical reflection itself taken now as a remnant of "humanism." One must, of course, continue to hear the sounds of those resisting, to study the history and structure of a "regime of truth" so long attached to enlightenment ideals hard to separate from anthropologism, racism, sexism, statism, and the like. But if one will take seriously the critical responsibility betrayed, as Gramsci shows, by Loria, then one must somehow turn once more against not only the apparently residual but powerful forms of reaction but also against the apparently emergent forms of a new "oppositional" consensus that, as Donald Pease has shown about the "New Historicism," merely functions to contain resistance within a state institution, within the academy. But having shown this betrayal of the clerks over and again, critical work must turn its back on its efforts and participants to do work—sometimes in the same institutions—the betrayal does not allow. Above all, critical work must see that resistance cannot be carried out on the terrain the institution establishes, debating its role in the institution's terms; but rather, resistance—alterity— must take the form of struggle in the form of displacement: producing knowledge of kind and content that, as was the case thirty years ago when "theory" came to the United States, is once again greeted as "barbaric" and "a threat to civilization" but now by the new oppositionalists as much as by the NAS'ies. In other words, critics must bring themselves into relations with materials and questions of an order so different as to be unrecognizable as criticism within the academy. One thinks only of Yeats, then, in answering the inevitable professional questions "So what should we do? What will it look like?" "What rough beast" must be the answer to the academics.

ACKNOWLEDGMENTS

Chapters 2, 5, 6, 7, and 8 appeared, sometimes in slightly different form, in the following publications. I thank the editors and publishers involved: *Criticism Without Boundaries,* ed. Joseph A. Buttigieg (South Bend: Notre Dame University Press, 1987); *Contemporary Literature* 26 (Spring 1985); *Minnesota Review* (Fall 1983); *On Foucault, Humanities in Society* 3 (1980); *October* 53 (Summer 1990).

I wish also to thank again my colleagues on *boundary* 2, Jonathan Arac, Joseph Buttigieg, Margaret Ferguson, Nancy Fraser, Michael Hays, Daniel O'Hara, Donald E. Pease, William Spanos, and Cornel West, for providing that rarest of intellectual qualities, a community of different and debating scholars. I want also to thank my Pittsburgh colleagues, especially Gayatri Chakravorty Spivak, Marcia Landy, Carol Kay, and Dana Polan, for providing a work context that seems often to be unlike any other. I wish also to acknowledge the kind support of the University of Pittsburgh Research Office in completing this manuscript, especially for funding Andrew Wood, a graduate student at the University of Pittsburgh, who prepared the index. I must also thank Meg Sachse, the Managing Editor of *boundary 2*, whose efficiency and perspective make an impossible task look easy and overwhelming crises mere problems.

I owe a special debt to Terry Cochran, the Director of Wesleyan University Press, for his editorial advice throughout the process of constructing this book—though, of course, I am responsible for its flaws. I want to thank him too for sharing his thoughts about criticism and culture with me over the past few years. In a typically postmodern fashion, we almost never see each other, but I feel I have learned a lot from him nonetheless. The same can be said of Wlad Godzich, a rigorous critical polymath whose depth of understanding and commitment gives him influence.

Carol M. Bové is a feminist whose psychoanalytic critical abilities I cannot equal; this puts her in a strong position to molest my writing, a position that, thankfully, she exploits only rarely. For that patience and forbearance and for sharing most things with me, I thank her again.

This is the first book manuscript I have had the pleasure to assemble with my child sharing my time and workspace. It is hard to imagine a greater (and sometimes more trying) joy. But as they say, children teach. And so I have dedicated this book to my daughter who, I hope, later in life will understand and not be embarrassed by it.

Wexford, Pennsylvania   P. A. B.
September 1991

In the Wake of Theory

CHAPTER ONE

Introduction: In the Wake of Theory

๛ During the late 1970s and the 1980s, various political, cultural, and intellectual forces combined to bring the moment of "literary theory" to an end in the United States. There are many stories that could be told about this, many histories as well. They would tell about the effects of professionalization; of the strange combination of events—Reagan's election and the Arab-Israeli conflict, for example—that would lead such otherwise divergent figures as Edward W. Said and William Bennett to take up positions "against theory";[1] of the persistent establishment of pluralism, as in the work of Gerald Graff and Wayne Booth; and of the anti-theory movement among neoconservatives and neopragmatists. This would be an important story and, depending upon who tells it, it would be a story of sadness and defeat; of celebration and restoration; or of ironic indifference—especially among the newly empowered for whom the fate of theory is a passé issue. In my work, I generally tell a sad story of the defeat of criticism by institutions, of knowledge and seriousness by posture and fashion, of memory by amnesia. Of course, I could tell a story of partial success: of reforms in canon formation, critical method, and problems of representation that have occurred since theory helped make it possible to speak of "difference," "subject formation," "discourse," "the other"—problems of gender, sexuality, race, class, and ethnicity. I am moved when I hear a Cornel West or a Stuart Hall or a Gayatri Spivak tell a version of this story, for I hear then of struggles for freedom and for justice; we should all rejoice when we hear the voices of those energetically resisting the imperialism and inequalities of Western societies.[2]

But what of theory itself? Can we and should we now theorize its end? its aftereffects? In the pages that follow, I am going to take a fairly close look at certain passages from Heidegger's *Being and Time* in order to clarify some of the mistakes that have been made by those who have reacted "against theory" and to suggest how complex the difficulties are for those hoping to develop new ways of theorizing within a present social, political, and cultural set of circumstances different from those that confronted and provoked an earlier effort at theory. For many who remember the political turmoil, the imperial horrors, and the treason of the clerks that marked the theory's period in the United States, from 1964 to 1981, or in France, from the early 1950s—the Vietnamese and Algerian wars—to the early 1980s, it might seem strange to say that present circumstances confront any efforts at new forms of theorizing, of criticism, with harsher circumstances. In the United States, however—and the recent disastrous war in the Persian Gulf shows how what happens in the dominant circles of the United States still matters overwhelmingly throughout the world—the diminished liberal consensus that, through affirmative action, civil rights reform, the women's movement, and other aligned progressive movements, provided the backdrop and political energy for the oppositional dimensions of the theory movements—these are now gone or diminished or fragmented. As the reactionaries like to say, this has left the defeated radicals of 1968 in the university. I try to suggest in some of what follows, however, that the oppositional efforts that characterize the radicals' work has such complex ties to the forms, histories, politics, and ideologies of just what they oppose that their (often successful) resistance dissipates much of its force repeating the gestures and extending the value of their opponents. Of course, one effect of the breakup of the liberal consensus according to which the radicals could work in the university has been the reactionary effort to take back the schools. Stuart Hall has irresistibly argued that Thatcherism has been a consciously hegemonic enterprise, in other words, that the neoconservative reaction has understood Gramsci all too well and attempted to dominate key points in society all at once.[3] The same could be said of the original Reagan agenda and, in basic ways, as the Pentagon's control of a compliant media organization in the Gulf War shows, nothing has changed under Bush. But we might say, once more invoking Gramsci, that the political force of the combined radical, liberal civil rights, antiwar, and women's movements forced the state—then under the guidance of Richard Nixon—to adopt strategies of "passive revolution." The state reformed itself, making real and necessary concessions that, in a sense, show the state to be weakened momentarily. One concession in this "passive revolution" granted "radicals" a certain limited but real place in the academy. With a changed mainstream consensus and with less organized direct pressure on the state, its guardians have begun to revoke those concessions; hence we see attacks on "multiculturalism," on the tenuring of young radicals, on the funding of the humanities, and on figures important to the last waves of theory, especially Martin Heidegger, Paul de Man, Stanley Fish, Edward W. Said, and recently Gayatri Spivak.

But since the radicals often have not done enough either to understand the ways their continued involvement with and dependence on not only such overt dominant practices and ideologies—such as "professionalism"—but such complex and essential practices as "history," some of the neoconservative assault is, I think, unnecessary. Of course, in saying this, I am merely extending Said's 1978 argument, but this time to include not only the "textual radicals" but the "historical" and "neopragmatists" as well. (Readers can make their own judgments upon what seem to be famous cases of careerist exploitation of marginal and oppositional positions.)

We need, I think, completely to rethink our intellectual practices and positions. We cannot or should not rest secure any longer in either the (limited) successes we have had or continue to fight for in such matters as "revising the canon."[4] We must continue the struggles, of course, but we must also be aware of how, in doing so, we sometimes devote our energies to struggles on the enemies' chosen terrain. One cannot, of course, simply "rebut" Bloom or Bennett or Paglia or de Souza; one must also discredit the errors, sloppiness, and polemics in their pronouncements. But the efforts must be linked both to the organization of radical forces within the academy as well as to those social groups producing new cultural and political arrangements either to the side or against the mainstream. This is to say that we be cannot be satisfied with merely demographic changes in the academy, in the form of either "tokenism" or "essentialism."[5] For that way lies cooperation with structures that are not now prepared to make concessions.

There are important oppositional intellectuals attempting to develop their work in relation to the emergent, minority subcultures in U.S. society. One thinks of Cornel West.[6] And there are, as I will discuss somewhat later in this chapter, oppositional historians trying to identify marginal movements, to tell different histories from different places about the U.S. past. And, of course, all of these writers are working "theoretically," even when their writing reflects an "activist," nontheoretical bias. From their work, new theoretical reflections will develop new roles for intellectuals, teachers, critics, and scholars.

But there remains a place, it seems to me, for the interrogation of the main figures, texts, and events of mainstream European and American culture. At times, questions will be hostile; at times, they will look for lost possibilities: they must, however, always be allowed. One cannot finally decide the West has nothing whatsoever to offer and so can be forgotten, not if one lives in the United States or in a world effectively contaminated by the imbroglios of dominant U.S. politics: witness the Gulf War's murder of hundreds of thousands and the hypocritical U.S. rejection of Palestinian claims to equal treatment with Kuwaitis. (The United States, we remember, would have no "linkage.") At least one must know the West's past and its continuing effects, its determining force; at most, one can look in the West's past for what I will call later, following Heidegger, the possibilities of Dasein, the fact of the ways human being was, they ways not told by those who survived, to paraphrase Benjamin. But the look at the past must come from the present, aim at it, and keep the future in mind: what else is the memory of possibility for? Hearing the subcultures, looking at the past, aiming at the present for the sake of the future. At times this means, if nothing else, an effort at memory to clarify what is happening in the present; to show how, for example, possibilities are closed down in a present move that *claims* to be "progressive." It is in this spirit that I turn now to a rather close look at certain limited moments in Heidegger. I am recalling some of his work; aiming at certain premature foreclosures in the present—neopragmatism and neohistoricism—in the name of a future that others are not making elsewhere.

II

In "The Worldhood of the World," part III of Division One of *Being and Time*,[7] Heidegger conducts an analysis of "theory" and "praxis" in relation to his themes of "concern" and "circumspection" (*Umsicht*). I point to this passage in hopes that it might help us with an understanding of how it is with theory that it can, as it were, come to its own end in the anti-theoretical neopragmatists and neoconservatives. Previous efforts to account for the "death of theory" have been largely political and historical stories—some of which I have told. Yet it remains to be asked if there is something about "theory" itself, as it were, that accounts for its inscription within the instrumental institutions and discourses of various "against theory" movements and moments.

It has been my thesis that it would have been too much to expect that "theory-work" somehow would or could stand outside the given realities of our time and place. I have argued that theory repeatedly shows itself, even and perhaps especially in oppositional mode, to be a kind of thought and work that is not privileged to remain outside the instrumental or professional or hegemonic operations of the institutions and discourses it so readily presents and criticizes, and furthermore, that the consequences of that inability are great: oppositional work sooner rather than later loses it resistant edge and reproduces the structures of power it depends upon for its own survival. Indeed, efforts to claim that theory might somehow have a privileged social, cultural, or political position within the fragmented and competing academic discourses and interests of postmodern America—these are self-evidently impossible to sustain. Many of us involved in theory have quite precisely tried to show some of the implications for theory of an inscription within those structures, ideologies, and discourses and also to show them to be inescapable. Indeed, in *Intellectuals in Power*, I argued at some length that the very discursive structures of humanistic critical work simultaneously make possible and restrict, draw limits to, any oppositional critical efforts.

In the essays that followed that book (a few of which are collected in this volume), I tried to show more specifically some of the institutional political effects of oppositional intellectual work's inscription within criticism. In this essay, however, I try to get at something a little different, something like what we might call the "ontological ground" of theory's inscription within the politics, discourses, institutions, and intellectual roles it claims to describe, reveal, make present, and critique. I return to Heidegger[8] to draw out of his work—especially as it deals with the facticity of Dasein as "thrown"—an understanding of how and why theory, because of the kind of "sight" it is, namely *Umsicht*, cannot but exist in a relation that entangles it in the instrumental. All efforts to think theory as a pure alternative to practice itself or to specific forms of unexamined practice are mystified failures. They exemplify the inscription of theory and theorists in the structures they hope, at best, to oppose but actually instantiate.

In *Being and Time*, Heidegger takes Kant as the best example of philosophy's efforts to think through to a conception of theory—intuition—as a pure relation to the objects of knowledge, to what Heidegger calls "present-at-hand." Any conception that privileges theory as a mode of work able to achieve "distance" from practices and methods, from constitutive discursive effects and institutional or ideological determinations echoes Kant's notion of "intuition." Furthermore, as Heidegger's rethinking of Kant's claims makes clear, no such conception can hold because "theory" and "practice" stand not as opposites—nor do their corollaries, such as "sight," "distance," and "proximity"—but as inseparable ways in which Dasein has its Being in the World. And, as such, their structured interrelationship can be understood only in a repetitive analysis that traces their interweaving and overcomes both the binary oppositions between them and all of the hierarchical relations that might exist within those binaries. As I shall also try to show, such overcoming means not only that theory cannot but fail in its efforts if conceived in the tradition of "intuition" but also that neopragmatist efforts to negate and displace theory with "practice" also cannot succeed; indeed, they are reductive of Dasein and of Dasein's ways of Being in the World because they themselves rest upon and have an interest in propagating the false hierarchical binary, "theory/practice."

There are, of course, many reasons for and many ways in which critics propagate this binary relation. Particularly since the deaths of de Man and Foucault and the revelation about Heidegger's and de Man's associations with fascism, theory, as it has been practiced in the United States, particularly as "deconstruction," has come under

attack for its failures to understand "history," to produce real historical knowledge, and successfully to elaborate the political, sexual
problems of gender, race, class, and ethnicity. In addition, it has been
partially displaced by efforts at "cultural studies,"[9] which, following
Raymond Williams, concern themselves with the forms and practices
of our life together.

Heidegger's work indicates that both progressive and careerist efforts to go in the wake of theory, to work pragmatically on certain
problems of our lives and their histories, and to produce knowledge
about them, about their representations, about their "constitution,"
and about their "theoretical" uncertainties—these efforts will always
proceed precisely in the wake of theory: harassed by what Heidegger's analysis suggests is an inescapable structural fact of Dasein. Heidegger's work shows that "theory" can never be "pure" and so seems
to support the turn away from theory. Arguing against Kant (as a
figure of philosophy) that the search for "intuition" can neither be
completed nor can it successfully ground "theoretical" efforts to gain
distant and controlling knowledge prior to an engagement with the
world, Heidegger also argues that by the same token, "anti-theory"
cannot but be theory. It is merely part of a movement that tries to bury
theory prematurely. It holds a wake before it's due. In trying to kill
theory, "anti-theory" is the mark of the humanistic intellectuals' rush
to leave it behind. And what has the rush left us with? A plethora of
succeeding and competing, fragmented critical projects, each and
every one trying to address some issue of liberation, politics, or history. And this state of affairs even has its own name and theory: postmodernism as pastiche. And it is always in a hurry, rushing always to
revise its own positions and practices to achieve new authority and
produce new "knowledge."

Rather uniquely, Heidegger tells us something of how and why this
set of circumstances had to occur; why "theory" conceived as the distant guide of practice could not but leave this chaos in its wake; and
why the various frantic fragmented efforts at practice and history—
which too often rest upon presumably well-understood critical axioms—are so perfectly part of the structures of reproduction they
claim to oppose. Heidegger has thought these questions ontologically
so that we can turn back to something in his work—which was foun-
dational to theory—to discover a kind of proleptic analysis that was

ignored and that might now help us understand not only some of what has happened but something of how we might choose to theorize again. Heidegger gives us once more old terms to take in a new way: terms like *circumspection* and *deliberation,* which help us locate the projects of most critics in the wake of theory and point to some new way to think theory's return, to think it as it casts a glimpse toward what is most needful.

III

One can take Walter Benn Michaels and Steven Knapp as exemplary instances of the "against theory" movements as they eventuate in some of the preeminent forms of New Historicist and neopragmatist thinking. One can carry out a critique of their work that shows it to be pure ideology; it is a kind of thought in which, as Althusser says, "the 'dominant' ideas . . . were playing their 'dominating' role to perfection, ruling unrecognized over the very minds that were trying to fight them."[10] Such a critique would, however, belong to the genre of political, historical stories often told before, and I do not want to repeat them here—at least not in exactly the same way.

Taking Knapp and Benn Michaels as convenient instances and putting them next to an important moment in Heidegger reveals—and goes beyond—the truth of the "ideology" charge by showing how viciously circular their arguments are. More interesting, however, it discloses how theory itself has at least one feature that links it to "pragmatism" in such a way that we understand more fully its own death, appropriation, and negation.

There are at least two ways of approaching Knapp and Benn Michaels's texts. (As a matter of economy I will abbreviate this as KBM.) The first is Foucauldian and would take the form of an old injunction put in a new way: know thyself!—and the genealogy of your discursive and institutional position.[11] Of course, this is precisely the sort of critical, historical obligation that those influenced by "analytic philosophy" most strongly resist and resent.[12] Were KBM genealogically to question the "obviousness," the "self-evident legitimacy" of the terms of their writing, of their critical "style," then it would be possible to ask them to account for the ways in which operations of power led them to speak as they do and, furthermore, to explain how the ways in which they write and "think" have come to be considered "legitimate" by (some) others who read them. In other words, it would oblige them to attend to the participation of the discourse that speaks to them in what Foucault has taught us to call "the regime of truth," that is, the interwoven connections of incommensurable and irreversible power effects in discourses and institutions that produce the "truth." For KBM, the "givenness" of their speaking is what Gramsci calls "common sense," the surest mark that such speech is "ideology."[13]

A second approach to a critique of KBM (which, I hope it is clear, I am taking as influential because it was and is "exemplary") lies in Heidegger. In #15, "*The Being of the Entities Encountered in the Environment*," Heidegger carries out an analysis of "presence at hand," "readiness to hand" as ways of Dasein's Being in the World. This analysis depends upon the corresponding phenomenological concepts of "equipment" (*das Zeug*) and "circumspection" (*Umsicht*). Heidegger also rethinks what the Greeks called "pragmata," that is, "that which one has to do with in one's concernful dealings (praxis)" (*BT*, 96–97). In the process, he clarifies relationships of "sight" existing between what is called "practical behavior" and what is called "theory." (Etymologically, of course, the Greek word *theorein* means "to see" [*BT*, 99, n. 1].)

Heidegger's analysis shows that the exemplary figure of KBM mistakes one part of Dasein's Being-toward-the-World for all of Dasein's Being-in-the-World. In essence, KBM writes as if Heidegger and those who theorize and philosophize after him had not existed. They do not recognize that basic to Heidegger's work is the demonstration that Kant mistakenly assumed it to be the a priori case that Dasein can be in the world only in terms of the schemata.[14] The entire Heideggerean argument shows the ontological primordiality of the ready-to-hand (*zuhanden*) to the present-at-hand (*vorhanden*) as Dasein's way of relating to the world.[15] Heidegger thus undercuts the Kantian claim to be in the world only by virtue of the categories. Yet the primordiality of the ready-to-hand does not eventuate in pragmatism, for to believe that it did would be to mistake one dimension of Dasein's Being-in-the-World for the ontological totality of that possibility. As Heidegger's preliminary analysis shows, it is possible ontologically, as part of the Being of Dasein, to be in the world, in relation to the world, "theoretically"; it is possible to do just what the KBM position denies: "If we look at Things just 'theoretically,' we can get along without understanding readiness-to-hand" (*BT*, 98).

KBM make an argument against theory by assigning a Kantian conception of intuition to theory and, once having done that, assert that it cannot be held: "Theory in a nontrivial sense always consists in the attempt 'to stand outside practice in order to govern practice from without,' and this strong ('foundationalist') kind of theory is the kind whose coherence we deny."[16]

Indeed, the neopragmatist and antioppositional KBM position makes a fundamental error in its reductive binary thinking about the relations between "theory" and "practice." KBM argue that in theory there is "distantiation," whereas "practice" alone presents a sort of truth of or in immediacy, in action.[17] This neopragmatism exists by virtue of a binary opposition that annuls theory in advance as folly. The fundamental problem with KBM, however, is that their dualisms are naive. The distantiation they assign as a quality to theory is, as sight, also an aspect of the "practical."

Heidegger's analysis of how Dasein develops the distantiation of theory in which, or by virtue of which, the "present-at-hand" emerges, reveals that the particular form of Dasein's concern (*Besorgen*) that grounds "theory," "intuition," or "science" is a specific way of seeing. Heidegger calls it *Umsicht*; his translators call it "circumspection." Heidegger's analysis of *Umsicht* shows that "sight" in the form of "looking around" and "looking in order to" is present in practice: if sight is the basic sense and category of "theory" and "intuition," then it is so only because and as a transformation of "circumspection"'s ontological priority in the constitution of the ready-to-hand.

"Sight" is not, as it were, the same in all aspects of Dasein's Being in the World, but as a fundamental existential element of Dasein's Being, it allows for a rethinking and overcoming of the traditional as well as neopragmatist binary relation between theory and practice. Heidegger restates and clarifies the "philosophical" problem in order to overcome it:

No matter how sharply we just *look* [Nur-noch-*hinsehen*] at the "outward appearance" ["Aussehen"] of Things in whatever form this takes, we cannot discover anything ready-to-hand. If we look at things just "theoretically," we can get along without understanding readiness-to-hand. But when we deal with them by using them and manipulating them, this activity is not a blind one; it has its own kind of sight, by which our manipulation is guided and from which it acquires its specific Thingly character. Dealings with equipment subordinate themselves to the manifold assignments of the "in-order-to." And the sight with which they thus accommodate themselves is *circumspection*. (*BT*, 98)

Heidegger thus differentiates the two kinds of "sight" involved in *Vordhandenkeit* and *Zuhandenkeit,* and he repetitively elaborates upon this difference. Initially in the analysis *Umsicht* is that sight not hospitable to theory, and it is primary to theory as *Zuhandenkeit* is to *Vordhandenkeit.* Of course, Heidegger does not leave the analysis at this preliminary point, which seems to sharply delimit theory from practice and, indeed, make theory derivative of practice. Most readings of Heidegger's work argue that the analysis of Dasein passes beyond the limits of this preliminary understanding of *Umsicht* as a form of concern (*Besorgen*) proper to *Das Man,* in order to reveal and come into "care" (*Sorge*) as Dasein's fullness of Being.[18] Indeed, as they evolve, Heidegger's arguments deny to the instrumental or pragmatic reason the primordial claims of immediacy and proximity by showing that common sense wrongly opposes theory and practice by blinding itself to the circumspect nature of practice. Moreover, the sight that guides practice (*Umsicht*) remains in a primordial relation of Dasein to the world as manipulation—in and by which the world remains as Thingly. In other words, "circumspection" is the ordinary relation to the world as equipment, as "pragmata," which, as such, is always necessarily blind to its own form of sight (*Umsicht*), assigning what it considers to be the secondary and, indeed, impossible relation of "sight" (*Sehen*) to "theory"—itself formed etymologically as "sight." In other words, "circumspection" establishes the world as Thingly, blinded to its own sight; and, in the process and necessarily as a state of circumspection, a fabulous binary opposition between "theory" and "practice," between "sight" and "immediacy." Heidegger's great achievement is to recover sight (*Umsicht*) from the blinding effects of Dasein's circumspect relation to "pragmata." By so doing, he names the kind of "sight" (or "theory") involved in pragmatic circumspection, breaks down the false way in which *Umsicht* concerns itself to maintain itself in the constitution of the world as

Thingly, and retrieves the possibility of different kinds of "sight"—
all of this by phenomenologically and hermeneutically analyzing the
ontology of Dasein. KBM could not have seen any of this for, in their
rush to remain in "practice," they represent and reproduce Dasein's
circumspect Being-toward-the-World: "To lay bare what is just
present-at-hand," Heidegger writes, "and no more, cognition must
first penetrate *beyond* what is ready-to-hand in our concern. *Readiness to hand is the way in which entities as they are 'in themselves'
are defined ontologico-categorially"* (BT, 101).

At this stage in the analysis, we might say that theory tries to leave
the "ontologico-categorial" behind. But insofar as "theory" is sight,
it cannot accomplish this without repeating the blindness of "circumspection." As circumspection maintains the world as Thingly, blinding itself to its own "sight" (*Umsicht*), "theory" cannot, as it were,
comfortably assert its pure and primordial access to "presence" in a
relation that requires the simple binary opposition of "theory"/
"practice" constituted by circumspection. Theory, Heidegger shows,
is entangled with circumspection precisely in its efforts to overcome
the place *Umsicht* creates for it. I mean to say that theory cannot accept the circumspect interpretation of its form of sight as intuition or
controlling distance—that way lies the downfall KBM predict and depend upon in an effort circumspectly to defeat it.

Heidegger extends his analysis to show more of how the relations
of theory and practice emerge from circumspection. As we have seen
in the exemplary KBM, circumspection—as practice—cannot see itself as sight, as a disposition that constitutes the world as Thingly and
its manifold as subordinated to the *Umsicht*, to the "in-order-to."
"Nor," says Heidegger, "is it itself the sort of thing that circumspection takes proximally as a circumspective theme" (BT, 99). Within
circumspection, then, the opposition between theory and practice
stands both as common sense and as philosophy (wherein, of course
it may be a problem dialectically to be overcome or pragmatically subsumed). Heidegger repeats the relation in its ordinary form to deny
and overcome it:

"Practical" behavior is not "atheoretical" in the sense of "sightlessness."
The way it differs from theoretical behavior does not lie simply in the fact
that in theoretical behavior one observes, while in practical behavior one *acts*
[*gehandelt* wird], and that action must employ theoretical cognition if it is
not to remain blind; for the fact that observation is a kind of concern is just

as primordial as the fact that action has *its own* kind of sight. Theoretical behavior is just looking, without circumspection. But the fact that this looking is non-circumspective does not mean that it follows no rules: it constructs a canon for itself in the form of *method*. (*BT*, 99)

"Theory" first appears as a particular form of sight, distantiated and "penetrating." If the ready-to-hand is proximate, it is also appearance. But this preliminary understanding—even if it is that of philosophy as well as common sense—of the relation between theory and practice does no more to interrogate theory than circumspection does or can do to understand itself. As a result, Heidegger's text moves from this preliminary analysis by rethinking how the ready-to-hand stands in relation to the world. The key to his analysis in this section is the notion of "work" which leads, in turn, through the concept of Nature to the process of discovery—which itself is properly linked to another form of sight, "envisaging" and what Heidegger will later call "deliberation" (*BT*, 410).

For circumspection "work" is the "toward which" of things, not the process of laboring. The "work," like the Thing in general, exists as such within a world taken as equipment; but because in the work there is always "a using *of* something for something" and "a reference or assignment to 'materials,' " when we use a work the "environment," even as Nature, "is ready-to-hand along with it" (*BT*, 100–101). "Circumspection," in other words, is not merely instrumental and anti-theoretical, as circumspection—that is, common sense or philosophy—might make one believe. Dasein is in a relation of concern to the world and its entities. *Umsicht* must, therefore, be understood as having the potential to make the world available beyond its own instrumentality in what Heidegger calls "penetration":

Our concernful absorption in whatever work-world lies closest to us, has a function of discovering; and it is essential to this function that, depending upon the way in which we are absorbed, those entities within-the-world which are brought along in the work and with it (that is to say, in the assignments or references which are constitutive for it) remain discoverable in varying degrees of explicitness and with a varying circumspective penetration. (*BT*, 101)

What we might call "mere circumspection" shows itself to have a capacity for "penetration" that might "discover" entities within-the-world. But this is a movement of *Umsicht* from within itself, which suggests that if circumspection overcomes its own "sightlessness" it does so in the form of a discovering and penetrating look. As such, it fulfills the capacity of circumspection, but, equally as such, it is not "pure theory," but it is the ground of theory nonetheless. More important, however, this structure of penetrating circumspection makes possible the philosophical claims for "theory," "intuition," and "presence" as the ground of knowledge, indeed, of "presence" itself as the ground of the ready-to-hand. In other words, the "penetration" that circumspection produces to approach "presence-at-hand" makes possible the theoretical and metaphysical claim for the priority of presence. For Heidegger, such an account is an error: "Such an Interpretation would overlook the fact that in this case these entities would have to be understood and discovered beforehand as something purely present-at-hand, and must have priority and take the lead in the sequence of those dealings with the 'world' in which something is discovered and made one's own" (BT, 101). Heidegger critiques this metaphysical claim for theory/intuition by once more analyzing the being of "sight" to show how the claim that readiness-at-hand rests ontologically upon presence-at-hand is an effect of Umsicht. Heidegger interrogates how the philosopher or theoretician must see to make the metaphysical claim that rests the former upon the latter: "To lay bare what is just present-at-hand and no more, cognition must first penetrate beyond what is ready-to-hand in our concern" (BT, 101). This necessity, however, contradicts the fundamental Heideggerean demonstration that all cognition is founded and so results in metaphysics. Theory, then, cannot but be metaphysics insofar as it is circumspective penetration.

Heidegger accounts for theory not logically but genetically. He continues to rethink theory (and intuition) by analyzing it as a way of existing, not merely as what it has been revealed to be so far: a method of penetration overcoming mere instrumentality, to establish the essential that is the ground of practice. Were theory merely that mode of penetrating insight outside a separate sphere of practice, then KBM would be correct in their assertions that theory conceived in that way cannot be coherent. Heidegger's thought preserves the figure of penetration as a guide to understanding theory, but he interrogates it to understand "how theoretical discovery 'arises' out of circumspective concern"; what are the ways in which "circumspective concern with the ready-to-hand changes over into an exploration of what come across as present-at-hand within-the-world" (*BT,* 408–409).

"Theory" should not be thought of as "privation," for it is not a mere "holding back" from manipulating, from circumspective penetration. Theory is not "the *disappearance* of *praxis.*" Heidegger calls "tarrying" the kind of looking one does when holding back from manipulation. It is a kind of "looking around." At this point in his argument, Heidegger voices the crux of his analysis so far. He has shown that theory is not in opposition to praxis; that sight is not solely assigned to theory (or science as knowledge); and that the effort to "penetrate" appearances and the ready-to-hand to reach presence as present-at-hand is itself part of the circumspect way of Being in the World. By contrast, Kantian metaphysics—as well as common sense and pragmatism, or what we might call "first level" circumspection—rests precisely upon the claim that intuition—or theory as science—is another, privileged kind of "sight" than *Umsicht,* one that brings knowledge into direct relation to the object. Heidegger quotes this sentence from *The Critique of Pure Reason:* " 'To whatever kind of objects one's knowledge may relate itself, and by whatever means it may do so, still that through which it relates to them immediately, *and which all thinking as a means has as its goal* (author's italics) is intuition' " (*BT,* 410). Heidegger rethinks intuition by rethinking what it means that Kant and all others who defend "theory" from "practical impurities" invoke "sight" (*Sehen*) as the guarantee for "the investigative discovery and disclosure of the 'things themselves.' " Those who stand in the Kantian tradition would have it that " 'Seeing,' taken in the widest sense, regulates all 'procedures' and retains its priority"—that is, over circumspection, *Umsicht.* Rather than put the Kantian assertion that all thinking has intuition as its goal, Heidegger insists that "if we are to exhibit the existential genesis of science in accordance with the priority of 'seeing,' we must set out by characterizing the *circumspection* which is the guide for 'practical' concern" (*BT,* 410).

Heidegger follows neither the philosophical nor commonsensical approach, which lets theory stand as apart from or in opposition to circumspection. Rather, an understanding of theory as a way of existing requires taking circumspection as the site to interrogate the origins of theory itself. Rethinking circumspection leads Heidegger to insist that to retain the preliminary understanding of *Umsicht*'s relation to the world as equipment. Heidegger stresses that this is not a relation between Dasein and the world as a mere compendium of things. Rather, in taking the world as ready-to-hand, Dasein goes beyond instrumentality and has "a primary understanding of the totality of involvements within which factical concern always takes its start" (*BT*, 410). This understanding takes the form of a "survey," which itself subordinates and guides *Umsicht* in its relation to the "equipmental totality of the current equipment-world."

Both Kant and KBM argue, for different reasons, that theory is distantiation, a form of controlling sight, unlike the proximity of practice. Heidegger rethinks circumspection to say how theory emerges genetically into another form of sight, which we might call "proximate envisaging" or "deliberation." This form of sight is a potentiality of Dasein's being as Care, not of Dasein as *das Man*. "Such a survey," Heidegger writes, "illumines one's concern, and receives its 'light' from that potentiality-for-Being on the part of Dasein *for the sake of which* concern exists as care." Theory emerges from circumspection as proximate envisaging, not as a pure form of knowledge guided by method and procedure—by "sight" (*Sehen*). In proximate envisaging, in deliberation, there is neither sight as "in order to," as manipulation, nor sight as penetration, as the creation of metaphysics. There is rather sight transformed into a seeing that discovers by closing distance and creating proximity. The "light" that grounds this sight is a potential of Dasein itself—namely, Care—and not method. Moreover, Heidegger's argument has overcome circumspection's penetrating instrumentality and metaphysics so thoroughly that it reveals itself as the ground of discovery, of a sight that "*brings* the ready-to-hand *closer* to Dasein." This is what Heidegger calls "deliberating."

Heidegger's discovery of deliberation is crucial for any thinking about theory. First of all, it lets us understand how theory comes into being as a way of existing; second, it reveals something of the status of theory as itself disclosing one's facticity; and third, it indicates that theory can stand in a relation of "presence" to what is absent, that is, to what is not then ready-to-hand. Theory emerges as circumspection surveys equipment and, in deliberative concern, brings things closer by interpreting what it sees. Therefore, "circumspective deliberation illumines Dasein's current factical situation in the environment with which it concerns itself"; that is, theory comes in and as a result of situatedness, which it discloses.

Most important, however, is Heidegger's explanation of how theory can seem to be the distanced form of metaphysical knowledge—intuition—which KBM mistake it as being. "Deliberation" might appear to be metaphysics by virtue of its seeming ability to make present, in theory, as it were, what is absent. Heidegger's own rethinking of the metaphorics of sight, light, and distance seems to imply that when there is deliberation something that has been sighted *at a distance* is brought close; that is, deliberation produces a representation that brings to present something that is absent, or present only to "sight." Heidegger's analysis preserves this rhetoric of metaphysics but overcomes it in showing that deliberation grounds the "existential meaning of a *making present*."

... deliberation never merely "affirms" that some entity is present-at-hand or has such and such properties. Moreover, deliberation can be performed even when that which is brought close in it circumspectively is not palpably ready-to-hand and does not have presence within the closest range. Bringing the environment closer in circumspective deliberation has the existential meaning of a *making present*; for *envisaging* is only a mode of this. In envisaging, one's deliberation catches sight directly of that which is needed but which is un-ready-to-hand. (*BT,* 410)

By this point in his analysis Heidegger has moved to a notion of sight as "envisaging," which, as he says, "does not relate itself to 'mere representation.'"

Theory, it would seem, reemerges in this thinking as an "envisaging" that "directly" "catches sight" of what is needed. Heidegger has offered a very powerful account of why intuition cannot provide a conceptualization of theory adequate either to Dasein's potentiality-for-Being or to the genesis of theory as a way of existing. Intuition's immediate apprehension of objects gives way to glimpses of what is needed as these are accomplished, through deliberation, in a situation where the environment exists, near and far, as equipment. Yet this equipmentality of *das Zeug* does not negate the possibility of theory (pragmatism) nor assign Dasein to mere instrumentality, nor even to theoretical "penetration" behind the ready-to-hand in order to reach the present-at-hand conceived as the ontological ground. Yet theory is always and everywhere a potential of Dasein's Being-in-the-World; it is always situated; it always reveals Dasein facticity, that is, historicality. It is always thrown and fallen. It is inseparably part of the complex modes of sight in *Umsicht*—no one of which is ever "finally" transcended. Heidegger has discussed structures of Dasein. With deliberation there is always also manipulation and penetration. Theory is not intuition, but it is also not only envisaging. Within circumspection it is looking around, "in order to," penetrating, deliberating, and envisaging—catching sight of what is not ready-to-hand but is needful nonetheless.

Indeed, one might argue that in this complex set of relations among kinds of sight in *Umsicht* lies the inescapable fact that theory could never be unavailable for the sorts of manipulations and appropriations by circumspect critics, professions, and institutions that we have seen since the 1970s. Indeed, it is in the nature of theory to be complicit with this circumspection. It would be naive to think otherwise. There is a sort of ground to theory's failure that alone makes possible its value: catching sight of what is needful.

IV

In differentiating his own work from that of Jameson, the paradigmatic Marxist, and Lyotard, the paradigmatic poststructuralist, Stephen Greenblatt takes a position that, not surprisingly, parallels the neopragmatist KBM. Greenblatt claims that Marxism and poststructuralism are unsatisfactory critical models, not so much because of the contents of their claims but because of the kinds of claims they are. "I propose," he writes, "that the general question addressed by Jameson and Lyotard—what is the historical relation between art and society or between one institutionally demarcated discursive practice and another?—does not lend itself to a single, theoretically satisfactory answer of the kind that Jameson and Lyotard are trying to provide."[19] Greenblatt, of course, indicts these ideologically different critical efforts for having their common root in a "theoretical" enterprise. He feels that "history" is too complex and too "contradictory"—this touchstone of Marxist thought is present throughout his indictment—for criticism ground in what he, like KBM, takes to be the basic impulse of "theory." "Theoretical satisfaction . . . seems to depend upon a utopian vision that collapses the contradictions of history into a moral imperative," writes Greenblatt, while noting that this collapsing is not an accidental effect of the specific works and theories under discussion. Indeed, he asserts that "this effacement of contradiction is not the consequence of an accidental lapse but rather the logical outcome of theory's search for the obstacle that blocks the realization of its eschatological vision" (PC, 5).

If KBM draw what we have now seen to be a naive opposition between "practice" and "theory," one that does not interrogate the common relations between the terms of their desired hierarchy, the same might be said of Greenblatt, and so his work is of no interest on those grounds. It becomes important, however, because in its invocation of "historicism" over and against theory's failure in "utopian reduction," Greenblatt repeats KBM's moves on a level of potentially greater danger than their mere invocation of "pragmatism." Greenblatt returns "history" to an intellectual arena from which theory had tried to drive it. We should recall from as long ago as 1970, when Paul de Man lectured on Nietzsche, that the *bête noir* of "literary theory" has been historicism, especially in its association with certain structures of power in the state and its institutions and in relation to certain notions of the self as well as certain forms of intellectual discourse. Indeed, Michel Foucault, from early in the 1960s made a special effort to understand the modern linkage between history writing, the disciplines, and the state and subject formation.[20] The "new historicism," while depending upon a certain version of Foucault's work, seems not to have made a very careful critique of his relation to historicism.[21] More interesting, however, is the "new historicist" failure to examine closely the reasons for the theoretical interrogation of "history" and "history writing." Greenblatt, in a move all too typical of the current U.S. critical profession, seems to feel that he can simply—literally without argument or demonstration—indict two theorists for simplification and then infer from that assertion another equally unproven claim, which in turn indicts and dismisses all theory—this in the name of "contradiction." That Greenblatt does not make careful arguments is not, however, the issue, no more than Greenblatt himself or the "new historicists" are the issue. Rather, what matters somewhat more is the fact that this set of assertions typifies the way much of the U.S. academy now works and furthermore that—as I will again argue—since theory is inescapable and since the theory movement is now over, it is necessary to recoup an understanding of theory work that can go forward beyond the reach of such dogmatic forgetfulness as we find in KBM and the "new historicism."[22]

V

In *Being and Time*, Heidegger develops a number of different understandings of "history" and places them in relation to sets of philosophical and political concepts and practices. My argument does not require a comprehensive treatment of Heidegger to establish that the "new historicist" claims do not escape the matrix of theory and that the simplifying and traditional ways in which they move against theory have no grounds, resting on thin appropriations of the relations between theory and history.[23]

That there's likely to be nothing "new" about the "new historicism" is now a cliché of hostile critics.[24] But that this "oldness" can be found in a failure to differentiate "histories"—the Germans, we remember, had different words, which we translate by the same one—suggests the scope of the problem and, as it were, the reason to look again at Heidegger.[25] The "new historicism," of course, draws much of its legitimacy from the opinion that "theory" is somehow a white, European, male bastion that, in Stuart Hall's formulation, destroys the subject and history at the very time when new subjectivities—of women, minorities, decolonizing peoples, peoples in resistance, such as the Palestinians, and others—are emerging into "history" or are forming and recovering their histories.[26] Suggesting another look at Heidegger seems to fly in the face of this idea. But if the "new historicism" is part of a modernizing project of historical reconstruction, as some of its analysts suggest,[27] then it is appropriate to see how Heidegger's critique of history in relation to modernity poses problems and opportunities for a newly thought theory intent, quite precisely, on *not* effacing complexity or the struggles of repressed groups for subjectivity.[28]

In #76, *"The Existential Source of Historiology in Dasein's Historicality,"* Heidegger makes a distinction between two notions of "history," *Historie* and *Geschichte*. He does so, in part, to specify how the "historical sciences"—Heidegger will go on to discuss Dilthey—have their ground in Dasein's historicality and how this in turn is rooted in temporality. Heidegger's interest in establishing this set of relations has to do with the problem of the nature of Dasein's historicality and the way in which this is or is not itself adequately understood in a historicizing manner. The key text in *Being and Time* makes this very clear: "Whether the *historiological disclosure of history* is factually accomplished or not, *its ontological structure is such that in itself this disclosure has its roots in the historicality of Dasein*" (*BT*, 444). It is enough to say about this passage that it suggests the impossibility of carrying out the "new historicist" project of denying "theory" a place in "historicist" work. The "new historicism" lacks a "theoretical" analysis of the status of "history" (or "practice") as one potential of Dasein's Being-in-the-World as well as an understanding of the ontology of Dasein—of subjectivity, of human agency—which shows that a category of Dasein's historically developed Being is not, in itself, entitled to claim itself as a privileged instrument for the understanding of Dasein as a historical being. "Historicism," in other words, is an effect of Dasein's historicality and the latter is not, as such, accessible to the former.

The "new historicists" err in the same way as the neopragmatists, failing to understand the ground of historicism within a "nonhistoricist" capacity of Being-in-the-World. Foucault can be used to illustrate some of the difficulties involved. In his work of the early 1960s, especially *Madness and Civilization* and *The Birth of the Clinic,* Foucault unearths something of the "historicality" of Being (subject) within modernity that would account for the coming into existence of the historicist project.[29] Foucault creates the effect, for some readers, of what seems to be an effort to write a history of history-writing. Rather, I believe, Foucault tries to get at what Heidegger here is theorizing: the problem of understanding "historiology's" "historical" existence. Foucault, of course, wants an explanation that avoids the ontological terms, but his efforts nonetheless rest on Heidegger's rethinking historicism's inability to gain access to what—ahistorically, if you will—grounds historicist possibilities, namely Dasein's historicality rooted in temporality. What, we might ask, must it mean to think "historiography" nonhistoriographically, given that history in this sense is—in terms of the earlier parts of my commentary—merely one form of *Umsicht,* one form of circumspection?

As critics argue about the "new historicism," part of its appeal derives from the fact that "theory" is or was felt to have denied "historical" access to the processes of "subject" and "identity" formation. But, as my sketchy remarks suggest, "historicism" cannot successfully serve such efforts without finding a way to overcome the "new historicism's" anti-theoretical biases. In Heidegger's words, before we could feel comfortable with the effort, we would need an answer to the question "what guarantee do we have in principle that such a factical procedure will indeed be properly representative of historiology in its primordial and authentic possibilities" (*BT*, 445). The difficulty the historicist faces in attempting to provide an answer to this question can be located in a long line of thinkers originating at least in Hegel and the German romantics. Heidegger's revisions of that tradition can be put aside for the moment since the point of my remarks is to suggest, somewhat ironically, how Greenblatt's "new historicist" claims simplify, reduce, and indeed reify the actualities of history and historiology.

Following a series of rather easy remarks on the methodological difficulty of determining the correct status of the "objects" of historicism, Heidegger's description of the theoretical problems within historicism comes to a momentary conclusion: "*historiological* disclosure temporalizes itself *in terms of the future*. The '*selection*' of what is to become a possible object for historiology *has already been met with* in the factical existentiell *choice* of Dasein's historicality, in which historiology first of all arises, and in which alone it *is*" (*BT*, 447). In other words, to put the matter simply, as Heidegger does in one of his more Nietzschean moments, "the historiological disclosure of the 'past' is based on fateful repetition" (*BT*, 447).

Given Heidegger's efforts to overcome various dualistic structures of thought within a general hermeneutics, it would not be sensible to read him as charging historicism with relativism, perspectivism, or subjectivity.[30] Rather what matters for Heidegger is that historicists do not understand theoretically what grounds precisely the actual "Objectivity" of historicism's claims. In a sense, the answer to that problem lies in what Paul de Man called "allegory" and what Heidegger calls "theme" but that, in both instances, is an effect of Dasein's Being-in-the-World:

For the Objectivity of a science is regulated primarily in terms of whether that science can confront us with the entity which belongs to it as its theme, and can bring it, uncovered in the primordiality of its Being, to our understanding. In no science are the "universal validity" of standards and the claims to "universality" which the "they" and its common sense demand, *less* possible as criteria of "truth" than in authentic historiology. (*BT,* 447)

The perspectivism or relativism that belong to old and new historicism—whether engaged with "poststructuralism" or not—means that its "Objectivity" can never be founded on positivist assurances but on its ability to thematize its object—"uncovered in the primordiality of its Being." Historiology, in other words, is a mode of circumspection in its attempt to present its objects and as such is within the complex and inescapable play of *Umsicht,* which means that historicism cannot uncover Dasein in its temporality, as past or as future. It would seem a poor ground—in its anti-theoretical form of circumspection and pragmatism—on which to imagine or attempt to form the disclosure of new subjectivities in the present for the future or to recollect forgotten Dasein as what was "once there" from a past for a future.

This failure is anti-theoretical historicism's major error and it returns my argument to what is needful. If what is needed is the making present or emergence or recovery of (new) subjectivities, of Dasein, which once was and must be again or must come to be, then "theory" must be reinvented in reply to that need—indeed, perhaps to suggest as new theory of the subject itself. Perhaps "theory" was, as Said repeatedly suggests, too "aesthetic," too "professional" to be oppositional or radical in a more than dilettantish way. There is certainly much evidence to justify that idea. But "new historicism" runs all of the same risks and perhaps others. While there is no doubt that, in the efforts at struggle, resistance, and subject formation, "history" has a role to play, a role made necessary by Dasein's very historicality, it must not be a history that is itself too much part of its time. On this point, Heidegger's eloquence suggests, among other things, that the recent fashion of "new historicism" is not only an ideological tool whose capacity for resistance is weakened by the professionalism of some of its U.S. practitioners but also that historicism divested of critical theory—and we must remember that Greenblatt's formulation coalesces with the "against theory" schools of "right" and "left"— is itself mere aestheticism: "If the historian 'throws' himself straightway into the 'world-view' of an era, he has not thus proved as yet that he understands his object in an authentically historical way, and not just 'aesthetically.' And on the other hand, the existence of an historian who 'only' edits sources, may be characterized by a historicality which is authentic" (*BT*, 448).

There is, of course, a curiously forgotten debate within and about the moment of "high theory." It had to do, of course, with the theorists' claims that their works were or are "historical." In a way, the historicist move to surpass theory—always taken paradigmatically as "deconstruction"—relies upon the unchallenged opinion that theory could not be serious in its claims for its own historicality. Yet *Umsicht* is certainly a temporal and historical category; Dasein as circumspection cannot but be historical in its equipmentality (*das Zeug*) just as it cannot be "intuitive" in its production of knowledge, although it becomes clear how within the structure of the "aesthetic" intuition elides with historicism. The point, of course, is not only that "historicist" procedures have no special claim on the historicality of Dasein but that nonhistoricist modes of being, knowledge, and writing can be historical: "Thus," says Heidegger,

the very prevalence of a differentiated interest even in the most remote and primitive cultures [and here he echoes Hegel's "Preface" to *The Phenomenology of Spirit*], is in itself no proof of the authentic historicality of a 'time.' In the end, the emergence of a problem of 'historicism' is the clearest symptom that historiology endeavors to alienate Dasein from its authentic historicality. Such historicality does not necessarily require historiology. It is not the case that unhistoriological eras as such are unhistorical also. (*BT*, 448)

What is needful, then, is historicality, but it cannot be found in a historicism that attempts to arrogate what is needful to itself, that indeed mistakes itself for historicality and for Dasein's complex possibilities of Being. It should not believe that it is itself a sufficient large and magical caldron in which to mix a future in response to Dasein's real and differentiated efforts to come into being in various futures. What historicism must always attend to is, as Heidegger might say, the *possibility* of Dasein, as it leaves the traces of its having been, as this turns toward and suggests the possibilities of what it might be.

CHAPTER TWO

The Function of the Literary Critic
in the Postmodern World

ᘓᔍ The major modern forms of aesthetic and moral
literary criticism are now illegitimate. The professional study of the
"form and meaning" of enduring works of "great beauty" and
"moral value" can no longer be justified in those terms alone. Those
who feel it can (or should be) need to explain the declining role of
poetry and literary education in America and must, in so doing, confront the fundamental political and economic forces that marginalize
the humanities and the poetic imagination. They must not do this
only in theory, so to speak;[1] they must also lay down a practical plan
that they can show has some chance of succeeding in the face of all of
the cultural and institutional forces that oppose the continuation of
critical intelligence and imagination in what many like to call our
"postmodern world."[2]

These residual humanists—they must *prove* they are more than residual—should also confront the all-too-painful personal realities of
the profession, especially the intellectual and pedagogical inertia and
irresponsibility of those very common professorial figures who not
only fearfully mock serious intellectual practice as "theory" but retire
into the semiemployment of their "teaching," "scholarship," and
above all "administration," safely away from hard work, the public-
intellectual sphere, and the intransigent political and cultural issues
facing our society. There is a nearly endless list of these issues that
quite specifically impinge on the skills and supposed values of literary
criticism: one thinks of such immediately "critical" topics as the
"death of the subject," narrative problematics, the instabilities of in-

terpretation, and the like, to say nothing of the socially more important but professionally more distant issues of the culture industry, the colonization of the unconscious and the third world by the new "information industries,"[3] the ever-increasing ties between knowledge and research and the military,[4] the challenges to the great explanatory models of the Modern period, and the need to find ways to theorize the decentered politics of the age of internationalized capital.

Even though we live in an age that increasingly exercises both hegemony and domination in and through sign-based structures, the literary academy not only has failed to reorganize itself to address the new social and intellectual problems created by these structures, but it has returned to "core curricula" and tried to minimize the influence of "radicals" within the academy.[5] Even worse, so-called men and women of the sixties have adopted a high moral tone (exploiting the communal rhetoric of the sixties?) to speak of their "love of literature" to justify their own decisions to operate the most repressive and anti-intellectual elements of university bureaucracy—often as failed critics whose professional survival has been a fluke of demographic history: that is, they were hired and tenured at a time of teacher shortages, have accomplished little, and block the way of other, better-trained, more intelligent, less self-centered, and politically more concerned scholars.

Of course, when speaking of the profession as a whole, my description of this situation is exaggerated and requires considerable amplification to be demonstrative; nonetheless (especially when speaking of very many academicians who have made their careers by running programs), it is, I feel, reasonably accurate. When one considers, for example, the existence of a group like Physicians for Social Responsibility adapting traditional medical concerns for health and life to counter the campaign of misinformation undertaken by bureaucrats, manufacturers, and others who profiteer in the "rearming of America," the absence of an institutionalized (and often even individual) response by literary humanists who are—supposedly—most caring of humane values and most able to examine the workings of sign systems, history, the creation of images, the manipulation of audiences, and so on—this absence is most amazing but also understandable.

Indeed, many (but I think not most) literary scholars and cultural critics do address these and related issues in their work and do help their students to acquire the skills and knowledge to treat them as well, but we must keep in mind the force of Louis Althusser's remark: "those teachers who . . . attempt to turn the few weapons they can find in the history and learning they 'teach' against the ideology, the system and the practices in which they are trapped . . . are a kind of hero. . . . [The majority] do not even begin to suspect the 'work' the system . . . forces them to do, or worse, put all their heart and ingenuity into performing it with the most advanced awareness."[6]

In a recent conversation with a distinguished critic who chairs a comparative literature program and directs an undergraduate humanities program, I rediscovered an all-too-common anticritical dimension to so-called American pluralism. This critic was willing, he said, to allow those he calls "deconstructionists" and others who "do that kind of stuff" to join the literature faculties of his university as long as they did not become dominant, as long as no "critical mass" was established that would shift the "balance of power" in the faculty. Why? Because he and his friends believed that all literary critical points of view should be represented on faculties; that no single point of view has a monopoly on the truth; and that it is only collegial if each and all can do their own thing. A majority of "contemporary" critics would not be acceptable, he felt, because they would attack pluralism itself (it is not clear that he has not overestimated his differences from the majority of "contemporary critics").

I refer to this incident not to illustrate the sad state in which we find liberalism in this unaware critic's pluralism but to draw attention to his anticritical position: no possibility exists, as far as he and others like him are concerned, to demonstrate the greater desirability of any critical position over another; they are all equal as forms of professional practice. This is the sort of position we are accustomed to associate with the careerist antitheoretical defenders of a pragmatic professionalism. What is interesting about this conversation is that it suggests that such pragmatic positions give ideological voice to the "silent majority" within the profession itself. What is most disturbing about this convenient arrangement between the leading representative figures and the purchasers of their books is its reduction of the critical mind to a nihilistic ascesis that is largely explainable in class terms. Since such an explanation would take more space than I have available, let me simply say that this "critic" had reduced the value of critical reason in intellectual life, education, and culture to a consumerist aesthetic of personal taste, "tolerance," and competition for rewards. He articulated a position as likely, I submit, to threaten civilization as any of the so-called advanced theories of contemporary criticism. Above all, his words represent the dominant institutional attitude toward literary criticism, an attitude that has become its purpose: gratification and the acquisition of exploitable skills.

II

American literary critics are not very likely to study nor to write such about the purpose and nature of their institutionalized discipline. Texts like Ohmann's *English in America*, Graff's *Literature Against Itself*, Said's *Orientalism* and *The World, the Text, and the Critic*, parts of Hartman's *Criticism in the Wilderness*, or Lentricchia's *After the New Criticism* and *Criticism and Social Change*[7] are not only an odd lot but noticeable because, to varying degrees, they all attempt—in their different ways—to relate the ends of literary study to the important social and intellectual issues of the time as these are reflected in the works and practices of other disciplines.

One might be able to imagine an occasion when texts of Iser or other so-called "reader response" critics interested in interpretive communities and competence models could be useful in addressing such issues; but until today no one has found a way to overcome the essential ahistorical, professionalized, and idealist tendencies of these "methods" and "positions" to turn them to any social, critical purpose. The task of making such texts useful is complicated by the existence of books like Culler's *Structuralist Poetics* or *On Deconstruction*. Yet without critical reflection on the history and practice of institutional literary study and scholarly production within Modern and Postmodern societies, humanistic educators and intellectuals will be of no help in our current cultural and political crises. No matter whether, like Gramsci, one believes in the formation of organic intellectuals for revolutionary purposes or, like Habermas, in inventing principles of organization to adapt our system to its problems—or in some other similar position—the critic or literary intellectual must establish connections with others whose work can help us understand and act on our present situation.

Unfortunately, North American literary criticism has very few practitioners whose stature is such that their work is of significance to many scholars in other fields or who are important originary figures within our general culture, as are Marx, Freud, Keynes, Dewey, and perhaps even Chomsky. One can even suggest that, barring the nonacademic Edmund Wilson and with the partial exception of Lionel Trilling, no literary critic has achieved the position of general cultural significance enjoyed, for example, by Reinhold Niebuhr from the 1930s to the 1960s. Of course, we must admit that it seems unlikely that our more technocratic society could ever again need a general intellectual[8] to elaborate the ruling class ideology as Niebuhr once did or as Croce did even more clearly in Italy.[9] But it seems strange that in an information-based society that relies increasingly on the manipulation of symbols, signs, and testing data to control and exploit political and economic opportunities—often to the detriment of less powerfully placed people at home and abroad—literary critics, those most thoroughly trained in and supposedly committed to the study of such semiotic processes, have not seriously taken up a position of opposition to their repressive use.[10]

Academic literary study is, in some ways, of very recent vintage[11] and appears destined to a short life. It may well go on for years as a self-renewing professionalized institution often can—despite its difficulties in reproducing. Perhaps all of the recent agony over and theorizing about the profession suggests that its contradictions and distortions have become so pressing as to leave its more anxious members little to absorb their energies except efforts to find what can at best be a merely verbal legitimation of their position and function. Of course there are those who feel no anxiety at all: these are either the habituated time-passers whose "common sense" keeps them going or the successful professionals who might be established figures in elite universities or well-funded specialists in composition and pedagogy. Of course, at times all of these shadows combine in one misty figure.[12]

A thorough and convincing explanation of how and why the legitimacy of academic literary study has come to require this professionalized apology would demand a very long story indeed. Now it is enough to remember the originary work of I. A. Richards and to recall how "practical" criticism cultivated the delicate sensitivity necessary to the fine art of balancing paradoxes and other forms of verbal instability in a pattern of critically resolved or suspended stress. We should remember that Richards called this cultivation "training in discrimination" and that as a form of professional and cultural specialization it contributed to the division of labor. We might also agree upon one result of this divisive training: it took critical thinking up into "lit. crit." Despite the New Criticism's antagonism toward "positivism," it is possible to argue that the assumption of criticism into "English Studies" corresponds to a renewal of positivist tendencies in the social sciences[13] and a reduction in its critical heritage.[14]

All variations on such an analysis would have to end by saying that eventually this division of intellectual labor, so easily institutionalized in the American bureaucratic university, helped produce an anemic institution largely bled of critical purpose by its isolation from the increasingly semiotic and informational cultural and political issues that, paradoxically, critics were best trained to analyze.[15]

Literary criticism's doubtful legitimacy can perhaps best be seen in the results of its persistent strategy: questing for the "new" as a way of reinvigorating and restoring itself. That this strategy is, itself, a sign of the decay of literary criticism out of the contradiction of its origins can be seen in any quick survey of its forms.[16] A very preliminary categorization suggests that contemporary literary critics can be divided into three groups by virtue of the differing relations of their practice and ideology to the active forces of anomie and repression in our civilization. In the first of these crude categories we find those who know not what they do when they ignore the anomalies of their professional and social situation and train their students—or hope to—in the no longer marketable skills of their own specialized paradigm. Such educators are functionaries of an ideology they do not perceive as such: they take their position to be natural and unquestionable, although mysteriously and sadly under attack. They grow depressed.

The second group is allied to the first: they are the priests of the dominant ideology engaged in defining its power and expanding its influence. They study the "crisis" of our culture and profession but do so only to reform the "flaws" and "misdirections" that have, as they see it, led to the loss of stability, order, values, and "common sense." They frequently mistake elements of the third group—if I may be allowed a prolepsis—for the *cause* of the crisis they perceive. They cannot seriously think through the idea that the questioning existence of those they call "radicals" or simply "barbarians"[17] indicates the real illegitimacy of the social organization and cultural values they defend or, in their fantasies, hope to "return to." The members of this second group are, of course, the ideological favorites of the first group, at least of those in the first group whose intellectual life has not ceased altogether. The first group values the high priests of the reaction just to the degree that the latter deny the importance of the questioners or find a way to domesticate them. Not surprisingly, often the priestly class sustains the tillers of the first group by misinforming them. Two of their functions, in clear words, are to simplify and to lie.

Of the third group—which is multifaceted—many descriptions might be offered. I am most interested in one feature that easily distinguishes this third group from the other two: its members often critically study the history and structure of intellectual language and practice to draw attention to its effects and to the traditional intellectuals' interest in playing certain roles. At times they go beyond even such critical history and suggest different kinds of language and work more likely to be of use, especially to others, in their struggles against power and domination.

Such critics try to invent new tactics to reduce the ease with which intellectuals can be taken back up into the hegemonic institutions that, in large part, have formed them. Because of this need to resist the "acceptable" forms of language and practice, critics of the third group often produce work others call "alienating," "elitist," "threatening," or simply "absurd." Of course much "theoretical" work in criticism and composition is simply narcissistic, obscure, or pretentious and prissy. But the simultaneous complaint that such "difficult" work—for which their leaders tell them they need "guides"—is (bizarrely) "reductive," "egotistical," hateful of literature, or "ideological" suggests how contradictory is the majority position.

This tripartite schema is very crude. It not only leaves out of account those "heroes," as Althusser calls them,[18] who work anonymously to alter the ideology and practice their institution embodies, but it also does not consider those (few) members of the first group who change, who are open to a discussion of issues, and who try to acquire the skills needed to see the social order around them and their professional function within it. Most important, however, is this schema's failure to describe how and to what extent the work of the third group is caught up in the dominant culture's defining practices and languages that are, taken together, precisely those realities that most make possible critical work. Needless to say, my categories would have to be refined to account for those whose work appears to place them in the third group but is actually merely subjective and sometimes exploitative private enunciation.

Of course, there is always the question of uniformity of views within each group. This question is an admirable extension of pluralistic[19] middle-class concerns for the individual as well as an important call for scholarly responsibility. Unfortunately, I cannot assume that responsibility here. Although specificity and precise detail are always crucial, I feel that in this case it is even more important to understand the role and ideology of contemporary literary critics by seeing how they represent and practice their intellectual functions. Within the third group this becomes a central question because one must make judgments on the relative effect of the various critiques and tactics suggested to resist and modify the ruling but illegitimate ideology of domination.

III

Any discussion of the role of the intellectual must begin with Gramsci who, recasting Marx's *The German Ideology,* best explains how the praxis of both the detached, disinterested mandarins and bureaucratic, technological functionaries supports the "hegemony" of the ruling class. Every emergent social group "creates together with itself, organically, one or more strata of intellectuals which give it homogeneity and an awareness of its own function not only in the economic but also in the social and political fields" (*PN, 5*). He goes on to suggest how useful this ideology is to the ruling class:

. . . every "essential" social group which emerges into history out of the preceding economic structure, and as an expression of a development of this structure, has found (at least in all history up to the present) categories of intellectuals already in existence and which seemed indeed to represent an historical continuity uninterrupted even by the most complicated and radical changes in political and social forms. . . . Since these various categories of traditional intellectuals experience through an *"esprit de corps"* their uninterrupted historical continuity and their special qualification, they thus put themselves forward as autonomous and independent of the dominant social group. (*PN*, 6–7)[20]

Gramsci's comments help us to see that modern idealism and American pragmatism have their historical origins in the social practice of traditional intellectuals whose misperception of their own "autonomy" legitimates their claims and actions and so their cultural force and value. In addition, this misprision blocks any investigation into the historical, social origins and positions of their own functions in society: they are, on this matter at least, ahistorical and nonreflexive. Since in literary study these idealist and pragmatic intellectuals are in a dominant position, I want to stress both this point about their blindness to the social origins of their beliefs[21] and the range of possible critiques that can be made of it. For example, when we invert what seems to be the direction of cause and effect, we discover, as Nietzsche had prefigured in *On the Genealogy of Morals*,[22] that to maintain their legitimacy these intellectuals must create a defense that blocks their own and others' investigations into their origins and purposes. In other words, in purely functional terms, traditional intellectuals are not and cannot be "autonomous" because to protect the illusion of their privilege and the structures it assures and depends upon they must rule out of play certain areas of investigation and so restrict the development of critical, especially political knowledge. (There are many ways in which they hinder others' research. Essentially they all come down to denying their legitimacy.[23]) It follows from this that idealist theories of knowledge are among the highest and most necessary defenses of such intellectual functions: the illusion of traditional intellectual autonomy "can be connected," Gramsci suggests, with "idealist philosophy" (*PN*, 8).[24] Habermas helps us to see how easily intellectuals tend toward an idealism: their social legitimacy depends upon the illusion of autonomy, and since, as Habermas insists, we make a validity or truth claim simply whenever we make an assertion, intellectuals can make legitimating representations of themselves (and their group's interests) only to the extent that they can claim them to be valid products of autonomous seekers after truth.[25]

Gramsci's concept of the intellectual corrects this representation in two ways: first, by referring all intellectual activity to "the ensemble of the system of relations in which these activities (therefore the intellectual groups who personify them) have their place within the general complex of social relations" (*PN,* 8); and, second, by reversing the division of labor:

The problem of creating a new stratum of intellectuals consists therefore in the critical elaboration of the intellectual activity that exists in everyone at a certain degree of development, modifying its relationships with the muscular-nervous effort towards a new equilibrium, and ensuring that the muscular-nervous effort itself, in so far as it is an element of a general practical activity, which is perpetually innovating the physical and social world, becomes the foundation of a new and integral conception of the world. (*PN,* 9)

Gramsci's notes are a valuable practical-historical formulation of the material power of intellectual activity in domination and resistance. More specifically, Gramsci helps us see the importance of education, especially humanistic education in the reproduction of the dominant mode of production in modern societies, that is, the mode of exploitation.[26] In the notes gathered as "The Study of Philosophy," Gramsci argues that it is mechanistic to believe that the unilinear succession of modes of production will lead inevitably to the revolutionary displacement of the bourgeoisie by the proletariat. This at-one-time historically necessary concept must be superseded by a more voluntarist model of social change that, especially in theorizing the party and the role of intellectuals, recognizes the cultural battleground of revolution.

The growing role of knowledge in social exploitation furthers the division of labor and, only seemingly paradoxically, reifies the potential for intellectual work. Intellectual functionaries are essential—especially if they are liberals—to the operation of the information-based and sign-oriented structures of our culture.[27] They are present at all levels of our bureaucratized society: "at the highest level," writes Gramsci, "would be the creators of the various sciences, philosophy, art, etc., at the lowest the most humble 'administrators' and divulgators of pre-existing, traditional accumulated intellectual wealth" (*PN,* 13). Following Weber and Marx and working along a parallel line to the Frankfurt School, Gramsci stresses the organizational nature of domination as a condition for understanding the key role of education, the development of what Alvin Gouldner and others call "cultural capital"[28] and the overproduction of intellectuals.[29]

The intellectual operation of the hegemonic organization requires a broad-based, humanistic education. But it also requires an elaborate structure of testing and tracking to elaborate "top intellectual qualifications" to distribute workers and rewards. The effect of this structure is to deny in practice what is claimed in theory: namely, the illusion of democratic access to and control of technology and high culture. The administrative hierarchy of education is a primary mechanism for subjugation and subjection, the reality of which should become obvious in its results: it promises access to and a share in the system, but also structurally "it creates the possibility of vast crises of unemployment for the middle-intellectual strata" (*PN*, 11). Gramsci goes on to draw the most important conclusion from his analysis of this structure: "The democratic-bureaucratic system has given rise to a great mass of functions which are not all justified by the social necessities of production, though they are justified by the political necessities of the dominant fundamental group" (*PN*, 13).

This means, of course, that the politics of culture is as important to revolutionary activity as the politics of economics. Culture, in other words, must be seen voluntaristically, as a mechanism for the defense of economic interest and political privilege. Not only does this insight imply that the battleground of political struggle must shift from that economic arena in which traditional Marxists are most accustomed to struggle, but it also implies that the politics of culture must, in large part, be a politics of the humanities, of the control of sign systems and their interpretation.[30]

Gramsci's analysis makes the inescapable claim that intellectuals are functionaries in class war. Humanistic discourses and practices, particularly those of philosophy and education, appear "above all as a cultural battle to transform the popular 'mentality'" (*PN*, 348). The aim of the hegemonic intellectuals is, in part through the middle-level functionaries, "to diffuse philosophical innovations which will demonstrate themselves to be 'historically true' to the extent that they become concretely—that is, historically and socially—universal" (*PN*, 348). The achievement of material and cultural priority ensures the "validity" of these concepts and the legitimacy of their practitioners.

The battle for domination depends upon the diffusion of organic intellectuals' concepts and their conflict with those of other groups. Another way of putting this is to say that language is an element in the political battle for hegemony—and, when put this way, it becomes clear how relevant Gramsci's remarks on the intellectual are to the practice of literary critics.

Gramsci's thinking about language begins from the American pragmatists and their Italian fellow-travelers. C. S. Peirce is especially important to Gramsci. Since the diffusion of philosophical concepts throughout society is essential to the establishment and maintenance of hegemony, "the question of language in general and of languages in the technical sense must be put to the forefront of our inquiry" (PN, 348). Gramsci modifies the Saussurian division between *langue* and *langage* in order to socialize and historicize the latter term especially: *langage* "is essentially a collective term. . . . Language also means culture and philosophy. . . . Culture, at its various levels, unifies in a series of strata, to the extent that they come into contact with each other, a greater or lesser number of individuals who understand each others' mode of expression in differing degrees" (PN, 349). Hegemony, then, is a function of language in its collective nature, or, as Gramsci puts it, "the general question of language" is "the question of collectively attaining a single cultural 'climate' " (PN, 349).

If culture is a question of language, as Gramsci suggests, and if hegemony and so politics is a question of culture diffused in and by language, then what shall we say is the role of the critic?[31] We can begin to answer this question by insisting that critical activity is more than "self-reflexivity," as many liberals would like to believe.[32] It should be always the dialectical reconsideration of concepts and methods based on the problems posed to criticism by the cultural environment. Critical education cannot be what it often sets out to be: the reproduction in the new generation of the knowledge, skills, values, and position of the predecessors and teachers.[33] Not only do many objective conditions, in fact, prevent this traditional form of educational reproduction, but such reproduction is inappropriate to the critical enterprise: critical training should produce an intellectual, not restricted, except tactically, to ironic negation,[34] who constantly thematizes his or her work as a practical process of creating cultural unity.[35] Such intellectual work can emerge only from what Gramsci calls the "liberty of thought," which, in turn, requires knowledge gained in resistance to the hegemonic censorship of alternative concepts. Without such resistance, a positive political critique cannot be produced. From a Gramscian point of view we must say that all such critiques have one essential condition: a recognition of what we might call the "interface" between philosophy (conceived as the highest form of articulated humanistic knowledge) and history. With this recognition as a point of departure, a new kind of critic is possible: one "convinced that his [or her] personality is not limited to himself [or herself] as a physical individual but is an active social relationship of modification of the cultural environment"³⁶ (*PN*, 350).

Were literary critics to take Gramsci seriously, they would carry out a thorough critique of the basic paradigms of literary education and especially its relation to the university.³⁷ They would, in addition, attempt to reconstruct that education along different lines. Such a critique would have to begin with an institutional history of "lit. crit." as an aspect in the reproduction of the hegemony of modern technological and cybernetic societies.³⁸ Critics would also consider what real social needs comparatively marginal figures like R. Blackmur and F. O. Matthiessen record and address in their work. In addition, one would have to judge the elements worth preserving in such hegemonic figures as I. A. Richards, W. K. Wimsatt, and Lionel Trilling.³⁹ In other words, taking Gramsci seriously would involve recasting critical studies so that they would engage constantly in dialectical self-revision and develop research strategies to study the ways in which the interrelated cultural strata of a society produce hegemonic and counterhegemonic representations in texts and other discursive systems.

A history of critical intellectual discourse and pedagogy might show, for example, that "lit. crit." institutionalized as "practical criticism" is one aspect of a disciplinary society that produces individuals who make themselves available to surveillance.⁴⁰ John Fekete has rightly suggested Richards's involvement with the defense of bourgeois interests and has begun an analysis of practical criticism's functionalism. His analysis might be extended, however, to trace the affiliations of practical criticism with not only the functionalist anthropology of Malinowksi but also with the sociology of Parsons and the proto-fascist elitism of Pareto.⁴¹ Alvin Gouldner details just how, in its various forms, functionalism practically and ideologically defends the bourgeoisie during and after the crises of World War I and the Great Depression.[42]

Reading Richards and practical criticism after Foucault illuminates the specific ways in which the newly institutionalized "lit. crit." implements the functionalist project. Most important, such a reading shows how practical criticism creates the "reader" as an object of knowledge positioned by its discourse and pedagogy to be subjected and subjugated to discriminating training. In Gramsci's terms, we might say that "lit. crit." is a way of intervening in civil society to enable a mass interiorization of self-disciplining techniques derived from the structure of the classroom and the values and exercise of the student theme or protocol. We could justly extend our sketch to implicate the basic concepts of the American New Criticism. We would see, for example, why the New Critics so valued irony and the image: in their assertion of the priority of these aesthetic qualities in modern theories of the text and critical reading, the New Critics simply enacted the turn away from historical reflection that might have made their discipline less effective as a defense of the hegemonic order. As we have seen from Gramsci's work, historically reflexive thinkers (like Croce) become aware of their own social and political function and become either oppositional or idealistic intellectuals. In their elaborate ironic readings the New Critics enacted the turn toward idealism that remains the dominant mode of North American literary criticism.[43]

III

Gramsci does not fully develop a theoretical model of how societies and their institutions survive, so we are left with our specific problem: how can the institution of "criticism" modify itself to regain its critical purpose. The essentially liberal and idealist emphasis on self-criticism, on "reflexivity,"[44] is by itself inadequate: it is a necessary but not sufficient attitude. At best it testifies to the existence of demanding problems within the intellectual, cultural environment and the felt desire for change. Gramsci does not tell us directly how the capacity for nonalienated, positive, nonspecialized criticism might develop nor how it will produce and disseminate a new ideological counterhegemonic unity throughout culture. But from Gramsci's theory of cultural politics and his notes on the intellectual we can learn how to set a direction for theorizing the adaptability of cultural institutions: each successive crisis in the development of society requires an available reserve of cultural capital, a capacity to reorganize the institutions of language and discourse to control and regulate the forces of production to legitimate and nonrepressive ends.

As Gramsci sees it, counterhegemonic forces always need an institutional structure to direct resistance and to reorganize the cultural possibilities of an old into a new and emergent society. For Gramsci, the vanguard party was the vehicle that would give political direction to the forces reorganizing economic and cultural production.[45] The party would serve this function because only it can produce the kind of intellectual able to lead the opposition to capitalist hegemony: "leaders and organisers of all the activities and functions inherent in the organic development of an integral society" (*PN*, 16). But it is precisely the role Gramsci assigns to the intellectual that suggests we should rethink the party's priority in his work.

In his post-1968 work, Foucault criticized the figure of the representative intellectual who might "speak for" and "lead" the "masses" as a potentially antidemocratic abuse of power. In what we might call "the structure of speaking for" the operations of power extend domination by making what is "known" into an object of science and an instrument of discipline.[46] Such "speaking for," we might say, reactivates the ideology of privileged subjects, points of view, and forms of language; it empowers certain determinations of will.[47] Foucault suggests that democratic forms require that the "representative intellectual" give way as a "representation" of intellectual authority and be displaced by the counter-image of the "specific intellectual." The latter, Foucault argues, always struggles against power locally, on a particular terrain, and does so in order both to sap and, if possible, to take power.

I have argued elsewhere[48] that one task awaiting the critic as specific intellectual is to reveal genealogically the role of the humanistic discourses in the formation and maintenance of dominant ideologies in Modern and Postmodern cultures. The genealogically trained specific intellectual can contribute an analysis of institutional discourses as these extend the disciplining power (which functions—at any given time—primarily in the interest of dominant groups) throughout an imperialist society and so the international order.

If Foucault is to be useful in refocusing these issues in Gramsci, one must keep in mind that after *The Order of Things* (1966) he thematizes neither the end of the subject nor the image of a new subject—much less a "method" to produce one. While the absence of such speculation might open Foucault to the charge that he undervalues the "utopian" element in culture or forms of resistance on the part of the oppressed, it more importantly, I think, allows him to cast off the traditional intellectual's assumption of responsibility for imagining alternative subjectivities and take up the task of the specific intellectual.[49] Such an intellectual must attempt to produce critical tools of use to those—on a national, local, or international level—who struggle against power as it subjugates them within constitutive systems of knowledge.

To be sure, these remarks inadequately represent both Foucault and his critics, but they do suggest one important democratizing modification of Gramsci's Leninist sense that the party alone can produce "leaders and organisers of all the activities and functions inherent in the organic development of an integral society" (*PN*, 16). A Foucauldian critique of this Gramscian figure would reveal its continuity with the often antidemocratic figure of the leading or representative intellectual to be found throughout high bourgeois, humanistic as well as bureaucratic professional practice and ideology. "The intellectual," Foucault writes, "spoke the truth to those who had yet to see it, in the name of those who were forbidden to speak the truth: he was conscience, consciousness, and eloquence." Foucault concluded, on the basis of his analysis of May '68 and the development of new forms of political resistance outside the working class and the Party—for example, environmentalists, gay rights, minority, and womens' movements[50]—that these specific Western struggles—and this is a temporarily necessary limit to the analysis here—no longer need traditional intellectuals "to gain knowledge" or produce representations (*LCMP*, 207). We might say that Foucault's theory, in contrast to Gramsci's, holds that the historical specificity of a high-tech, information-based society, in which even the most advanced industrial economies are subject to the operation of the law of value, needs not "organic" intellectuals to provide leadership but specific intellectuals to provide expertise and to decode and control the discourses and technologies dominant in such a society. Foucault derives his claim that traditional or leading intellectuals are antidemocratic "agents of this system of power" from many historical and contemporary factors, but it especially depends upon and reveals the fact that these newer forms of political resistance arrogate to themselves responsibility for knowledge and consciousness in structures outside the "leadership" of both traditional and organic intellectuals. They are to a great extent "self-informing" and aspire to be "self-determining." Consequent on the democratic possibilities present in these new political forms, Foucault offers the specific intellectual a new project: to name, reveal, and undermine the anonymous and obscure (although immediately present) operations of power as they negate such democratic possibilities.

Unlike Gramsci and, as we shall see, unlike Habermas, for Foucault, the intellectual's work must be regional and technical, specific and not totalizing; its aim is "to sap power, to take power" (*LCMP*, 208), not to represent others or bring enlightenment. Gramsci, we must remember, had insisted that "the new stratum of intellectuals" will lead to "a new and integral conception of the world" (*PN*, 9). While Foucault does not accept the leadership role assigned by Gramsci to the "organic" intellectual, his theory of the "specific" intellectual does coincide with the Italian's in one all-important regard, namely, in its stress on the way intellectuals join the service of the "truth of the collectivity" (*LCMP*, 208) by struggling against the forms of power.

In other words, the aim of Gramsci and Foucault, and, as I shall suggest, of Habermas as well, is to theorize (albeit in very different ways) an intellectual capable of practical political action against domination.[51] In post-'68 France, given the association of the PCF with the State and the critiques by Derrida and others of Foucault's own "representational" project in *Histoire de le Folie* (1961), Foucault was obliged to move away from both his own earlier problematic intellectual role as "archaeologist" as well as from Althusser's party.[52] After May '68 Foucault was able to say that Deleuze teaches "us something absolutely fundamental: the indignity of speaking for others" (*LCMP*, 209). This self-revising statement, which moves Foucault away from the position of the representative intellectual implicit in his study of madness, can be seen as also a turn away from the Gramscian project. The positive element in such a revision is clear: we must draw the conclusion from that position metonymically associated with "Deleuze" and "appreciate the theoretical fact that only those directly concerned can speak in a practical way on their own behalf" (*LCMP,* 209). While it may be that, as some like Gayatri Spivak have tried to argue,[53] this model of "self-representation" effectively reimposes Western forms of subjugation upon the third world in the process of theorizing it, it should be kept in mind that Foucault's idea is, in itself, a challenge to the often Gramsci-like position from which these critiques come. Even Gramsci's organic intellectual, we recall, spoke for "his" class (and the term was often gender-specific in Gramsci) only from the basis of a complexly elaborated universalist position which grounded the considerable specific analysis that needed to be done.[54]

The practical project Foucault's work suggests could take the form of a demanding inquiry into the genealogy, affiliations, ideology, and structures of the institutions that form our critics—one that not only deployed already existing categories of critical thought but was able to invent new ones useful to the struggle to redirect critical energies. The interventions of the specific critical intellectual into the humanistic institutions of power should be aligned with the forms of resistance of those subjugated by the operations of power as they work (almost entirely—despite their Reaganaut and Thatcherite populisms) in the interest of the dominant groups. Foucault's metaphor, drawn from the ideals of third-world nationalist struggles, has been too much sullied by first world terrorism to be easily used,[55] but the democratic sense behind it bears being recalled: specific intellectuals must be like guerrillas struggling with appropriate groups resisting on the local terrain of their domination. The object is "to attack an institution at the point where it culminates and reveals itself in a simple and basic ideology, in the notions of good and evil, innocence and guilt" (*LCMP,* 228). Despite the contrast between Foucault's concept of the "specific" intellectual and Gramsci's of the "organic" intellectual, the former's thinking does let us appreciate, in a slightly new light, both the values and limits of Gramsci's thought on this matter. It highlights one not-quite-so-Leninist aspect of Gramsci's thought: we can see that the concept of the "organic intellectual" not only demystifies the illusory role of the traditional intellectual, but in so doing it also potentially clarifies and approaches the recognition of the need for oppressed peoples to speak for themselves, to be allowed access to the acoustical systems, which, as Regis Debray might put it,[56] would allow them to direct their own cultures and to legitimate their subjectivities in resisting the subjugation of dominant discourses.

In theory, the association of the "organic" intellectuals with the bureaucracy of the vanguard party should not deny this need; but, as Gramsci develops the concept of the "organic" intellectual in relation to the intellectual potential of all human beings, it does tend, nonetheless, to reserve dialectical critical thinking to an elite representing the interests of the class in modifying the social environment. Although Gramsci insists that all human beings are intellectuals (*PN*, 9), his programmatic writing sometimes strikes a different and disturbing chord: "In the modern world technical education . . . must form the basis of the new type of intellectual" (*PN*, 9). Gramsci's theoretical commitment to the idea that all humans are intellectuals gives way to his political sense that resistance and the formation of a new hegemony require a leading elite, trained in science and other forms of technically advanced managerial disciplines. This idea is not the same as that of the "specific" intellectual because such technological "organic" intellectuals provide not only leadership in directing the movement of the masses as they develop through education in the party toward socialism, but they become, in themselves, the form and model of intellectual life per se. As I have already suggested, it is not only Foucault who is suspicious of the political consequences of this line of thought. Bahro, Konrad, Szelenyi, and Habermas have also made the point. But Foucault is particularly useful in suggesting how the possibility for reinscribing domination through the effects of knowledge and representation inhere even in the political structures of this organic model.[57]

Foucault's post-'68 conception of critical practice is more modest than that proposed by Gramsci. It is certainly less utopian than that suggested by Habermas or a number of American critics influenced by Anglo-American philosophical interest in consensus-making.[58] Foucault quite rightly insists that critical thinking should produce texts and analyses that name both the forms of knowledge and institutions through which power is brought to bear, especially as it operates in the interest of the hegemonic. But this critical practice can occur only alongside the other actions of those struggling in their own ways to sap regulating power on a local level. Gramsci has brilliantly seen that if the intellectual is to be conceptualized, the technical intelligentsia's role in the extension of state and civil oppression must be elaborated. But perhaps even this subtlety does not catch the manifold forms of power as it extends throughout society and across different societies in the structures of imperialism and neocolonialism. It remains tied to an essentially hierarchical model of bureaucracy linking civil society and the state, to a basically macroscopic conception of oppression that, above all, fails to consider the complexities of power-knowledge in disciplining society to maintain its own subjectivity—a process that, of course, has consequences far beyond the limits of Western national boundaries.[59] One might follow the implications of both Foucault and Althusser and suggest that Gramsci remains, on this point, and despite his critique of imperialism, within the modernist metaphysical concept of a transpersonal subject. On this matter at least, Foucault's analyses of Western disciplinary practices for constituting the subject within the microphysics of power suggest that Gramsci's work locates itself on the periphery of the dominant discourse of disciplinary subjugation.[60]

Foucault's work on this point suggests that the critical project cannot be restricted to the dialectical debate with the social environment, which essentially is what Gramsci proposes. But the project must also take on the genealogical burden of aggressively inquiring into the institutionalized discursive foundations of key concepts, figures, and their effects in the various modalities of power that create and sustain them. It would, in other words, mean giving a new seriousness and direction to Gramsci's notion of doing an "inventory" of the self.

In other words, Foucault's work extends Gramsci's insight into the centrality of language in social organization by stressing the necessity for the oppressed to speak for themselves, to produce their own representations, their own "subjectivities" "outside" the reach of subjugation or in resistance to it. While such a claim does not diminish the importance of the intellectual, especially of the critical intellectual struggling against an increasingly semiotic structure of dominance, it does change the intellectuals' role. It suggests that intellectuals recognize that others can struggle to create their own subjectivity independently of intellectuals' power to produce representations and, indeed, try to gain control of the knowledge-producing apparatus of subjugation in order to be independent of it. Critical action can not only disclose and undermine the discourse of oppression, but it can open space to help others form their own subjectivities in opposition to the discursive and institutional definitions generated and affixed by dominant structures and their agents.

Habermas insists that such social subjectivities can emerge only in a space where meaningful and undistorted communication is possible. He follows Weber in two important ways: a critical concern for the anomie of public institutions and a distrust of the party's claim that the state seizure of power will end class divisions. As a result, Habermas sees certain tendencies in modernity and especially postmodernity as a retreat from rationality, or, as he puts it, as *"an outbreak of new contingencies."*[61] Simply put, Habermas's project stresses that history is developmental and that successful societies produce intersubjectively "recognized norms or *rules of communicative action*" regulating the economic and cultural "distribution of products" (HM, 132). Habermas complements earlier revisionists of historical materialism by emphasizing the importance of rules for instrumental and strategic action in this distribution. He goes so far as to assert that development of the forms of production depends, in large part, upon intersubjective communicative norms. (Unfortunately, this causes Habermas to be sympathetic to certain pragmatist moments in the conservative liberalism of Richard Rorty.) Different societies, of course, organize themselves differently, and Habermas wants to conclude from this that "unilinear" Marxist models cannot account for these various forms of organization (HM, 139). One might extend Habermas's argument into areas of imperialism and theories of colonial and neocolonial resistance; but Habermas himself refuses to do this.[62]

Habermas himself, however, is concerned to argue that Modern Western societies cannot generate norms of intersubjective communication. His complex argument can only be briefly summarized: rules of intersubjective communication regulate the "specific forms of social intercourse, that is, the relations of production," but since these "express the distribution of social power . . . they prejudge the interest structure of a society" (HM, 138–39). In modern capitalist societies, Habermas concludes, such rules can only maintain economically exploitative relations (HM, 103). In Postmodern societies, we might say (elaborating on Habermas's thinking), the primacy of science, technology, and education in the organization of the socioeconomic system means the central problem is that of the relationship between society and what Habermas calls "internal nature" (HM, 165). And with this concern, Habermas converges with Foucault and suggests yet another necessary dimension for critical intelligence in Postmodernity: the critique of administrative attempts to produce and control motivation and meaning in a culture made anomic by the difficulties of generating and sustaining nonsubjugating intersubjective rules for communicative action and resistance. Habermas would have it that we must develop public-sphere institutions while always recalling the distinction between the idea of their necessity, that is, the idea of democracy, and the formation of institutions that allow that democracy to exist.[63]

Foucault has already contributed substantially to our understanding of how power has formed and disciplined the western subject to maintain domination. For Habermas, the intensifying (Western) transition from a classical, economically based illegitimacy to an information-based one would involve an intensification of those kinds of techniques Foucault has in part analyzed: "In a future form of class-domination," Habermas writes, "softened and at the same time intensified, to sociopsychological coercion, 'domination' . . . would be refracted a second time, not through bourgeois civil war, but through the educational system of the social welfare state" (HM, 166). (It would also require extending this project to include questions of imperialism and gender.) Habermas envisages a chaotically vicious cycle of struggle "between expanded participation and increasing social administration" (HM, 166).[64] He pessimistically concludes this line of thought with a vision of the end of social evolution: "The structural scarcity of meaning" would in itself prevent the development of social adaptation. Learning would end, killed by subjugating representation. Societies could no longer form adequate motivations. Limits and contingencies—which Habermas associates with the Postmodern— would increasingly appear as society failed to regulate communicatively its own relation to internal reality.[65] We might say that, for Habermas, the guerrilla-like struggle to sap power so that the oppressed might speak for themselves is only one element in what one might call "an analytics of dissolution." Or, as I have tried to suggest elsewhere, we see that this line of thought brings Habermas to the point of calling seriously into question the adequacy of any critical practice that identifies itself solely with negation.[66] No doubt such a denial also, at one time, brought Habermas to charge indiscriminately that Foucault and Derrida "on the basis of modernistic attitudes . . . justify an irreconcilable anti-modernism."[67]

Momentarily putting aside Habermas's defense of enlightenment reason[68] lets us develop a sense of what might be the composite aim of critical work today: Critical intelligence involves a demystification of intellectuals' sense of their independence, a constant genealogical self-criticism, and research into specific discourses and institutions as part of the struggle against forms of oppressive power, forms of surplus-value extraction—if one talks about the international question in those terms. Yet critical intelligence should be all this with an eye to the possibility that such critique, in our time, may not get beyond an increasingly anomic struggle against more subtle but more powerful forms of domination and allocation of motive and meaning—especially within the worlds of Western intellectuals. This means, inter alia, that Western intellectuals must confront the historicity of the current surplus of ideological production as an essential condition both of right-wing authoritarianism and of the general critical inability to understand and destroy the system that depends upon that surplus as well.

Critical research should operate in this complex of problems because they are some of the issues that demand attention in our culture. They are increasingly linguistic-based problems of ideology and representation. They touch more and more the ability of intellectuals marginal to the dominant group and of subaltern groups to speak, to be heard, and to understand the discursive relation of the psyche or "internal nature" to society. If literary study affiliates itself with these other modes of critical work, not only will the profession and institution be modified, but perhaps it will also help ease the shortage of critical intelligence in a society now so easily manipulated by the image-producing agencies of politics and corporations.

CHAPTER THREE

Notes Toward a Politics of "American" Criticism

It is certain that they [American industrialists] are not concerned with the "humanity" or the "spirituality" of the worker, which are immediately smashed. This "humanity and spirituality" cannot be realised except in the world of production and work and in productive "creation." They exist most in the artisan, in the "demiurge," when the worker's personality was reflected whole in the object created and when the link between art and labour was still very strong. But it is precisely against this "humanism" that the new industrialism is fighting. "Puritanical" initiatives simply have the purpose of preserving, outside of work, a certain psychophysical equilibrium which prevents the physiological collapse of the worker, exhausted by the new method of production. This equilibrium can only be something purely external and mechanical, but it can become internalised if it is proposed by a new form of society, with appropriate and original methods. . . . It is in their [American industrialists] interests to have a stable, skilled labour force, a permanently well-adjusted complex, because the human complex (the collective worker) of an enterprise is also a machine which cannot, without considerable loss, be taken to pieces too often and renewed with single new parts.

—Antonio Gramsci, *The Prison Notebooks*

ﻙﻥﻁ **O**ne should never write in the abstract about the nature of "oppositional criticism." "Criticism" of any sort must always be concrete and specific no matter how theoretically informed. "Oppositional criticism," particularly, cannot be defined or theorized so much as it must be enacted. Only because academic criticism is carried out so often in a professionally and institutionally social space could one even imagine a "general theoretical discussion" of "oppositional criticism." Whenever oppositional critical work is done, it is always specifically placed (conjunctural) and so cannot be treated as a matter of "theory" rather than as the concrete form of practice it must be to be itself. Furthermore, if, as R. P. Blackmur always had it, criticism is a social gesture, highly contextualized, or "overdetermined," then it cannot be "defined" or "debated"; it cannot be "represented" except by and as an enactment, a "dramatization"—in Blackmur's word—that engages specifically with the object of its critique. There are several reasons why "oppositional criticism" must be enacted rather than abstractly "theorized." Most important among them is the fact that the "profession" has an uncanny ability to adopt its seemingly most stringent critics by recycling their values and methods, transforming them into new "fashions" for replication and reward. That this could be the fate of "oppositional criticism"—if the notion is taken up in the abstract and made merely the subject of articles without consequence—no one should doubt. The genealogy of the "oppositional" makes it readily available for such recirculation.[1] "Oppositional criticism" should not be confused with an attitude of generalized dissatisfaction with the profession or the culture; it is not merely a weak effect of alienation and commodification. It should, I think, be differentiated from any proverbial articulation of attitudes toward values, institutions, and "life situations"; one thinks here of a tradition that extends from Kenneth Burke to Wayne Booth.[2] Nor does "oppositional criticism" train us to see literature as a way better to deal with the problems of modern life.

To catch something of the force of an "oppositional critical" act, one must first of all see it as an act and in action; one must see it engaging critically with some element of the empowered structure of the society and culture against which it takes up its stance. One must see it not as just a "force for change and betterment" but as a relentless even if sometimes admiring but implacable agonism, as an indecorous enemy if you will. One cannot, therefore, speak merely generally to the topic "what would 'oppositional criticism' of American literature and culture be"; one must "instantiate" that criticism for, in its "oppositional" position, it cannot exist as a series of generalities, of prescriptive statements laying out a program, method, or set of "values." We cannot forget that Marx and Nietzsche teach intellectual warfare: Critical instruments are weapons—even for those who argue so hard to deny the fact—especially so despite the ease with which many professionals concede the fact. "Oppositional criticism" can be found only at those places where these weapons are brought to bear on just the entrenched values, interests, and practices

of professionals and institutions important to the academy and so to
its effects upon and roles within the larger socius.

It is with these thoughts in mind that I give attention in the following pages to some of the work of Sacvan Bercovitch. His institutional
distinction and his critical ambition bring him to attention as a figure
to interrogate if one wants to mark some of the limits and possibilities
of the criticism of "American literature."[3] Pointing to some of these
limits and possibilities helps develop an image of "Americanist" criticism as emerging from a set of assumptions, values, practices, technologies, institutions, and languages—all relatively systematic, all
interrelated—that suggest a link between a certain kind of rationality
and certain more material, historical interests of a sort that need to
be opposed for the political consequences of their link with that rationality. They need to be opposed if the possibility of a different order and organization of knowledge, self, and society is to be recalled
and perhaps made possible.

II

Never before has so much of the study of "American" literature
and culture been as critical of the classical forms of "American" writing and the dominant forms of "American" society as it is now. Bercovitch puts the matter succinctly when he says that the new
generation of "Americanists" does not separate the "America of the
spirit, represented by our classic writers, from the realities of American life, represented by ideologues and their victims."[4] Of course, in
this day and age, the right wing does not want for followers who
might challenge this "New Americanist" critical history.[5] The conservatives quite precisely bemoan the "New Americanists'" double
ideological challenge: to the established disciplinary, discursive procedures that, in fact, depend upon the separation of the two forms of
representation Bercovitch names and to the liberal, pluralist ideology
that that discipline's discourse reproduces and distributes in a normalizing relationship to the State and the constantly "new society"
produced by "American" capitalism.

Everyone now knows the names of the books and critics that the
profession feels have broken open the canon of "American" literature

and reformed the ways in which that literature and its place in "American" cultural history is to be thought about.[6] Most agree that feminist revisions of history and feminist readings—including concerns with literacy—as well as objections to the "androcentric"[7] discourse of "American" studies itself, have done most to reorganize the production of knowledge about our culture. Feminism has shown how women and their writing have been excluded from and by the valued realm of the "classic" and so extended the hermeneutics of suspicion to the term itself. In the process, an entire body of literary and cultural production has been recovered from the historical amnesia enforced even by such generously powerful texts as *American Renaissance*,[8] and they have helped us to understand the power structures and determinative effects of the gender bias of "American Studies'" discourses themselves. In addition, of course, recovering the work of "scribbling women" has paradigmatically helped us understand how polymorphous, how differentiated, how filled with resistance and alternative forms of creation the once apparent monolith of "American literature and culture" has always been.

Feminism, of course, has not been alone in this remaking of "American Studies." The new attention to minority—black, Hispanic, and Amerindian—writings has drawn our attention to the international nature of our history, to its founding involvements with other cultures of Africa and Latin America, as well as to our society's long history of extermination and imperial aggression. In the reading of black women's writing, many critics feel that the questions of class, race, and gender can be uniquely studied to get a clear sense of the workings of powerful, authoritative, and complex structures of oppression and resistance.

It would seem, in other words, that in the very recent past, "Americanists" have come far toward meeting Edward W. Said's definition, more than a decade old, of real oppositional criticism: it must be "actively generated out of a genuine historical research," and it must be "ultimately fixed for its goals upon understanding, analyzing, and contending with the management of power and authority within the culture."[9] There is now enough critical energy being devoted to critiques of the origins of "American liberalism" in relation to the "self" in laissez-faire economics that we have no fear that the relations—

sometimes oppositional, sometimes supportive—of our literary masters to the often awful forms of "American" political and social life will ever be forgotten.

Jonathan Arac has said that Sacvan Bercovitch's *American Jeremiad* should make it impossible for anyone to use easily the word *America*.[10] And, indeed, obsolete as well as neoconservatives agree that the "New Americanists"—perhaps like the flag burners of whom we have recently heard so much—have no respect for the achievements of "American" culture and society. Often these conservatives disguise themselves as pluralists.[11] And as "pluralists" they are often challenged, in turn, by ideology critique and by historicist recoveries of the "real differences" that exist within but are often forgotten by the recorders of "American" culture. For the most part, though, the future of "American" criticism of "American" literature and culture seems secure; we are, in a way, talking of generational change here, and the future, of course, belongs to the young.

III

Bercovitch suggests some of the problems and possibilities in the New Americanism: "America" has a habit of making it new, and although making it new—through ideology critique or historical recovery or whatever powerful critical device—cannot be trusted to provide us with any way out of the wilderness of the "American" ideology, it can move us toward "an alternative future" (A, 439). Summarizing his sense of the value of the essays collected in *Ideology and Classic American Literature,* Bercovitch is unusually optimistic: "I would like to think . . . that among these ["the richness of the problems at issue, the methodological and practical challenges involved in these inquiries"] is the challenge of alternative ways of intellectual, moral, and political commitment" (A, 439). Bercovitch clearly *would like to think.* . . . But what are the problems that lead Bercovitch to express this relatively minimal (and desperate) desire in the face of his critical intellectual analysis—an analysis that suggests quite precisely the opposite outcome to this "New Americanism"?

Bercovitch remains interesting because—from the center of the profession, as it were—he so clearly and usefully lists what he takes to be the definitive problems molesting any "Americanist" critical

project. As he puts the issues they do seem compelling; that he sees
them molesting even the authoritative work of the brightest "New
Americanists" gathered in his volume attests to the gravity of the issues in his vision and to the compulsive force of his final expression
of desire. Yet the problems he imagines are not the final problems.
Were we to mistake them for the most basic problems, we would lead
ourselves to two unsatisfactory results: a persistent concern with the
epiphenomenal that would be always preliminary to an "American"
criticism; or, more dangerously, to institutionalizing a politically and
aesthetically reductive model of critical practice. We would replicate
the already established discipline by not querying its precise genealogical, discursive relations—even in its "oppositional" moments—
to the state, to the dominant forms of rationality, and to the institutions of "American" culture. In other words, and to put the matter
crudely, to take Bercovitch's problems as "radical" would allow us to
avoid describing, theorizing, politicizing, and where possible, resisting and reorganizing the forms and institutions that treat "American" literature and culture as a "subject" of knowledge. That is to
say—and still too simply—Bercovitch's are problems of "content,"
of the "representations" "within" ideology, problems of "consciousness" that can be dealt with in "reforming" modes, by adjustment
and adjudication within the ongoing terms and institutions of
"American Studies," "American" culture, and the "American" state.
His "problems" are not radical precisely because they do not and cannot lead to a new set of rationalities and practices or to a new politics.
He can merely imagine the possibility that some "Truly New Alternatives" will emerge from the regular oscillation of Old/New that
makes up the jeremiad of "American" politics.

But how can one reasonably believe in this "possibility" or practice
a discipline whose forms of rationality allow for such imaginings? I
do not ask this question to object that Bercovitch seems to offer neither a plan for bringing it about nor a theory of agency that would
account for the desire. I ask it, rather, to draw attention to the fact
that one can believe in this possibility only if one accepts Bercovitch's
theory of "consensus" and "dissensus" formation—in other words,
his model of inner and outer, self and other, old and new—a model
of rationality we should all recognize as problematic. In other words,
one must first accept this possibility as such, even as utopian desire;

and that acceptance depends, in turn, upon working within an institution and discourse that aligns a form of reason and forms of power in ways that allow individuals to speak of these matters that determine what "American" literature and "American" critics can and might be. Michel Foucault's forceful phrase comes to mind: one must accept the "regime of truth"—in any or all of its variations—to be in a realm where what is thoughtful about Bercovitch's "Americanist" vision and project makes any sense. (The hidden question, of course, is, does one want to be in this regime, and if so, why?)

Bercovitch, as always, puts the matter eloquently, reasonably, and lucidly:

The option [for "American" critics] is not multiplicity or consensus. It is whether to make use of the categories of the culture or to be used by them. I do not claim that the essays here altogether avoid the peculiar cultural traps embedded in the quest for "America," in either its multiple or its unitary guises. Indeed, I am aware that what at the start of this Afterword I called a dialogue in the making has itself the makings, *in potentia,* of still another example of the special genius of the rhetoric of American consensus, which is to co-opt the energies of radicalism: to reabsorb the very terms of opposition into the promise of the New, that long-nurtured vision of Futurity that carries us forever back, through a procession of sacred landmarks . . . to the ideological premises of modern democratic liberalism. I am aware, too, that some of the central concerns . . . may be even more problematic than their treatments in this volume suggest. (A, 438–39)

If Bercovitch seriously means that critics must either "make use of the categories of the culture or . . . be used by them," he repeats an authoritative blunder that restricts "criticism" to endless repetition. It would be interesting to ask how it came to be possible that Bercovitch could put the matter in terms of this unquestioned dualism. For a moment, let us rather think of some of the consequences of what he has allowed himself to say: We have to imagine that critics—and all others, intellectuals in their own work, wherever that might be—are either always nothing more than the unquestioning agents of already inscribed categories or that somehow what privileges critics, indeed establishes their identity *as such,* is their ability to escape this determination and, by means of the knowledge of the categories, no doubt acquired through the practice of the "Americanist" discourse, not only rise above them but put them to some use—a use that in itself transcends, is outside, the ideological realm made up and disseminated by those very categories. But we have seen that Bercovitch's claims cannot be taken seriously without wondering what it is that allows him to propose such a simple opposition. Training as an "Americanist," as a "cultural critic" of his sort would not provide the grounds for choosing not to be a victim "of" the culture's categories. So what would be the source of the values and desires that would direct the operation of this critical use of the categories and where would they originate if not also in and from the ideologies and powers of these "Americanist" discourses? And why assume that these discourses provide a set of possibilities to "use" rather than "be used" when the correlations between this discourse and its culture have not yet been made clear? Why assume that these categories have any liberating possibilities at all when, as we see them at work in Bercovitch's "oppositional" practice, they allow him to deceive himself about the "freedom" he has to choose the model he proposes? To put it simply, what would be the source of this free critic's authority and whence such a critic?

So let us not quibble with Bercovitch's formulation; he certainly could not mean it if he thought more about it. Let us rather ask what it means that the thought was available to him, or rather, that, in this context, he felt it desirable to enact such an emprisoning representation of critical possibility—in direct contradiction to his voiced desire.

One can find a partial explanation for the appearance of this representation in the logic that interweaves Bercovitch's own professional, institutional position and the discourse of "American Studies." A detailed placing of that discourse is beyond the reach and purpose of this essay; but it is clear enough to say that it allowed Bercovitch to choose to study the "jeremiad" as a "cooptation" theory of "American" radicalism whereby all challenges to the "American" consensus shatter in the face of "America's" rhetorical, political uniqueness: "to reabsorb the very terms of opposition into the promise of the New." Donald Pease has laid out the consequences of this position.[12] Bercovitch's view of "America" as a "jeremiad," as a cultural machine for producing political "consensus," makes him suspicious of all critical claims to begin again, to stand outside the terms of debate. The logic of this suspicion, so the argument goes, is that one must postulate the possibility of being within that culture in order knowingly to use its very categories against itself. (The only other alternative—one Bercovitch does not examine—is to offer something "really new," which is itself, precisely, just the latest, empowered version or transformation of what has always come before.) The paradox is that we are to assume that this is a potential of the very same device that manufactures consensus, but we know it cannot be so; in fact, the user of a culture's categories must emerge as the specular alternative to the dominant forms of "America," as its ghastly (spiritual) other, somehow "in the world," as the Church Fathers would have it, but equally somehow not "of the world." In critical terms, we would say that not to be used by the culture means being beyond or outside it. This is what we sometimes call metaphysics, and it is a problem that theory has spent considerable time dealing with over the past twenty years.[13] It is also a problem that, cast in these terms, cannot be taken seriously in that no one can ever be "free" of the order of rationality of the time or of that order's relations—as technologies and practices, as intermediate rules of social combination—to the largest orders of power in a society.[14]

Bercovitch's institutional power and scholarly, critical decorum—the style of his writing and career—make him "representative" within "American Studies." At this moment, one can best see much of what "American Studies" traditionally allows one to choose to be as a critic by reading as closely as possible the work of precisely its most accomplished and thoroughly institutionalized figure. His "originality" lies, as it were, in his most fully extending the possibilities of his chosen discipline. One can read his text to say something about the empowered rationality of the very discourse he helps to extend and redefine; one can talk about how it exists, as he puts it, "in its theoretical fullness" (A, 438). The process is doubly interesting in part because Bercovitch takes it as a central part of his task to reflect upon the ideological consequences of the workings and techniques of this discourse in its society. As he elaborates on it, this critical and scholarly discourse seeks the "American" dream in "American" literature; it continually realigns "classic literary" and ideological forms of representation; it involves the all too common occurrence of a radical criticism emerging in relation to professionalized "American" institutions. "America" has produced, according to Bercovitch's figure of the "jeremiad," no radical discourse—aimed at "renewing" this culture gone wrong—that has not, because of its very desires, lost its energies in the mainstream of "American" culture, business, and politics. Hence Bercovitch's own desire to see in the essays of the "New Americanists" the possibility of "alternative" forms of historical study and representation—alternatives that will not, as it were, always already be positioned to become part of the consensus of "America."

Bercovitch's vision of the peculiarly "American" nature of the problems facing any radical emergent culture helps identify the limits of actually existing "American" criticism:

> I think, for instance, of the problem of locating our radical tradition in a literature obsessed with an *American* dream; or of the problem of locating that dream, considered as our *radical* tradition, in the realm of literature; or again, of the problem of locating a radical discourse about American culture in what is after all a rather *traditional* exchange among professional *literary* critics. (A, 439)

"Americanist" criticism has, in Bercovitch's view, made too much of the literary, taking it perhaps uncritically as the privileged site of cultural resistance to the oppression of U.S. society. In other words, this professionalized debate among academic literary scholars may indeed have invested the literary with a liberatory, critical possibility that there is no prima facie reason to believe it actually possesses. Or, to put the matter mildly, the literary—as represented by these academic "Americanists"—may not be the best evidence for the possibility that a radical alternative to the dominant order of "American" oppression, of the "ideologues and their victims," actually exists, has existed, or can ever exist in U.S. life and economy (A, 428). The critical error may lie in decoding or interpreting "American literature" as the expression of a dream for a better "America." This is not to say that this literature should be read as a collaborative enterprise or even one in a mixed or dialectical relation to the oppressive and nonliterary. It is simply to say that the institutionalized discursive practice, the habits and procedures of "Americanist" work have led to the consistent representation of "American literature" as an embodiment of utopian hopes, of aspirations for a fulfillment or recovery of lost dreams—or simply as a reservoir of unfulfilled potentialities.[15] "Americanist" discourse, in these simple terms, is part and parcel of the operations of "America." The discourse reestablishes "America" as the vision of the New; the discourse has legitimacy—no matter how critical it may be of actually existing U.S. society—only in an affirmative relation to "America" as the process of national self-affirmation and international self-assertion.

We can imagine alternative ways to conceive the critic's relation to culture so that the binaries that emerge in Bercovitch's work do not define a dilemma—but not, I would argue, unless the very nature of "Americanist" discourse is overhauled so totally—or perhaps put aside so thoroughly—that it might not be recognized as "Americanist" at all. But is this a possibility? Operating within the boundary of "Americanist" discourse, trying, as they say, to "subvert" it from within—it is against the seemingly easy possibility of this tactic that Bercovitch warns us. Stepping "outside" this boundary? How does one do this when "American" literature and culture have come to be represented as they are by an "Americanist" discourse so aligned with the operations of its own "cooptation" that that literature cannot possibly be seen again "for the first time"? But how can one use the categories of the culture against itself when these categories, these sets of representations and their systematic and asystematic organization are as powerful as they are, when they are so essential to making the critic who thinks he wants to be beyond them? What one would need to succeed at this transcendence would be a theory or myth of the self-originating critical mind. Or at least one would need a theory of the critic as "master" of the discourse(s) that have made that critic expert and competent. What would be the grounds for imagining such a critic in this day and age? And what would such a critic have to do?

That Bercovitch dedicates another of his edited volumes, *Reconstructing American Literary History,* "to the Memory of F. O. Matthiessen and Perry Miller" can be understood in several ways, any one of which might partially answer these questions.[16] In one sense, Bercovitch is the institutional successor to these luminous figures at Harvard, so the dedication is appropriate; in another sense, suspending consideration of their institutional position for a moment, these two men were the leading figures of their discipline, critics and historians whose founding and revisionary texts were authoritative and are, even today, the object of constant reconsideration. In any event, this dedication is a gesture of succession, of continuity with the master critics of the past.[17]

Is it true that "American Studies" seems to have had greater need for these authoritative critical masters and their texts than most other subdisciplines of modern literary study? If so, the reasons would not be hard to understand: the literature needed a founding authority; the nation needed its identity and continuity; in part both were provided by the professionalized, institutionalized success of the discipline in elite private, state, and state-related universities: this structure generates masters necessary to maintain discipline and to the power formations of training, rewards, and discursive regularity: leaders also align the discourse properly with the supporting state apparatuses. Not only in his own writing but in his massive and maieutic editorial enterprises, Bercovitch plays this role of the master in wonderful parts. I have focused so much on the "Afterword" to *Ideology and Classic American Literature* precisely because the essay exemplifies the power operations I am suggesting: Summoning new essays, reprinting already published pieces, asking for "reconsiderations" from older "masters," this "Afterword" positions not only a new generation in relation to an old—and mark how the inclusion of "old" masters means that generation here is a professional, not a chronological category—but all of the new in relation to his own sense of all relations between new and old and all of these and his own sense of what, as midwife, he seems to want to aid in delivering: "alternatives."

Taking his position seriously—precisely as it is marked by his dedication to Miller and Matthiessen—means that his work can point beyond itself, to what needs to be, but, as I see it, cannot be done within that enabling discourse of "Americanist" criticism. It seems to me implicit, for example, throughout the resonant and sometimes knotty work of Jonathan Arac, perhaps the most brilliant young contributor to the new *Cambridge History of American Literature* that Bercovitch is editing—it seems implicit throughout Arac's work that the "Americanist" position on matters "American" cannot be sustained; from *Commissioned Spirits* through *Critical Genealogies* to "'A Romantic Book': *Moby Dick* and Novel Agency," Arac—perhaps like Matthiessen before him—has tried for an internationally comparative position on "American" literature of a sort that simultaneously accords the historical, geographic specificity of the conditions of cultural production their full weight while neglecting neither the "global" nor theoretical view of the putative "American" subject at hand.[18] So the key, as it were, to Arac on Melville lies in Schlegel and Goethe! Arac's example can, of course, be compounded. Donald E. Pease is another instance of the limits of "Americanist" criticism; his work exemplifies another response to its crisis: Pease has so thoroughly made his own the work of Habermas and his predecessors that his vision of "America" is, we might say, as European as it is "Americanist." Bercovitch's writing points to this need in "Americanist" criticism and to his own hopes for a criticism beyond the "national." There is no doubt, I think, that the strictly "national" focus of "Americanist" criticism cannot be sustained; indeed, Richard Poirier has made a point of criticizing the "parochialism" of this criticism in a recent essay in *The London Review of Books*: "The result [of such nationally focused criticism] is a stifling parochialism exactly where there is most need for comparative studies involving other literatures of much longer duration. Principally, this has to mean literature in English. . . . Those who refuse . . . to inquire into 'the Atlantic double cross' . . . are not able in an effective way to speculate on a phenomenon of immense consequence."[19] Arac, Pease, and the others engaged in similar projects suggest the sort of paradigm shift that Poirier obviously feels is essential to provide the "New Alternatives" Bercovitch requires.

But if we recall our Foucault, if we recall the Gramsci with whose words I began this paper, we would understand that the radical change in the "regime of truth" necessary to shift us beyond the iterations of "American Studies" cannot occur without both a genealogical critique of the emergence of that discipline and its discourses (or the discourses that generate it; the question of priority is open) and a political theorization of the relation not just of the ideology but of the discursive and institutional relations of "Americanist" criticism—even in its oppositional moments—to the larger systems of representation essential to state and other forms of power in our imperial and oppressive cultural, social order.[20] Of course, such a set of critical investigations would require borrowing critical tools from any number of places other than "American Studies." It would also mean a willingness to theorize the discourse with no advance regard for its "accomplishments." This is not to say, however, that such theorization should have no interpretive sympathy for its objects: minus that sympathy even the critical understanding necessary to struggle cannot be achieved.[21]

A critical genealogical awareness of "American Studies" as a set of established and oppositional discourses and disciplines must be achieved if the criticism of U.S. literature and culture expects to distance itself enough from its determinant affiliations and its regulating rationalities to gain some control over the means of intellectual production inherited from the past and entangled with other practices and ideologies in the present. Of course, we must recognize the conundrum in what I am suggesting. The study of U.S. literature and culture cannot transpire without drawing on the textual, historical, and critical resources established in the disciplines of "American Studies." More important, a critique of these disciplines and their cultural, political placement cannot occur without the enabling, authorizing, empowered devices and insights provided by a number of critical discourses often affiliated with "American Studies" itself. As an example of the sort of problem that faces the intellectual self-consciously carrying out such a project, one thinks immediately of the similarities between "American Studies'" involvements with myth, typology, and historicism and the historicist edge to genealogical critique. As I see it, however, these problems need to be taken not as limits but as occasions and opportunities for reflection upon the issues that arise in attempting to carry out a critique with instruments entangled in the very "regime of truth" under investigation. One wants to say that such problems are occasions for genealogical, theoretical reflection upon "American" literature and culture as constructs of U.S. society; upon the formation by that society of the established and oppositional "Americanist"; upon the position of any agent attempting to carry out such a reflection—a reflection, we must repeat, enabled in part by those discourses themselves—upon the needs of the present that encourage, make possible, require, or call forth such reflection.[22] Perhaps the demise of the cold war and the weakening of "American" imperialism in a time of different global relations of power, race, gender, economy, and technology so alter the position of any "critic" that a set of complexly polyvalent, perhaps kaleidoscopic reflections and discourses alone can provide the conditions of critical practice.

Following Erich Auerbach, Edward W. Said has made much of the fact that the critic must be distanced from a dominant culture, must be an "exile."[23] That "exile" is the appropriate emblem for critical distance reflects a complex understanding of the material workings of "culture":

> I shall use the word *culture* to suggest an environment, process, and hegemony in which individuals (in their private circumstances) and their works are embedded, as well as overseen at the top by a superstructure and at the base by a whole series of methodological attitudes. It is in culture that we can seek out the range of meanings and ideas conveyed by the phrases *belonging to* or *in* a place, being *at home in a place.* . . . culture is used to designate not merely something to which one belongs but something that one possesses and, along with that proprietary process, culture also designates a boundary by which the concepts of what is extrinsic or intrinsic to the culture come into forceful play. . . . But . . . there is a more interesting dimension to this idea of culture as possessing possession. And that is the power of culture by virtue of its elevated or superior position to authorize, to dominate, to legitimate, demote, interdict, and validate: in short, the power of culture to be an agent of, and perhaps the main agency for, powerful differentiation within its domain and beyond it too. . . . What is more important in culture is that it is a system of values *saturating* downward almost everything within its purview; yet, paradoxically, culture dominates from above without at the same time being available to everything and everyone it dominates.[24]

One must not only understand national and regional "cultures" but also their interrelations and relations to "metropolitan" cultures in an imperial (whether colonial, postcolonial, neocolonial, or decolonizing) order to understand how differentiated the distantiation of critical exile has come to be.[25] Auerbach could write *Mimesis* in Turkey because his distance from libraries allowed the synthetic point of view on the topic of "realism" that defines that book. But when culture becomes so clearly a set of processes and values that define and enable both that culture's defenders and its opponents—that is, like Satan's hell, always in our hearts—then the possibility of exile becomes harder. One must be in exile in relation not only to the national but to the regional, local, and international effects of culture as well. Auerbach lets Said quote Hugo of St. Victor to the effect that exile and therefore critical perfection depends upon taking "the entire world as a foreign land." This remarkable asceticism in the face of the restrictive but enabling ravages of imperial nationalism—whether Roman, German, or American—makes it possible for the critic to occupy the paradoxical position of worldly transcendence, the old Christian position of "being in the world, but not of it." Or, to put it somewhat differently, "exile," as ascesis, is a demanding discipline of critical self-making.[26]

While honoring the values of distance and the experiences of exile that theorize it as a critical necessity, one must also wonder if the study of culture does not require an even more complex and difficult position: being in and of one's locale while understanding its needs and hence one's own projects in terms of a global or transnational set of interlocking perspectives. The best critical emblem for our time might be what Gayatri Spivak has taught us to call the "post-colonial subject," that is, the gendered intellectual engaged in agonistic analysis of global issues central to regional and national concerns and always motivated by an understanding of the complex position that any citizen of a postmodern cultural multiplicity must occupy.[27]

I want to suggest too crudely that "American Studies" taken as a field in its "theoretical fullness"—I realize this formulation occludes specific differences—has not yet reached the point of "exile" in relation to itself and its nationalist projects. This is an intolerable situation to be in because, like it or not, the citizens who carry out even "New Americanist" discourses do so precisely as persons whose own positionality—despite the appearance of their practice—is not solely determined or defined by their inscription within the professions that trained them (pace, Stanley Fish!). This has, of course, always been true as any look at the monuments of the subdiscipline would show. But it is intensely true now precisely because the historical multi-positionality of the critic is a determining "fact" that has already been partly theorized within criticism in the work not only of Spivak but of Foucault, Gramsci, and others.

Jürgen Habermas makes an important point in his recent essays within the *Historikerstreit*. Commenting on his own authority to oppose Andreas Hillgruber's study of the German army on the Eastern Front—despite his nonexpert status—Habermas claims his right to intervene as a citizen affected by the public consequences of Hillgruber's and others' works: "I am thus making the self-observations of a patient who undergoes a revisionist operation on his historical consciousness."[28] In other words, Habermas implies that professional academic productions emerge into general culture along vectors constructed and kept open by the ideological and institutional operations of the dominant powers within our societies. The intellectual—both in the specialized sense and the Gramscian sense of "everyman"— not only has the right to intervene in the so-called debates that travel along these vectors and, in the process, make up some important parts of our political, ideological culture but also the obligation to intervene given that the arrogant task assigned to the producers of institutionalized knowledge—especially of a historicist kind—is, as Habermas puts it, "to treat historical consciousness as a maneuverable mass in order to provide suitably positive pasts for the legitimation requirements of the present political system."[29] Of course, one sees in this remark some of the characteristic flaws in Habermas's own sense of the oppositional: It is not merely a matter of the "contents" of the "representations" of the "past" that should be our concern—although no doubt it makes a crucial human and political difference if World War II is seen as a common war against bolshevism or not— but of the structure of a persistent system, of our new social order, that, as such, needs a certain relationship between state, governments, ideologies, and varying sets of ideological representations, not only for its survival, but also, in the fullest sense of the word *hegemony,* for its mastery of all possible forms of radical opposition short of "revolution."[30] We might say in this context that Bercovitch has mistaken "hegemonic" operations of the extended state for "America": an understandable error, perhaps, but one that should not be repeated.

"American Studies" has always had admirable, important, and powerful oppositional figures and practices within and adjacent to it. In recent years, especially in its historicist, feminist version, revisionist critics have powerfully and crucially recovered the progressive energies of these figures and advanced the rights and identities of women and other minorities within the "American" socius and tradition. The work of Bercovitch and others, however, has reminded us of how "American" ideology and "American" discourses and institutions seem particularly well suited to disarm these radical challenges by bringing them within the "pluralistic" economy of everyday political conflict and debate, the sort of struggle that goes on always within a "liberal" state system. Gramsci, however, has helped us further to understand that unless the "opposition" to a given "hegemony" attempts to build a counterhegemony, to resist encirclement by the hegemonic institutions, the fate awaiting that "opposition" can be anticipated in the strategy of "passive revolution": "the gradual but continuous absorption, achieved by methods that varied in their effectiveness, of the active elements produced by allied groups— and even of those that came from antagonistic groups and seemed irreconcilably hostile."[31] In other words, critical work must be directed at or against the present; let it emerge, if it must, from a historicist sense, but let it always be, as Foucault says, "a history of the present."[32] The issue must always be the placing of "Americanist" work in the contemporary national and world order—a placing that puts at risk not only those terms themselves, but also the disciplines and knowledges built up as the condition for the critical engagement with the present. To put the matter bluntly, one must say that merely historicist studies such as those of the "emergence of the bourgeois self in post Civil War laissez-faire economics" matter hardly at all unless they are directed against both the present relation of the "regime of truth" to the structures of power and exploitation as well as all social, political elements that block the recovery of the "demiurge" of which Gramsci speaks so eloquently.[33]

I am suggesting that the critical preservation or reform of the discourses and institutions of "American Studies" is analogous to capitalism's maintenance of a stable work force, a certain "equilibrium," the collapse of which would threaten both the workers, who fear the loss of the only order they know, and the capitalists, whose dominance depends upon the workers' internalization of that equilibrium. "Passive revolution" prevents the dismemberment of the discourse and its institutions; it encourages their "transformation," a notion that must be seen in the sense Foucault gives it in *Discipline and Punish,* where he refuses the rhetoric of metaphysical agency and causality to mark the anonymity of power's operations.[34] Gramsci speaks of "puritanism" as an ethic essential to control of the "American" worker; we need only recall the State-led assault on "drugs," the critical invocations of "ethics,"[35] and recent calls by high government officials for more Puritan values of hard work and saving to have a sense of certain alliances between cultural institutions and the state's capitalist roles.

Criticism of "American" culture must set out to have the present as its subject and cannot proceed to any high form of criticism of the institutions of culture and the state without considered and consciously politically motivated examinations—descriptive and theoretical—of the "regime of truth" to which such criticism has and continues to belong. "American Studies" cannot change its paradigm simply by thinking it is treating new topics or loosening up the canon. It must change its own relations to the present but must first attempt to know them and to know its own place within relations as these develop the technical empowerment of specialized "critical" intellectuals. Without such theorized, material forms of knowledge, politically directed at a remaking of the regime of truth, such criticism does not deserve the name. At most it remains "scholastic" or "academic" in the weakest and most pejorative senses of those words. Criticism cannot and should not attempt to prescribe or even imagine the future, but it can and must take aim at the unequal, imperial, antidemocratic present if its work is to be of use to anyone in our world. Critics should never be good company.

Intellectual Arrogance and Scholarly Carelessness, Or, Why One Cannot Read Alan Bloom

ᏧᏍᎣ What is one to say of Alan Bloom's book and its success? It really is seemingly impossible to deal with the book by itself, without, as it were, thinking long and hard about its phenomenal sales, wondering who actually buys it, how many people actually read it—wondering if it appeals, as it were, only to the converted. One might wonder, too, if it does have its place on the best-seller list, in part, as rumor has it, because of the efforts by those in power and with access to the material means of production—like Bill Bennett and Norman Podhoretz, of whom it is said they bought and sent many, many copies.

Quite a few academic intellectual readers—but not all—seem to me to have problems dealing with the book. They are angered by it or amused, or they find it boring, badly written, unutterably simplistic and so cannot write about it except at great cost, wondering all the while if it is worth the trouble. Some who have a certain sort of strong political concern write about it as a phenomenon that shows the function of the intellectual in our politicized culture. Others, who are powerful specialists in areas that Bloom claims to know well and claims to draw on for his inspiration—these write to correct him, to show that he is a bad philosopher or historian of philosophy. Their aims are mixed: sometimes to fix mistakes, sometimes to discredit him and so his entire use of philosophy and the ancients, in order, perhaps, in turn, to discredit his antifeminist, antihistoricist, and conservative vision. I am assuming in all of these remarks that most academics want, in some way, to write against Bloom's book, at least in substantial part, and are looking for ways to do so.

I am willing to pay attention to it because it is an exemplary instance of a certain kind of antitheoretical intellectual practice, of a certain kind of nostalgia for a kind of intellectual that the postmodern U.S. society seems not to need much anymore. Bloom seems to me to be of interest because he is part of a residual formation and so a sign of a desire on the part of many to overcome in a reactionary sweep the cultural consequences of living in an apparently fragmented civil and political society where the state no longer seems to have a unifying and regulatory function. We might say that Bloom's book is an effect of the Reaganism that so powerfully embraces it. I do not mean that it is an ideological weapon waved by Reaganauts against "liberals," "theorists," and other kinds of "perverts." I mean that Reaganism has paradoxically accelerated the effects of what critics since Jameson have called "Postmodernism" as the cultural logic of late capital. It has furthered the fragmentation and competition of elements of society—removing the state wherever possible from its role in competition, in relating national capital as part of a global economy of regional and international autonomy. Yet it has done all of this in the name of exercising a State authority against the critics of that capital and social order, indeed, against all of those who would speak against the American nation or against its State as it is in the hands of the Reaganaut adventurers and gangsters. Perhaps it only makes sense to try to read Bloom's book as a dark allegory of Reaganism, but even as such, it has interest only for its exemplary status—particularly as an anti-theoretical text.

We would be well served by considering what kind of text Bloom's *The Closing of the American Mind* might be. Literary critics who belong to a certain varied tradition of reading—and I think I am one of these—expect that when a humanist writes about the texts of others he will quote from those texts with some frequency, that he will, as we say, do a reading of them, that is, allegorize his understanding of their structure, significance, and value; we expect, in other words, that such a humanist, who intends to make a claim upon our reason and win our assent, will make a rational effort to show us that his understanding and judgment of texts can be supported both from the text and by reasoning inferentially from it perhaps to other texts or perhaps simply to conclusions about it itself. Best of all, we critics hope that we might see in this process some evidence that the texts under consideration have been convincingly construed. By this, of course, we do not mean we want evidence that the reader has produced the "correct," the one, only, and true meaning or even the meaning the author intended. We want to see, rather, that the reader has produced some sense in an encounter with the text and that that sense is likely to produce more, that it is likely to be judged as making an intelligible and imaginative claim upon our understanding of the text, of reading, and of literature itself. When these kinds of critics read Bloom, they are bound to be disappointed and frustrated. We can find no textual evidence, no argument, no analysis that would let us say that the book under consideration has itself won the right to make the statements it does about other books and cultures. This means, in sum, that critics simply cannot take this book seriously as any sort of intellectual production to which they will give authority. The book appears as a set of mere assertions about other books and events whose authority must be simply granted to Bloom, for the simple reason that his text makes no effort to be demonstrative, to have earned the right to make claims in an arena of debate, discussion, and dialogue. Above all, critics expect great (critical) books to take into consideration other readings of the material at hand, to question them, to show with evidence and argument where and how they fail to illuminate both the texts and issues at hand and to legitimate the methods and interests of the author. In other words, critics expect authors to earn their authority and to do so in terms of debate that treats specifics; or again, critics expect others who hope to be taken seriously in what they say about other complex cultural and textual phenomena—we expect others to show that they have dealt with the materials in ways that record and consider their verbal and historical complexity. And it is, most of all, on this last point that Bloom's book falls short. To fall short in this context means, of course, that the book appears everywhere and always to be made up of gross simplifications, of reductions of intellectual, philosophical, textual, cultural, and political experience.

Let me take one narrow example. Many years ago I had the fortune to speak at a conference in Toronto that brought together, in discussion of Plato, Alan Bloom and Hans Georg Gadamer. As I recall, Gadamer repeatedly charged Bloom with not knowing Greek, with being unaware of the historical nature of *The Republic* as an educational and political document, and of ignoring an entire range of scholarship on the text. Not being expert in Plato studies, and having little Greek, I could only feel then that Gadamer had the best of the debate: he could cite the text, explain its philological burden, recite the history of education's relations to politics in Athens. Now, my point is not that Gadamer is right and Bloom wrong; there might well be others entirely more right than either of these men. My point is that in reading Bloom's discussion of *The Republic* one cannot tell that there are other informed ways to understand Plato's text. Some of us know some of these other ways and know that they do not conform to Bloom's understanding. We want to know why Bloom's is right and why Gadamer's, for example, is wrong. A good critical paper would, as we say, have taken Gadamer's reading into account and shown why it was wrong. Bloom, perhaps feeling himself a distinguished Plato scholar, might have felt no need directly to consider alternative interpretations. But even so, a critic would have wanted to see how and why he developed his own sense of Plato, not only to learn how to read Plato correctly but also, by comparison, to judge where the other commentators have gone wrong and why—this is true whether one has read Bloom's predecessors at Chicago or not. (Claiming mere ancient authority is not how scholars do things in the Modern world.) In this way, authentic humanists remind us, scholarly community and understanding are developed and culture is enriched. It is a sign of the crisis under which Bloom writes that he so profoundly contradicts some of the deepest tenets of the position be claims to espouse.

Absent both any attention to any serious alternative understandings of *The Republic* and any detailed reading of the text itself, a critic can only feel that what Bloom presents is weak, reductive, and unauthorized—resting only on the authority of one of his teachers whose own claims are regularly and convincingly contested. Someone, for example, who has read Gadamer's historically contextualized essays on Plato cannot but feel that there are things about Plato that Bloom somehow fails to take seriously; the conclusion must be either that Bloom does not know the materials or he is closed-mindedly reductive. Of course, I have said nothing here that I would not have said to a potentially good student about what kinds of things he must do if he expects to convince an audience interested in fully understanding the complexity of masterful texts and classical forms of experience. All of this adds up, I think, to one of the two principal reasons why it is impossible to read Alan Bloom. Of course, one can gloss Bloom; the margins of my copy of his book are filled with corrections, exclamations, and examples that he does not consider, all of which would complicate or destroy his positions if he did. But more important, Bloom's work energizes no one; he can inspire no one to produce real criticism of the sort I tried to describe above. This should surprise no one. Bloom asserts that scholarship and creativity have nothing in common; professors, in particular, he tells us, have little or no creativity; this lack makes us inadequate commentators on the arts, which are, of course, creative. Perhaps one reason Bloom's own book so studiously avoids scholarship of any sort is to avoid appearing uncreative. Perhaps, however, it is unfair of me to say this since, as near as I can tell, for Bloom, philosophy's commitment to reason repeats the old separation from poetry—perhaps in this sense philosophy cannot and should not try to be creative—this may be the negative reason why, in Bloom's vision, it can be the ground for education and the university in a way literature cannot.

Indeed, I would go so far as to say that Bloom's separation of reason from creativity—while taking Plato strangely as his model—is a mark of the unreadability of Bloom's text. What I mean is very simple. It has been the position of literary criticism at least since Coleridge that criticism shares in the status of art itself. An important modern heir of Coleridge, R. P. Blackmur, refers to criticism as one of the arts. Simply put, in that tradition, one says that when criticism is as responsible to the alterity of the text as I suggested criticism expects itself to be when trying to make cogent statements—it is then itself an instance of creativity that has been summoned into being by the power of the texts its reads. Consequently, by being itself creative in the production of a reading, criticism will, in turn, produce further readings. Harold Bloom would call something like this "tradition that works," or Mishnah.

Alan Bloom's book is not readable in this way because it is not a reading. This is, I think, to say more than that it is not scholarly in a "scientific" sense. It is to say that the book, despite all of its claims of indebtedness to Plato, has not been inspirited or energized by any other text or author. It is not a generous or loving text. (Although perhaps I should say that Bloom's book has been inhabited by the ghost of Leo Strauss, on the model of "La Belle Dame Sans Merci.") R. P. Blackmur, whom I mentioned a moment ago, once wrote in a magnificent essay, "A Critic's Job of Work," that criticism can be itself only when it is in love with the object that animates it:

> Criticism, I take it, is the formal discourse of an amateur. When there is enough love and enough knowledge represented in the discourse it is a self-sufficient but by no means an isolated art. It witnesses constantly in its own life its interdependence with the other arts. It lays out the terms and parallels of appreciation from the outside in order to convict itself of internal intimacy.[1]

Without reading, without intimate knowledge, there is no love, there is no criticism, and there is no self-sufficiency. Paradoxically, there is also no interdependence with other arts or texts. Bloom's book is not readable because it is eros gone wrong; it tries for self-sufficiency, which can be achieved only through intimate dependency, through what Blackmur calls humility. Without this sort of loving independence, the text cannot be interdependent; it becomes, to use loosely very troubling words, it becomes sterile and unproductive.

In fact, it is Bloom's aspirations to authority and self-sufficient independence that make this book ungenerous, closed, and so unreadable on another level. All this can, I think, be seen in what amounts to very little more than a sophomoric debating trick: Bloom structures the book's assertions in such a way that any fundamental objections to his basic assertions can be dismissed as belonging precisely to the cowardly and empty forms of life, of false intellect that he hopes to outline, destroy, and replace. For instance, if I may return to my example from Gadamer's comments on Plato, one finds that Bloom's sense of Plato's defense of reason as philosophy depends upon denying any historicist reading of *The Republic* that, by contextualizing it, might let us see it as a historically situated document whose comments on and uses of reason are situated, occasional, historical in the specific cultural sense of political writings. Gadamer's arguments are not this crude, but my summary will serve because the matter at hand is Bloom's tactic of assigning all historicist readings, in advance, to the ashcan of antireason that underlies the collapse of university education in the United States. Bloom's story links enlightenment to suspicion of reason to perspectivism to historicism to nihilism. Any critique, then, that says simply, "Bloom, you're wrong, historically it was different," any such critique is meant to be placed by Bloom in such a position that it is automatically seen as illegitimate. Literary critics might see in this line of attack some form of anxiety or defensiveness, but to show it would require developing a reading of an unreadable text—a text that means to offer itself precisely as the final word on the matters at hand.

Let me discuss something that might suggest one of the origins of Bloom's work or perhaps one of the ways we should receive it. In his well-thought-of book *The American Jeremiad,* Sacvan Bercovitch attempts to sketch the tradition of political, spiritual writing in the United States. One important characteristic of the jeremiad is precisely its unwillingness to tolerate other opinions on the matters at hand. Bercovitch suggests that closedness has been constitutive of the tradition he studies:

> I approach the myth [of America] by way of the jeremiad, or the *political sermon,* as the New England Puritans sometimes called this genre, meaning thereby to convey the dual nature of their calling, as practical and as spiritual guides, and to suggest that, in their church-state, theology was wedded to politics and politics to the progress of the kingdom of God.

Bercovitch goes on to say that he aims to study the presence of the jeremiad in other forms of American writing as well: "doctrinal treatises, histories, poems, biographies, personal narratives." He adds that Perry Miller had told the story of the dark side of this impulse but goes on to say "that the Puritans' cries of declension and doom were part of a strategy designed to revitalize the errand [into the wilderness]." "I believe," Bercovitch continues, that "even when they are most optimistic, the jeremiads express a profound disquiet. Not infrequently, their affirmations betray an underlying desperation—a refusal to confront the present, a fear of the future, an effort to translate 'America' into a vision that works in spirit because it can never be tested in fact."[2]

I have cited Bercovitch—and shall do so again—only to one end: to recall to mind how Bloom, despite his evident rhetorical nostalgia for the "old world" and its ancient regimes, is primarily involved in the age-old business of articulating some sort of consensus vision around the term "America." (Of course, for the definitive discussion of this entire process, one need only see Donald Pease's remarkable book, *Visionary Compacts*.) It is, after all, "America" that arouses Bloom's concerns and anxieties: America's decline and fall and the chance for its resuscitation. And, of course, typically, Bloom appeals to the Fathers and their conservative heirs, especially Tocqueville, to legitimate his own vision of what is needed.

In a chapter entitled "Ritual of Consensus," Bercovitch stresses that throughout our history the very symbol of "America" has suppressed real class difference and conflict; he might have added other equally important matters of race and gender as well. Of course, the characteristic of the jeremiad that allowed for this suppression is the rhetoric of amelioration, what we might call betterment promised by the American way. In fine, even Bloom's Platonism works under the umbrella of and as a support to the consensus ideal of "America." What we might most easily see with Bercovitch's help is that all jeremiads require, as a condition of their reassertion and reactivation of the consensual force of "America"—they all require and depend upon an at least putative and often real diversity that can be defused either by charging it with anarchic anomie or by taking it up within a safe pluralism:

> Like biblical exegesis and the Puritan rhetoric of ambiguity, it encouraged multiplicity of meaning while precluding contradiction in fact. . . . a call for progress that enhanced the glories of the past; a nostalgia for a golden age that enforced the values of the present; and most important, a restrictive mode of consensus that throve on the diversity of sectarian belief, precisely as those diverse sects throve on the competitive systems they espoused. (*AJ,* 170)

Lest someone object that Bloom's concerns are universal and not simply American, let me end this little deviation into Bercovitch's work by allowing him one more word on the powerful effects of the jeremiad: "Of all the symbols of identity, only *America* has united nationality and universality, civic and spiritual selfhood, secular and redemptive history, the country's past and paradise to be, in a single synthetic ideal" (*AJ,* 176). In other words, and put crudely, Bloom no more indicts the competitive capitalist order that promotes the fragmentation and diversity he laments than could any other ritualist of "America"—especially in the age of Reagan and Bush.

Bercovitch's impressive study allows us to see another of the many reasons why critics, as I have already suggested, cannot read Alan Bloom: efforts to produce dedifferentiating documents of cultural consensus are inherently closed; that is, their very rhetorical, intellectual, and cultural function is not to reproduce erotically but to confirm and to deny—to confirm the desires of those who work to sustain the consensus by denying the need either to reconsider long-held images of the ideal or to admit as legitimate the felt and reasoned needs of others whose different histories threaten the representation of consensus and all of its works.

But Bloom's book remains unreadable in another way—I hope that it is clear that all of these ways are part of the same structure of closedness that I truly despair of ever making open. I have thought of many ways to suggest this last sort of closedness. Above all, I felt that it would be best represented as the closedness of neurosis that, of course, cannot be reasoned away. I am attracted to this representation because of the now commonplace post-Althusserian sense that ideology is structured like a neurosis. But I finally felt that this line of approach would be reductive and would too easily slide off the Teflon surface Bloom has constructed out of his closedness. So I thought instead of another, somewhat different problematic, a quite old one, in fact. Given that, as everyone says, Bloom has a vision of what has been, what is wrong or has been lost, and what needs to be done or what would be better, I wondered if he were at all troubled by the authority, the status of his vision. Bloom would no doubt be suspicious of any psychoanalytic treatment of his vision—and so I will make no effort at the obvious on that basis. Let me instead recall a stronger tradition of visionary awareness, one that seemingly has impeccable conservative credentials, namely, those of T. S. Eliot. Speaking of Dante, Eliot tells us how the Florentine's achievement depended upon the existence of a nonmodernistic imaginative mode, namely, "vision." Dante has, Eliot tells us, "a *visual* imagination" because "he lived in an age when men still saw visions." We have lost the trick: "We have nothing but dreams, and we have forgotten that seeing visions—a practice now relegated to the aberrant and uneducated— was once a more significant, interesting, and disciplined kind of dreaming." [3]

But as Eliot well knew, visions were not always comforting things; they especially troubled reason trying to decide their authority. Let us recall, for example, the opening of Chaucer's late-fourteenth-century poem "The House of Fame." In the Proem to Book One, we recall, the narrator calls his hearers to order by playing the scales across the many ways in which a vision can be taken:

> God turne us every dreem to goode:
> For it is wonder, by the roode,
> To my wit, what causes swevenes,
> Either on morwes or on evenes,
> And why th'effect folweth of some,
> And of some it shal nevere come;
> Why that is an avisioun,
> And why this a revelacioun;
> Why this a dream, why that a swevene
> And nought to every man licht evene;
> Why this a fantome, why thise oracles,
> I noot, but who so of thise miracles
> The causes knoweth bet than I,
> Divine he, for I certainly
> Ne can hem nought, ne nevere thinke
> Too bisily my wit to swinke
> To knowe of hir signficaunce,
> The gendres, neither the distaunce
> Of times of hem, ne the causes,
> Or why this is more than that cause is—⁴

Chaucer surely confirms Eliot's sense that in the past visions were indeed complex and hard-to-know things since the narrator not only endlessly tells us he does not know the origins, authority, or effects of visions, but he lists as many different and differently burdened types as he does here. We might say that Chaucer's narrator has a scrupulous tone that alerts us to the difficulty of knowing how authoritatively to take any vision that we might have. It is indeed hard to tell the difference between a revelation and a fantasy, between an oracle and a phantom caused by bad digestion. Chaucer's humor should be taken seriously in this Bloomian context because it catches a certain sort of ironic openness, a healthy skepticism about the status of one's own visionary productions. More important, though, it precedes Chaucer's great exposition of the character of a man who, troubled by the doubts caused by the need to deal with the problematic status of representations, becomes, as Talbot Donaldson puts it, "entirely persuaded of the truth of old books." Donaldson continues in a way that I think catches that closed Jeremiah we know as Alan Bloom:

These [old books] suffice him and he does not feel the need of any direct experience of the things of which he reads. When the eagle . . . offers him direct experience and—indeed—imposes it on him, the narrator rejects it . . . apparently he would much prefer to read about such exciting experiences than have to endure them. He behaves as if he were afraid that too much reality would force him to change the comfortable attitude he has assumed toward life.[5]

Chaucer catches the comfortable attitude of the dreamer toward ancient books in an image of metaphysical vision he allows him in his private dream; it is an image of transcendent knowledge. In his dream, the angelic interlocutor soars and carries him along:

> And with this word, sooth for to sayne,
> He gan upper alway to sore,
> And gladded me ay more and more,
> So faithfully to me spak he.
> Tho I gan I to looken under me,
> And biheld the airissh beestes,
> Cloudes, mistes, and tempestes,
> Snowes, hailes, raines, windes,
> And th'engendring in hir kindes
> Al the way thurgh which I cam.[6]

The narrator from his transcendent height then draws the moral of his dream vision by citing Boethius:

> And tho thoughte I upon Boece
> That writ, "A thought may flee so hye
> With fetheres of philosophye,
> To passen everich element,
> And whan he hath so fer ywent,
> Thanne may be seen bihinde his bak
> Cloude, erthe,—and al that I of spak."[7]

Chaucer's narrator is driven by his uncertainty over the status of his vision, which, as you recall, involves seeing the entire history of Troy played out before him—he is driven by the anxiety of doubt about what we might call his vision's "cognitive status," its "authority," if you will—he is driven to the final willful assertion that his vision is unquestionable, the confirmation of philosophy that, as part of the wisdom of ancient books, surely, in turn, confirms his vision. For as we recall, the narrator is told that every speech confirmed within the House of Fame is indistinguishable from its speaker: "That it the same body be."[8]

I am suggesting that, for reasons Bloom's discourse does not begin to address, his book is unreadable and closed: it takes the form of a naive dream vision, one whose origins are easily confirmed within the history of the genre—were one eager to make the effort to demonstrate rather than merely suggest the case. Also, there is a particularly American version of this genre, the one Bercovitch most usefully names the "jeremiad." It is always an impossible possible philosopher's song—as Wallace Stevens might have put it. By always and everywhere closing its eye to the present—invoking some past in the name of some future or some apocalypse—it inevitably remains a document of the present blind to its own genealogies, confused in its ambitions, naive in its claims, and ultimately unproductive.

Finally, one speaks hesitatingly of Bloom's book because it does not deserve the massive attention it has had orchestrated for it. Even in the time of conservative government by astrology, there must be more articulate, less superbly self-indulgent texts than this around which to rally right-wing ideologies. There are, of course, a number of serious people who will say we must deal with the issues this book raises even if we do not accept Bloom's precise formulations of problems and their solutions. I would ask such people that they recall that the one thing hegemony requires is to set the terms of debate. In the face of the likes of Bloom and his confreres, every effort must be made precisely not to join the conversation. Further: one must make every effort to deny the validity of the other question that necessarily follows out of my sort of remarks: what then will you put in Bloom's place given that "obviously" things are wrong. In response to that, one must say at least two things: first, that the neopragmatist and neoconservative ameliorative discourse out of which it comes is highly suspect; second, that there is already a massive volume of material of quite high quality addressing an entirely different set of issues, working with entirely different problematics (note: I did not say "problems") that it is precisely the effect of Bloom's work to displace. The answer, then, you see, is to point out that it is Bloom who is trying to provide an alternative to a given body of work that he finds distasteful. My position is simply that his work is so little convincing, so undemonstrative, so closed, so much an expression of desire, and so much self-manipulating fantasy that it does not deserve even the sort of putative attention it has received. The best thing to be done with Bloom's book is either to wrap it in the hooting silence it deserves or leave it to a polemicist of Marx's sort, who could, in *The German Ideology*, turn the Bloom of his time into Mad Max—as fitting a symbol of our time as Bloom's silly claim to hover above the agora allows.

CHAPTER FIVE

Closing Up the Ranks:
Xerxes' Hordes Are at the Gate

ల⚬ $\mathbf{M}$ost of the important essays of Edward W. Said's *The World, the Text, and the Critic*[1] were previously published, but it is a sign of the power and significance of Said's project that this is nonetheless the most impressive book of American criticism since Jameson's *Political Unconscious* (1981), de Man's *Allegories of Reading* (1980), and his own *Orientalism* (1978). In *Orientalism*, Said made an extremely powerful case for the need to redefine and reshape literary critical practice by illustrating how literary critics can turn their powerful explicatory tools on forms of language usually excluded from the academic canon and how by asking different, nonacademic questions grounded in the worldly concerns of the present, literary criticism could become somewhat less marginal and help demystify the relations between knowledge and power. In *The World, the Text, and the Critic,* Said makes a more extended case for how what he calls "secular criticism"—that is, criticism practiced against the dogmatic and comforting closure of being at home within the dominant culture and practiced without systemic assurances that answers can be found to all cultural problems—can "think of itself as life-enhancing and constitutively opposed to every form of tyranny, domination, and abuse" (29). Not only does Said make a moving theoretical and political case for such a criticism, but he finds compelling historical instances of such critical practice in Swift, whose work Said discusses at length in two essays, and crucial literary evidence of texts insisting on their own status as worldly events in authors such as Conrad, Wilde, and Hopkins. In addition, he writes at length of the relative strengths and weaknesses of the oppositional projects of Derrida and Foucault—both of whom fail by succumbing to the temptations of system—as well as of the massive cultural studies of Schwab, Renan, and Massignon. Said also maintains his career-long antipathy to religious thinking in his assertion that critics comfortably placed within the class-based nationalism and ethnocentrism of the dominant culture they represent and reinforce are as dogmatic as the religious can be. Said finds discomforting evidence for the increasing desperation and conservatism such dogmatic criticism implies in a number of books by various critics—Kermode, Frye, Bloom, and Girard—whose work marks "a dramatic increase in the number of appeals to the extrahuman, the vague abstraction, the divine, the esoteric and secret" (291). While Said does not give us an extended discussion of this problem, it is clear from what he says elsewhere that such concerns with "mystery"—as in Denis Donoghue's *The Arts Without Mystery* (1984)—turn critics dangerously away from the historical sphere of human labor and mark the limits of Anglo-American literary scholars' willingness to deal with problems of power and social life, especially within critical institutions that reward depoliticized fancy and fantasy.

Said's critique of the present state of critical practice is meant to be all-inclusive. He repeats charges against Derrida that he has been forcefully elaborating at least since his Gauss Seminars at Princeton: Deconstruction is a serious project to be studied and understood, but it is both an unnecessary ascesis of critical power and a conservative rarefication of cultural production, which in its textualizing obsessions is absolutely reductive: "Western thought is something more differentiated, incorporative, and, most important, institutionally representative than Derrida seems to allow" (209). (How Said would deal with Derrida's very recent papers on educational institutions and the nuclear arms race is not clear.) But it is not only the critical systematizers, represented by Derrida, whom Said charges with abandoning critical practice. While Said does attack critical systematizers and academic institutions that support them, his critiques of those operating within "culture" are more important, more devastating, and, from the point of view of the academic study of literature and those who—so badly—support it, much more dangerous. One should recall that to operate unreflexively within "culture" is the practice of the vast majority throughout the profession, not just at Harvard, as Walter Jackson Bate would have us believe, and that the majority's sense of its own interests appears in the ongoing personal and institutional resistance to all powerfully negative critical thinking—excoriated, stupidly but effectively and uniformly, under the signs "deconstruction-ism" or "theory." This majority resistance often takes the form of the very employment and tenure discrimination Bate has urged upon university administrators nationwide. Stanley Fish has contended that not too deeply underlying Bate's concerns for what he sees as the central role the classics should play in constituting a stable and value-laden culture is a strong sense that the barbarians are within the gates—of academic study—and that the interests and authority of those at home in or defending that culture will suffer: "It is this prospect [of endless critical difference] that distresses Bate, not only because it will further fragment an enterprise whose coherence he believes to be in danger but because it will disperse the power and authority that was once centralized in Harvard and its sister institutions" ("Profession Despise Thyself: Fear and Self-Loathing in Literary Studies," *Critical Inquiry,* 10, no. 2 [1983], 355).

Bate's little essay, "The Crisis in English Studies" (*Harvard Magazine,* 85 [1982]), is, of course, only one in a long and tiring line of essays by "humanistic" scholars who, since Picard debated with Barthes and Abrams with Miller, have argued that theory, deconstruction, or professionalization, by virtue of seeming to be a danger to the institution of literary study as the "humanists" would like to conceive it, is a threat to civilization itself—which usually means Eurocentric, male hegemony. But Bate's essay marks a change in that tradition of anxious protest; it comes at a time when reactionary protest is increasingly successful. It is not simply to correct Bate or combat his "prestige" that powerful figures within the profession such as Fish and Paul de Man ("The Return to Philology," *TLS,* 10 December 1982, pp. 1355–56) have chosen to contest his claims. Said makes the point that it is not coincidence that literary criticism extends cultural and systemic modes of practice in the age of Reagan. While Said's comments on this point may be too unspecified and undiscriminating to be completely satisfying, there seems little doubt he is correct. The back-to-basics movements, the establishment of "core" curricula, shifts in NEH funding patterns, and other nostalgic and instrumental revisions have all lent support to the conservative "cultural critics" who have often been at the heart of these reforms. The strongest evidence of how their power has increased as a result of all of these institutional reactions could not have been available to Said: namely, how the "cultural critics" have closed ranks and through their spokesmen have uniformly attempted to discredit *The World, the Text, and the Critic* and, hence, Said's challenge to the dominant forms of critical practice. In other words, I take it that the attacks on Said in the leading cultural tabloids are an ideological attempt to disarm the "barbarians" by neutralizing the most serious challenge to the status quo.

Indeed, it must be said that Said's work is a far more serious challenge to the forms of institutional practice, reward, and replication than deconstruction has been until now. (Feminist deconstruction could potentially play a powerfully subversive role.) Said's position is especially challenging because he calls for the politicization of a major form of cultural practice at the very time when depoliticization of the public sphere, of civil society, is necessary for the forces of reaction to expel, to roll back whatever threats to ruling interests actually became embodied by the countercultural resistances of the late 1960s and early 1970s. We must not forget that Bate and others always locate what they see as the disintegration of culture and English studies at the time when—to the cultural critics' horror—such "marginal" phenomena as lesbian and Chicano literature gained a place in the academy and minorities and women made some social advances. We must also remember that these events were roughly contemporary with the introduction of structuralism and deconstruction into America. Even though I agree with Said that (nonfeminist) deconstruction, because of its reductiveness and its integration into the profession, is now more conservative than not in its effects on critical practice (see my essay, "Variations on Authority," *The Yale Critics*, ed. Jonathan Arac et al. [Minneapolis: University of Minnesota Press, 1983], 3–20), we must not forget that the cultural critics saw it as subversive and dangerous.

In other words, in an era when Reagan can effectively assert that "America is back!," when militarism expands with no significant opposition, and, as Stanley Aronowitz has pointed out, when the terms of public discourse are determined by the right, literary critics' desires to return to the "good old days" must be seen as an acculturated part and parcel of a larger political movement. "Culture," Said tells us, "furnishes us with systems of authority and with canons of order whose regular effect is either to compel subservience or to gain adherents" (290). It is the compulsive aspect of this reified "culture" that, when activated in the interests of dominant groups, becomes authoritarian and a threat to criticism—no matter whether that activation is consciously directed, as it now often is, for reactionary political motives or exercised habitually, as the common sense of ideology. Said's stress upon the "authoritarian," positive closure of the "culturally comfortable critics" makes him especially threatening now, at a time when humanists like Abrams and Bate can accept Derrida. This same stress makes Said's work useful to those who want to change the profession so that it can not only grip the world more effectively but also do so for politically progressive purposes, that is, to further what we might call participatory democracy.

Following a description of the dangers of systemic thinking "predetermining" all problems and answers, Said himself makes an important positive statement in the name of the negative: "Criticism . . . is always situated; it is skeptical, secular, reflectively open to its own failings. This is by no means to say that it is value-free. Quite the contrary, for the inevitable trajectory of critical consciousness is to arrive at some acute sense of what political, social, and human values are entailed in the reading, production, and transmission of any text" (26). There is no one, except perhaps the most dogmatic ideologue, who could not—publicly—affirm this skeptical attitude. Yet if taken seriously, its consequences are far-reaching; it suggests questioning not only explicit systemic and dogmatic but cultural predispositions as well. Such a move not only is difficult but can be politically and morally destabilizing. It threatens the "self-evident" values of the "humanists'" "basic premise": "the Renaissance tradition of *litterae humanioris*," writes Bate, "has long served as a kind of hub to the wheel, giving a necessary center to the emerging spokes of more specialized approaches, which, without that center, lose their original purpose and function" ("To the Editor," *Critical Inquiry*, 10, no. 2 [1983]: 365–66). Bate puts forward no self-reflective arguments for this claim; his assertion is rather "authoritative," that is, dogmatic in

Said's terms because unreasoned and meant to appear to rest on a "consensus." Bate's anxiety is not simply that that "consensus" no longer exists, but that admitting the likes of lesbian and Chicano literature into the academy reveals that there was no "consensus" at all, merely an order of things maintained by and for an empowered elite who suppressed and excluded others—in the name of all the best. . . .

David Lodge notices that Said's position is a challenge to this basic and usually unquestioned "humanistic" premise ("Adventures Among Master-Theories," *TLS*, 4 May 1984, p. 487). But Lodge dismisses it as unthinkable, as an obviously undesirable consequence of Said's flirtations with Foucault and Gramsci: "it is a route that leads further and further away from literature and literary studies as cultural institutions, and may actually demand their extinction." Two things must be said in answer to Lodge's anxiety: if these institutions are as dogmatic, ahistorical, and closed as Said says (Lodge has not rebutted that claim), their demise might be desirable, and our discussion of their demise might be irrelevant—since so-called market forces are having the effect Lodge fears; but if these claims are true, as I think they are, and the reviews of Said are evidence of it, then changing the institutions so that critical thinking is what goes on there, even at the risk of their stability, would be a positive effect of Said's position. Critical thinking, in other words, is broader than those interested in the traditional institutions of literary study usually would have it be. Consequently, Lodge is unable to see Said's arguments as attempts to reground the discourses about literature within larger critical processes and to reshape literary training so that its practitioners can carry out these broader practices more effectively. That Lodge confuses Said's call for such a reconfiguration of critical practice with the end of literary study is not only startling but reveals that the institutional and ideological interests Lodge represents are indeed as closed and dogmatically self-confident as Said asserts. Lodge has created a false opposition; Said wants neither to destroy the study of literature nor to "revitalize" it for either "cultural" or "professional" reasons. Said would rather find ways to return the critic to the political task of a situated interrogation of past and present discourses and institutions—but so that such interrogations always emerge from and are directed toward matters of human consequence on the present occasion. I would suggest that Lodge's own professional and ideological commitments not only keep him from seeing this restorative dimension of Said's work but would lead him, if he were consistent, to oppose it—despite its evident "humanism."

But while the cultural critics might absorb Said's assertion about skepticism—without, of course, attending to the materialist consequences of studying the production of texts—they cannot accept the fuller image of the critic, he goes on to propose, for in it critical negation becomes a primary cultural activity with a political purpose: "I take criticism so seriously as to believe that, even in the very midst of a battle in which one is unmistakably on one side against another, there should be criticism, because there must be critical consciousness if there are to be issues, problems, values, even lives to be fought for" (28). Said goes on to say that if criticism is to be truly "oppositional," as it must be to be criticism, it must not only avoid dogma and system, but it must find "its identity [in] its difference from other cultural activities." As a result of this crucial claim, Said's critic should never be at home in the institutions of criticism and should be their severest enemy: "In its suspicion of totalizing concepts, in its discontent with reified objects, in its impatience with guilds, special interests, imperialized fiefdoms, and orthodox habits of mind, criticism is most itself and, if the paradox can be tolerated, most unlike itself at the moment it starts turning into organized dogma" (29). Some may find Said's implicit description of academic literary study too unnuanced; I am, however, startled by the accuracy of its bold outlines. Others implicated in the sketch must sense its accuracy as well, that is, if the uniform hostility of the response is any measure.

In the widely circulated literary tabloids, *The New York Review of Books, The London Review of Books, The New York Times Book Review, TLS,* and *The New Republic,* Said's reviewers not only have been hostile, dismissive, and condescending but, along with those in journals like *The Hudson Review,* have adopted a univocal position whose orchestral effect is to submerge Said's challenge to the interests of the professoriat and those they serve. What is truly remarkable, I must add, is how totally inappropriate the reviewers have been to Said's work; or, better, how totally appropriate their choice has been by editors of journals whose public voice in the sphere of *litterae humanioris* gives them great power—greater by far than *Diacritics* and *boundary 2,* where intelligent, critical reviews of Said have appeared.

While culturally comfortable critics who write (regularly) in these (paying) journals may not discuss the material mechanisms of the production, reading, and distribution of texts, they apparently—along with their editors—understand such things. Since Said is attempting nothing less than to contest for the authority and legitimacy of the critical profession, the material fate of *The World, the Text, and the Critic* is more important than any theoretical or scholarly judgment passed on it. All such judgments, when they are made by the culturally comfortable critics or, should we say, more directly, by the ideological representatives of the cultural interests of a hegemonic capitalist and imperialist class exercising disciplinary power—such judgments are empowered in part by virtue of where they appear and of the "consensus" they seem to emerge from. They aim to delegitimate Said's political, intellectual challenge either by characterizing him as a barbarian (and an Oriental one at that) about whose incompetence the record needs to be set straight or by slapping him on the back as a long-lost fellow amateur and Victorian essayist who simply needs to drop all that "theoretical"—read "high intellectual" and "political"—rhetoric. Said knows that he is in a contest for authority, not only with the systematizers like Hillis Miller and their popularizers like Jonathan Culler but also with the "normal" practice of professional literary study that self-destructively fetishizes "Eurocentric humanities"—he could have added "phallocentric"—"because they are either old or they have power, they have been handed on in time or seem to have no time, and they have traditionally been revered, as priests, scientists, or efficient bureaucrats have taught" (22).

In light of Said's specific attack on the "cultural critics'" very ground of being, their antagonism should not be unexpected. What makes their response dangerous to the critical intellectual life is that it marks a major push by the mandarins and their centurions "against theory." In a perceptive response to Walter Benn Michaels and Steven Knapp ("Against Theory," *Critical Inquiry,* 8, no. 4 [1982], 723–42), Daniel O'Hara warned that their essay marked both a desire and an attempt to return to good old-fashioned practical work carried out with common sense, that is, a reaction against the "destabilizations" of theory production and a recuperation of untroubled belletristic biography, commentary, and explication as the criteria of "critical" work ("Revisionary Madness: The Prospects of American Criticism

at the Present Time," *Critical Inquiry,* 9, no. 4 [1983], 726–42).
O'Hara's Juvenalian satire went unanswered precisely because it
caught the shape of the emergent. Signs of this reaction are everywhere. At a conference at Notre Dame (April 1984), Cornel West argued that, given the collapse of realistic and reductive premises in
philosophy, Richard Rorty's turn to American pragmatism little disturbs the philosophy profession because it successfully obscures the
critical need for philosophers to confront sociopolitical history in a
materialist way; it closes down new possibilities for critique and organic intellectual practice as quickly as the crises of modern philosophy open them up. The celebrity Rorty has achieved among literary
critics indicates, in turn, their immense desire for "pragmatic" solutions to cultural problems based upon the resources available to the
"community" from within its own "comfortable" and exclusive traditions. Jonathan Culler's work and celebrity present further evidence
of the same "cultural" desire. Not only is Culler's entire career an
exercise in the "pragmatic," that is, "guiding" and "clarifying" and
"making available," but his recent guides explicitly call for a return
to "doing readings," informed by or armed with whatever distilled
categories of *nouvelle critique* the reader wants to apply or "get a grip
on." Further evidence can be found on an entire spectrum of intellectual work, a spectrum perhaps best defined by quick reference to titles
like *The New Centurion* and *Act and Quality.*

When this massive right-wing, often anti-intellectual, priggish, and
belletristic apparatus gathers to weaken Said's position, then, given
Said's prominence among critics trying to change the profession and
put it at the service of those hoping to further democracy, what we
are seeing is more evidence of the reaction's drive to extend itself
throughout those intellectual institutions where resistance and "the
negative," or "negation," as Adorno used to say, can still survive. It
is only the negative that makes possible the defense of life. Said puts
this powerfully in seeing criticism to be ironic, capable of negating
what is—negating in the name of something higher but something
higher that is in history, always situated, always confronting and
emerging out of an occasion. Given the dangers posed to the rest of
the world, to our own minorities and oppressed, by the dominant
forces of our own societies, given the truth, for example, of the Frankfurt analysis of the intentions of mass culture and the culture indus-

try—despite whatever Utopian elements appear in resistance to it—
then it becomes the yea-sayers who are the barbarians within, threatening, in the service of forces they are ignorant of, to destroy the possibility of negation. The culturally comfortable critics often identify
themselves as heirs of Arnold. In doing so, they equally often forget
that, in part, Arnold meant his normative definition of culture to
point out the shortcomings of his society's own dominant values,
manners, and traditions. Raymond Williams, in *Culture and Society*
(1958), and George W. Stocking, Jr., in *Race, Culture, and Evolution*
(1968), both reminded us long ago that a critical attitude toward
one's own culture requires more than "critical detachment." It requires some substantial dissatisfaction with current values. It requires
an attitude and experience of alienation, a subject Said discusses at
some length in taking Auerbach's exile in Turkey as metaphorically
paradigmatic of all oppositional critical work (5–9). Arnold would
have felt that those comfortable with current cultural values and traditions were philistines.

   William H. Pritchard provides a uniquely clear example of the anti-
intellectual and smug laziness at the "sensitive" heart of the culturally
comfortable critics. In a bantering, condescending, and critically silly
essay in *The Hudson Review*, Pritchard, one of the journal's editors,
takes the bull by the horns. Note the exclusionary violence in his
words: after telling us he is an "amateur"—one should hear the correct intonation—he goes on to explain that his aim is to separate "deconstruction" as much as possible from "enthusiasm" for the "old
values"; he admits that this is "a bad way to behave if you believe that
pluralism ought to be the *roomy, inclusive* word for one's philosophy
toward *alien* modes of approaching literature. . . . It may even be appropriate," he goes on, "to speak up as a professional colleague of
these critics and teachers who is, by careful standards, rather mini-
mally educated in the literatures of decon [despite the reference to a
bug-spray, Pritchard is referring to the work of de Man, Derrida, etc.]
. . . yet knows there's a reason for my not 'keeping up' in the way I
keep up with the things I care most about" (*The Hudson Review*, 36
[1983], 541; my emphases). Pritchard's essay indiscriminately belit-
tles all theory as "deconstruction"; it also encourages "business as
usual" but, perhaps it is needless to add, not on the scholarly model
of an M. H. Abrams or an Erich Auerbach or on the verbally alert

model of an Empson or a Burke. Dealing with the problems of culture, as Said might say, requires little intellectual effort for Pritchard: "All one needs is an active mind, a good chair and a lot of time to sit in it." Even the arguments of an Altieri or Hirsch are redundant for him: "speak boldly of what . . . Frost or Stevens was 'getting at' . . . and maintain that a good poem is one in which that intention, that meaning, is vibrantly, originally, beautifully stated" (548).

Except as an example of Said's general contention about cultural critics, how does Pritchard's ungenerous little piece involve him? Pritchard's essay is a review of *The World, the Text, and the Critic* and Jonathan Culler's *On Deconstruction* and so, ironically, continues the paradoxical linkage of Said and Culler begun in 1975 when *Structuralist Poetics*, with its ability to "dispel confusion," won the James Russell Lowell Prize from the MLA, rather than Said's *Beginnings*. Pritchard's essay is interesting only because it exposes the strategies for dealing with Said, especially by taking advantage of the comparison with Culler.

First of all, Pritchard uses Said's critiques of unworldly theory mockingly to dismiss deconstruction (this was an unacceptable prospect Said anticipated in his critique of Derrida as long ago as his Gauss Seminars); second, he misuses Said to show how long ago "we" knew all about what "theory" "tries to teach us." So for Pritchard, when Said writes "theoretically," he writes badly, "without polish," and he wears out "our" patience with old news badly dressed: Pritchard advises that we bemoan and discard this Said. He is always valuable when he explicates literary texts, but even then, "one can only regret Mr. Said's too-extensive acquaintance with theory and theoreticians" (544). Third, and most important, Pritchard trivializes Said's critique of culture:

He seems to be trying to climb out of the marmalade and get back in touch with "existential actualities," with life, politics, society, manners. I can only encourage him in this endeavour by suggesting, even if he chooses not to take up once more the book I understood him to be writing years ago about Swift, that there is Anthony Trollope or John Henry Newman to benefit from his consideration. Since he has paid in full his theoretical dues, why not head off on a road not quite so traveled these days? (544)

Inscribing Said within this underlying narrative of the prodigal son is an important tactic in the way that the cultural critics deal with

Said. They are prepared, for their own interests, to welcome this "Harvard man" back into the fold—or so it should be made to appear. Beneath the prodigal son motif are actually enacted a temptation scene and a condemnation scene. They aim to recapture surely not Said but others who might follow after him and who, they hope, might accept their ideological normalizing and domesticating of his project. But the condemnation of Said appears in the figure of Culler, who functions as the professional ideal: "For inside the formidably thorough, patient, well-read person of Jonathan Culler beats an unproblematical heart of common sense" (547). Some who "keep up" better than Pritchard might contest the first part of that sentence— five books within eight years?!—but not the second.

The effect of this obfuscation is, I contend, to reveal all of the dangers of criticism Said suggests exist in our institutions today. Were Pritchard alone in these anti-intellectual, commonsensical pratings, the issue would be moot. But John Bayley, in *The New York Times Book Review* (February 27, 1983, 11, 18–19), makes the same moves. He too opposes "amateur" to "professional," dismisses the critical investigation into the relations between power and knowledge (but links "that silliness" with Fish, not Said), accuses Said of "turning from" theory for purely careerist motives, and attempts Said's own cooptation by announcing that "Mr. Said's prospectus does often sound like a return to amateurism by professional means, as it were: a return to the world by renouncing the critical devil in the text" (11). Bayley lightly passes over Said's linkage of new critical conservatisms with Reagan to affiliate Said, preciously, with Henry James—"the critic's only weapon, the exercise of his intelligence"— thus obscuring Said's political and institutionally reformist and contemporary purposes. Finally, Bayley aligns Said with Victorian essayists (E. S. Dallas?!), praises and regrets "the real book" inside the one Said actually wrote—"relaxed and discursive, original, immensely learned"—and ends in another version of the prodigal son: "It is a singular reflection on our academic culture that, to establish what is simple or obvious, Mr. Said's book has to masquerade as yet another daring display of critical theory" (19). Similarly, Claude Rawson, in "Textual Harassment" (*The London Review of Books*, 6 [5–18 April 1984], 12–13), finds that while Said wants to break out of the grasp of theory and argues that one must and should, Said himself cannot:

"Said's new book expressly insists on the opposite proposition that 'texts . . . are events,' but in practice constantly reverses the equation" (12).

Denis Donoghue's response is, at first sight, more generous: "the essays provoke due interrogation of contemporary literary theory, and exact from the reader the care and conscientiousness the questions at issue warrant" (unfortunately not, as we have seen, from all readers) (*The New Republic*, 18 April 1983, p. 30). After abstracting a brief quotation from Said, however, Donoghue, exercising one of a reviewer's oldest prerogatives, decontextualizes his quotations and comments: "Put like that, his position sounds fairly conventional. . . . Still, it is my impression that Professor Said would prefer to be called an old-fashioned historical critic rather than to settle for the weightlessness of the particular theorizing he has come to dislike" (31). One hastens to add "perhaps," to ask if he would prefer it to the particular lightness of such writing as Donoghue's own; one also rushes to ask what happened to Said's own self-characterization as ironic oppositional critic. Why can't Donoghue fairly represent and discuss the alternative Said proposes to Hillis Miller's type of work as well as to Donoghue's own? He quibbles that Said should not have taken so long to see the "error" of Derrida's and Foucault's ways (Donoghue saw those long ago): "I am surprised that he is surprised by, say, Foucault's insistence upon the anonymity of power" (32). The surprise continues. Said discussed the problems of Foucault's theory of the anonymity of power immediately upon publication of *La Volonté de savoir* (1976), especially in differentiating himself from Foucault's critique of the subject. Donoghue moves to further the cooptation and dismissal of Said's challenge by remarking its lack of novelty— Burke said it long ago—but Donoghue gives himself away a bit here, expressing anxiety that Said's work will become powerful enough to produce "Saidettes." The feminine diminutive is worth mentioning. Would "organic intellectuals" who appeared in the academy working with, "after," or along Said's lines, who would try to engage in constant oppositional critical practice—would they be "Saidettes" just as "Derridians" are what they are? Hardly possible, except that we see that, by making such a gesture, Donoghue feels that he can close the differences between Said and other presumably discredited critical fathers like Derrida and Foucault.

The harshest and most ungenerous critique of *The World, the Text, and the Critic* is Irvin Ehrenpreis's "Three-Part Inventions" (*New York Review of Books*, 30 [19 January 1984, 37–39). Ehrenpreis attempts no cooptation, only dismissal. Said, he would have it, gets his facts wrong, can't reason clearly, and can't write English. Is one justified in hearing an almost unnamable slur in the way Ehrenpreis chooses to make the last point? "Said's prose style, in keeping with his limitations as a scholar or critic, is marked by unfortunate idioms" (39). Ehrenpreis does catch Said in some imprecisions and shortcuts that must be acknowledged; yet again the question arises why Ehrenpreis, so totally unsympathetic to Said's project, agrees to review, or is asked to review, this book. Why, too, does he fail to engage critically the arguments of the book, choosing instead to amplify errors or dismiss what are interpretive disagreements as mistakes? E. P. Thompson and Eric Hobsbawm both warn that radical intellectuals must be careful in their scholarship. Given the enormous pressures on Said's time and energies and given the occasional nature of critical essays—about which Said says much—dismissing his book for inconsistencies and incompletions, in other words, reading it as if it were an encyclopedic treatise, is inappropriate. Hobsbawm's warning holds as true for critics as for historians: "One's got to be academic because there are people who will be watching you and trying to catch you out" (*Visions of History,* MARHO [New York: Pantheon Books, 1983], 32). By writing occasional essays, Said opens himself to Ehrenpreis's attack, which is all too clearly an example of what Hobsbawm describes. Ehrenpreis musters the old standbys of academia to dismiss the text without consideration: it is unresearched, imprecise, badly written, and so on. When one expects Ehrenpreis to engage with Said's argument, one finds name-calling and subversion: "As a literary theorist, Said disturbs one with his lack of precision. Where an argument begs for sharp definition and cogent reasoning, Said becomes wordy and vague" (38). When one expects arguments from Ehrenpreis for his critical values, he gives us evidence of their mean-spiritedness. Ehrenpreis's attack is meant to dismiss Said's project by painting it as patently not worth reading.

Hobsbawm points out that *TLS* has mounted an attack on Christopher Hill at a time when the decline of radicalism in the universities makes such radicals vulnerable, when the forces of reaction have reappeared to roll back the advances of the last democratic moments. I am suggesting that the same is true in the broad-based attack on Said and, through him, on others who, after the 1960s and early 1970s, are trying to preserve and further the little that has been won. But the forces of reaction are clearly united: Pritchard names those who should be admired, rather than those "problematizing" critics of recent years: "Hugh Kenner, Robert M. Adams, Irving Howe, Christopher Ricks, John Carey, John Bayley, Helen Vendler, John Hollander, R. W. Flint, Paul Fussell" (548). In a not surprising act of consensus-making, Rawson puts forward a similar list: "Hugh Kenner, Denis Donoghue, Geoffrey Hill, Robert M. Adams, Michael Foot, Norman Brown, J. Middleton Murry, George Orwell, Andre Breton" (12). Despite the strange eccentricities of Rawson's list, one is struck by the overlapping names, the presence of favored authors and reviewers of the tabloids I have mentioned (Robert M. Adams?), and the coincidence that some of Said's reviewers are on these lists.

The World, the Text, and the Critic has struck home, evoking a chorus of dismissal and petty praise and eliciting a set of aggressive tactics from the cultural critics newly assured of their hegemony within litterae humanioris—especially now that the Yale Critics have been largely silenced. What should be evident is that, given the willful anti-intellectualism of a Pritchard or the blatant exercise of power by Ehrenpreis and others, the cultural critics are the barbarians, the threats to a progressive and humane civilization. They need to be beaten back.

While I have my own reservations about Said's version of the critical intellectuai (see "Intellectuals at War," SubStance, nos. 37/38 [1983], 36–56), they reflect minute differences from Said compared to those from Ehrenpreis, Donoghue, et al. Joseph Buttigieg has argued that Gramsci's exemplary worldliness "needs to be restored to literary criticism today" ("The Exemplary Worldliness of Antonio Gramsci," boundary 2, 11, nos. 1 and 2 [1982–83], 36); Said has attempted this. Buttigieg also warns that such worldliness can be easily "dissipated" by becoming "fodder for academic debates." The World, the Text, and the Critic has fallen victim to its enemies; its friends will not do it justice merely by reinscribing it, no matter how generously, humanely, or complexly, back into theory. Before that happens, its challenge to and response from academia must be described. I have tried to do a bit of that here. Only then can it be used to modify the profession, to carry out the democratizing political work these culturally comfortable critics oppose.

But what I have done here is only a beginning. Were one to take seriously Said's assertion that "the inevitable trajectory of critical consciousness is to arrive at some acute sense of what political, social, and human values are entailed in the reading, production, and transmission of any text," then one should investigate and report how editors chose these reviewers, on what basis, and to what ends. Given that many of these reviews appear in journals of general interest, such as *The New York Review,* where literary criticism is only one of many interests; given, that is, these journals' concerns with issues of more immediate political and cultural resonance than "lit. crit." usually has, one would like to know if Said's involvement in public, political matters—especially his studies of media presentations of the Middle East and of the "orientalism" of many of Israel's supporters—played any role in determining the choice of reviewers. (At this point it is worth mentioning that Rawson disfigures his discussion of Said's book by constant reference to Said's own arguments about the need for Palestinians to create an effective narrative of themselves, their dispersal, their exile, and experiences. ["Permission to Narrate," *London Review of Books,* 16–29 February 1984, pp. 13–17.] Rawson simply cannot conceive how cultural identity and political power are affected by and in narrative structures.)

Beyond these broader questions, which, unfortunately, cannot be investigated here, let alone answered, it is nonetheless possible to suggest one potential consequence of these reviews that might have an effect on the university. In *The Partisan Review,* Michel Foucault pointed out that the university has two functions: "to put students out of circulation" and to "integrate" them into the values of a society. Foucault goes on to say that once the status of the university becomes problematic—to students and faculty—"universities must increasingly provide rituals of inclusion inside a system of capitalistic norms." "The upper-middle class," he says, "needs, for its economic development, knowledge, the university, the faculty and students" ("A Conversation with Michel Foucault," 38, no. 2 [1971], 194–95, 200). Said's call for a skeptical critical consciousness flies in the face of all of the recent reactions—core curricula, professionalization, the financial and tenure crises—that are meant to secure the university to the dominant interests by stabilizing study in canons and instrumentalism. He urges a skeptical critical consciousness that is, moreover, materialistic, political, and unencumbered by narrow ideological commitments. Such a consciousness can frighten the reaction, especially given the key role the humanities and a developing sense of the obsolescence of traditional literary studies played in the alienated consciousness of student rebels.

Taken in such a context of recent history as well as of present interests, the conservative professoriat's attempts to isolate, diminish, and exclude Said's call is only logical, in keeping with its own—alienated—interests. Radical feminist critics and others involved in minority or Marxist studies also challenge the reimposition of the canon and the authority of those attempting it. We all know the academic difficulties such groups face. To some extent they are successfully marginalized and denied access to the cultural apparatus. Said, however, is different. Unlike Jameson, for example, whose announced political and ideological commitments might be seen to "place him" outside the main traditions of the academy—and many, including Said, have warned that Marxism is in danger of becoming a literary subdiscipline—Said operates within and against the academy, employing the most powerful intellectual weapons it provides to grip it, in order to demystify and change it. And Said has had some access to the public media. But Said is particularly dangerous for the cultural critics and a traditional academy in a specific way: he can be the conscience of the academy and can appear to be the best it can produce. He is, after all, a passionate humanist, literate, eloquent, and productive; these are the academy's own announced values, and they cannot be easily deprecated. Indeed, because Said embodies these values, he is not only authoritative and legitimate—within the academy's own terms, and hence, the applicability of the prodigal son motif—but he is also exemplary, seductive, and convincing.

As a result, simple dismissal of Said is not an effective strategy; Ehrenpreis's review undermines itself because its self-evident polemic fails to acknowledge, even grudgingly, Said's virtues. Nor can the cultural critics simply place Said on the margins, as they might even a Jameson or Derrida. More complex strategies of cooptation, diminishment, and correction are needed to neutralize the very space that

Said occupies; but such a tactic must fail on one level since Said's representations are vectors of force empowered by the ideals of critical practice that he, unlike the cultural critics, takes seriously. This tactic can "succeed" against Said only if the cultural critics are willing—as they apparently are—to diminish further the active, negative possibilities of criticism. When Donoghue urges that there be no "Saidettes," he is urging an ascetic—and, following Nietzsche, one must say, resentful—reduction of the power of criticism. Such an ascetic move is, not surprisingly, nihilistic. Nietzsche warned us long ago of the life-denying practices of the "yea-sayers." In our day, they have aligned themselves with the political and social forces of reaction in a way that spells a risk for us all.

CHAPTER SIX

Celebrity and Betrayal: The High Intellectuals of Postmodern Culture

℮∿◌ Regis Debray has awakened to a nightmare: the social and political condition of postmodern intellectuals is betrayal. *Teachers, Writers, Celebrities* dispels all traces of aura from intellectual life and production by analyzing the social reality of the Western intelligentsia and its relation to mass media and the system of commodity distribution.[1] Although Debray's focus is contemporary France, his "zoology" of the "intellectual animal" illuminates the situation of the intellectual in all postmodern Western societies. Before Debray, Gramsci and Althusser had both presented the inevitable complicity of traditional intellectuals with the ruling class in maintaining hegemony and manning the ideological state apparatuses such as the church, the schools, and the universities. Yet in so doing, both Gramsci and Althusser reserved for the intellectual a leading role in the process of cultural and economic change. Gramsci, realizing the depth and power of cultural control of the nation by the forces oppressing the people against their own self-interest, called for the workers to develop their own intellectuals to represent them, to theorize and organize their position, and to educate them critically to loosen the hold of cultural illusion on their will and consciousness.[2] In other words, Gramsci called for his own reproduction—scholar, critic, politician, organizer—as the intellectual exemplar for his time and named this reproduction the "organic" intellectual.

For Gramsci, the organic intellectuals of the working class could assume their leading role only with the aid of a traditional humanistic education in the classics. Indeed Gramsci's insistence that education in the humane classics alone suitably prepares the intellectual to understand the cultural-historical situation might be seen either as a historically and politically appropriate response to the amnesic, decadent education that government "reform" promotes or as a nostalgic, idealistic limit on Gramsci's "philosophy of praxis"; but in either case, Gramsci's own inscription within the discourse of a classical tradition—even if only to go beyond it in a new proletarian hegemony—suggests genealogically the cultural priority he ascribed to the intellectual in revolutionary practice. Most important criticism of Gramsci's conception of the intellectual focuses upon his distinction between traditional and organic intellectuals and his demystification of the apolitical, ahistorical illusions of the former.[3] Also, his highly innovative suggestions about the workers' need to develop their own organic intellectuals, which have such far-reaching theoretical and revolutionary implications, have been the subject of great interest. But what is, perhaps, most obvious in Gramsci has not been much mentioned, namely, the very way in which his novel revisions of intellectual theory, despite and because of their transumptions and reversals, actually preserve the "aura," the leading role of the intelligentsia. As many scholars have shown, intellectuals are a product of bourgeois society; they are a replacement for the church as a form of legitimation and are sustained economically by the surplus of industrial production.[4] While the distinctions between intellectual functions at different cultural-historical moments should not be forgotten, useful critical consideration should be given to the powerfully entrenched ideology and position of intellectuals even in some of the most subtle revolutionary theory. To what extent does the persistence of this leading intellectual role limit such theory and practice, and to what extent is it itself historically justifiable in our contemporary, postmodern world?

A brief look at Althusser might begin to expose the nature and importance of the problem I am suggesting. Althusser, while insisting that ideology is ahistorical, a permanent and inescapable feature of social reality, reserves for the Spinozist or Marxist intellectual the honorable task of acquiring scientific knowledge of the devices of ideological recognition that always already constitute individuals as subjects. Since ideology is inescapable, the intellectual pursuing such scientific knowledge is, for Althusser, always in a heroic aporia:

"Now it is this knowledge that we have to reach, if you will, while speaking in ideology, and from within ideology we have to outline a discourse which tries to break with ideology, in order to dare to be the beginning of a scientific (i.e., subject-less) discourse on ideology."[5]

It might be puzzling to find Althusser calling for the end of the subject in keeping with his antihumanistic, structuralist politics while, at the same time, deploying such classically humanistic metaphors of supervention and "daring." There are many ways to explain this apparently minor problem: a residue of Hegel, the unpleasant fact that texts escape authorial control—perhaps it is an example of the very aporia Althusser is describing. But it is difficult to believe it is only the latter because this daring supervention is supposedly the way out of the aporia toward a "scientific discourse." Could this textual problem be part of the ideology of the intellectual as essential provider of knowledge and meaning needed to lead, or as Gramsci might say, "direct," society to a better world? The uncertainty of Althusser's text, despite itself, preserves the "intellectual" as privileged subject. Surely in the modern world, especially in France, the intellectuals come to Althusser (and Gramsci as well in Italy) already constituted as the social fraction legitimately expected to criticize, interpret, alter, and supplement culture in the name of party consciousness, man, or progress. In any event, the intellectuals are the producers of value, meaning, and symbol, and they maintain their traditional dominant position in two of the most influential theorists of intellectual practice in our period.

The aim of Debray's book is to deny legitimacy, once and for all, to this intellectual fragment of our postmodern society by showing how, as a direct result of mass media and the dominant role of the laws of distribution in late capitalism, the intelligentsia is the greatest danger to the people. The paradox of Debray's situation, one of which he is at least partly aware, is that such a revelation about the intellectuals is itself an intellectual act and hardly a marginal one since it has a long and distinguished genealogy behind it of which Althusser and Gramsci are among the finest examples.[6] But unlike his predecessors in this tradition, Debray does not reserve a sanctioned space for politically or morally correct intellectual practice. In his analysis, he does find remnants and residues of previous and more valuable, because less market-oriented, forms of intellectual behavior and existence. *Le Monde* is one of these: "No change of government is capable of making the people of France regress into barbarism, but the disappearance of *Le Monde* really would imply the end of civilization and its probable replacement by one objectively regressive in comparison" (*TWC*, 174). To prevent *Le Monde*'s demise is impossible, it would seem, for the internal laws of the mass media implacably drive society to a more and more culturally impossible state. The nature of intellectual life and behavior and the social organization and fragmentation of the intellectual fraction of bourgeois society make it impossible for intellectuals to provide symbolic value, complex information, or critical intelligence to society. It is the peculiar achievement of Debray's book to make the case for this position compellingly clear despite the aporia of his own intellectual reflection on intellectuals.

In his substantial introduction, Francis Mulhern questions how Debray can sustain his own position in light of this aporia (*TWC*, xxvi). The answer, of course, is that he cannot, not if "sustaining" means standing outside the object critiqued, finding and analyzing an "independent" position. Mulhern does not, I think, realize that he is still operating within the old ideology of intellectual privilege, demanding rightly, from that perspective, that Debray be held to account for the very possibility of his own position. What Mulhern seems not to have understood is what Debray shows so tellingly: Debray's position is not simply his critique of the intellectuals and their necrophiliac romance with the necromancy of the mass media but above all the reflection of the degenerate and distorted—by classical criteria whose passing Debray mourns—features of all critical intellectual work in a postmodern world precisely as these can be seen in his own work—in the irony of his celebrity, in his unavoidable reliance upon and inscription within the structures of betrayal he reveals. Debray shows that the reality of postmodern intellectual life is betrayal not only because intellectuals commit treason against the people's interest for the sake of their own self-interest but because the structure is such that the very critique of that betrayal must always hand itself over to the very media it critiques and give itself to the very structure it tries to date and designate. Put simply, what Debray shows most cleverly and importantly and what, to some extent, Mulhern misses is that ambition motivates the critique of ambition—or seems to; there is no difference; the effect on the intellectual's career can be the same, that of a desire for influence and the like. The clearest evidence for this awkward position is not the activities of the successful intellectual celebrities but the remorse, frustration, and anger of even the most moral and disinterested scholar whose favorite book or article meets, not with ridicule, but with silence or faint praise. Mulhern accuses Debray of not specifying clearly his use of and nostalgia for a classical French discourse of reason. Debray, I believe, does do so repeatedly; but more important, Mulhern's comment reveals that he has not fully seen Debray's tactics and situation. Taking Debray seriously means it is foolish to read him unreflexively—that is, only with the criteria of the very classical reason he shows is now lost—or to hold him to the highest standards of academic prose, when the final demonstration of his work is that all of those standards and criteria have been cheapened to mere formal manners and—despite their internally consistent disciplinary organization—no longer determine intellectual success or failure in a mass-media, mass-market economy for cultural products. Nonetheless, Mulhern's response is worth commenting on both because it introduces Debray's work to English-speaking readers and so may be highly influential and because it reveals the persistent ideological illusion that in the postmodern world intellectual discourse can be held strictly to standards of reason, verification, and independence, which are themselves products of earlier times and no longer representative of the way intellectuals legitimate their power, positions, and activities, that is, produce, advertise, distribute, and defend them. There is, then, a strange but revealing discordance between introduction and text, between Mulhern, the author of the brilliant *The Moment of "Scrutiny,"*[7] and Debray. Mulhern, who seems to be calling on Debray to legitimate and account for the possibility of his "critically enlightened" position in the face of the symbolic and critical immiseration produced by the plethora of media images—which Debray states is seemingly inescapable—turns out to be the blinded party to this textual union. Despite his deployment of a "rational" discipline, "mediology," in his attack on the intellectuals, it is the impossibility of doing what Mulhern desires—reason has become a weapon in power structure—that Debray's book thumpingly insists upon, tattooing his critique with high ironic apologies for being like those he attacks: his purpose is "to elicit from the risk that the doors of intellectual legitimacy will be closed against us, a desire to dismantle the mechanisms that dictate to whom and to what these doors open; and to see the conditions on which they do so" (*TWC*, 3). And, of course, it must be pointed out that while Debray mockingly worries about the doors of influence closing to him, he is himself a leading intellectual political celebrity in France: "famous" since his capture by Bolivian forces in 1967 at Ché Guevara's killing; the object of a political and media blitz to free him, as Genet had been freed earlier, from a thirty-year jail sentence; a leading participant in the events of 1968 and one of the most insightful commentators on those events;[8] a leading member of the P.S.F.; and finally, a member of Mitterrand's government. The irony of Debray's celebrity and his roots in the Ecole Normale only validates the demonstration he affords us of the scene of general intellectual treason in postmodernity. He has already been handed over to and made famous by the market.

Teachers, Writers, Celebrities is a history, a theory, and an analysis of intellectual social formations and their relationship to and determination by the forces of cultural production and intellectual-political influence. As a history, Debray's book examines the social role and structure of French intellectuals from the Third Republic to the present. As a theory it explores the contradictory social existence of the intelligentsia as an "animal of power," successfully adapting itself and its interests for survival in different economic and technological environments. As a historically concrete analysis, it "x-rays" the internal structure of the intellectual group and details the nature of its interactions with other social forces that it serves or supports. All of this is done within the context of Debray's attempt to develop the "science of mediology," which involves both tracing "the symbolic function in Western societies," the direction of its forces, and its relation to the state and also theorizing the idea of "medium" itself and "the new political and cultural technology introduced by the modern *mass media*" (*TWC*, 1). *Teachers, Writers, Celebrities* is a fragment of a larger, multivolume project to be published as *Traité de médiologie*. Althusser's influence on Debray shows itself in those aspects of mediology that look like a "positive" science and Lenin's and Gramsci's voluntarism is reflected in those features of mediology that allow its practitioners to operate on the world. Indeed, Debray closes his text with a willfully optimistic call for the use of mediology against the social decay caused by the cultural impoverishment of postmodern symbols: "the alternative to decadence is a more positive policy of exchanging the criticism of weapons for the weapons of criticism with regard to the mediocracy around us" (*TWC*, 245). Debray hopes to form mediology into precisely such a weapon: "A rational discipline like mediology (which aims to be rigorous and must show itself to be so) can help fashion tools to make reality intelligible and weapons to transform it; inasmuch as it acknowledges the real, it can also serve those who find advantage there" (*TWC*, 2). The danger that the "positive" science of mediology can be used—as semiotics is used by ad agencies—by the very manipulators it hopes to understand is not the greatest limit on mediology; the double bind that catches up the mediologist himself or herself inscribes the mediocritic into the mediocracy itself. Debray always recalls the tight spot oppositional intellectuals are in because of the inescapable imposition by the mass media of its own market logic on cultural production. Debray ends his text by reminding us (and himself) of the probable futility awaiting such a critic because of "the aporia in which any discursive critique of the media finds itself—the object of criticism (and a boycott is part of the very wording) has the material ability to reduce the subject to nothing by withdrawing it from circulation" (*TWC*, 245). In the face of such limits on individual or even "scientific" critical efforts to bring about revolutionary change, to reverse the cultural decadence of postmodernity, and to name those in complicity with that decay, Debray turns his "optimistic will" away from high intellectuals toward an unspecified sense of collectivity and direct action. How this is possible in light of the almost Frankfurt-like pessimism of his analysis of mass culture's effects is not specified. But mediology is neither a utopian nor an apocalyptic projection; rather it shows clearly from within its own degraded cultural position—and even more clearly because of its awareness of this position—that intellectual life has no independent identity or history but that it is always, in all forms, a function of the material world in which it is inscribed. Debray's text presents a broader version of Althusser's reading of philosophy: "Philosophy, like religion and ethics, is only ideology; it has no history, everything which seems to happen in it really happens outside of it, in the only real history, the history of the material life of men."⁹ It is the very fact that nothing happens *within* intellectual life that Debray is getting at when, à la Balzac in *Lost Illusions,* he does a "zoology" of the intellectual animal. It is the adaptation of this unchanging fauna of modern and postmodern culture to various economic and technological means of cultural production that allows him to generate a theory of the intellectual broadly applicable beyond France to all advanced Western elites. It is also what allows him to write of Hegel, Balzac, and Nietzsche that "the naturalists of the human mind saw though [the men of culture whom Balzac calls the *gens des lettres* and Nietzsche the "camels of culture"] sooner than the historians of society" (*TWC,* 3). Not only is this "zoology" something of a departure from the classical French discourse of Linnaeus, Cuvier, Buffon, and Geoffrey de Saint Hilaire which, according to Mulhern, underlies Debray's book, but this ironic tilt toward these ironic "naturalists" and away from "historicism" allows Debray to establish the most important of all conditions for his study: that the intelligentsia as such exists despite intellectuals' liberal pluralistic claims that they/we do not constitute an object, a social fraction. Establishing this point of departure allows Debray, of course, to elaborate his theory of the intellectual—this modern and postmodern creature—which, in turn, reinforces the credibility of his contention, after Balzac, Hegel, and Nietzsche and despite "official" assertions to the contrary, that the "intellectual animal" exists. In fact, Debray goes so far in showing the social reality of intellectual life's dependence upon the illusion that the intelligentsia does not exist that, for him, the surest sign of someone's participation in the intelligentsia is that person's insistence that it does not exist.

Before he can carry out his history, theory, or analysis of the intellectuals, Debray must show that the object of his study has a social reality. This is not a structuralist project for Debray; that is, he is not, after Kant and Saussure, constituting the "object" of his "science," nor is he applying philosophical categories to an aspect of "human existence." He is demystifying the liberal ideology that denies intellectuals a corporate existence by generating concepts about that existence whose legitimacy can be measured by the degree to which they make aspects of social reality intelligible. More specifically, mediology is intended to illuminate the intellectuals' pursuit and defense of power and show how they/we are constituted as a social subject in these relations to power.

The intellectuals are organized hierarchically into high and low intellectuals with different social lives, political commitments, and mutual relationships. Just as Gramsci extends the term to include technical experts, Debray uses "intellectuals" to include teachers, ad executives, government policymakers, media executives—all of those who distribute, repeat, or modify cultural symbols and images or who administer the systems for such distribution. The "high intellectuals" or "intelligentsia," who are Debray's primary concern, are distinguishable from the proletarianized mass of intellectual workers by the role they play in society, especially vis-à-vis the mass media, and so are culturally more important to society than the relatively anonymous lower intellectuals. They are more important because they have more power and because their careers and positions are the logical fulfillment of intellectual life in any phase of modern or postmodern society.

The high intellectuals or intelligentsia are negatively cohesive because individual members are always in competition with each other for power but according to rules and manners that code the struggle to prevent serious, damaging, long-term effects upon the *group's* position (*TWC,* 17). By definition not homogeneous, the intelligentsia is not a class, caste, or corporation but a "social category" (*TWC,* 21). Needing each other to promote their positions and careers, intellectuals nonetheless cannot organize collectively. The higher up the ladder of intellectual power one goes, Debray shows, the chance declines that some sort of meaningful collective or union will exist among intellectuals, except as a means of self-promotion. The social reality of the intelligentsia is extremely individualistic and alienated: "each member is irreducible to his neighbour and it is precisely that difference that makes him an intellectual" (*TWC,* 22). Of course, as intellectual work is more and more proletarianized and, for example, one composition instructor trained in tagmemics easily replaces another or is replaced by cybernetics, the ranks of the intellectuals who are individual, noninterchangeable practitioners of a "liberal" profession decline. Needless to say, the remaining elite assumes a different relation to social life than earlier elites had done prior to the rationalization of cultural production. But what always separates the intelligentsia from other intellectual workers is that it produces culturally significant symbols. The intelligentsia is defined as "those who *create* as opposed to those who administer, distribute or organize, those who invent as opposed to those who repeat." Debray cites Michael Löwy's description of this intellectual aristocracy as " 'direct producers in the sphere of ideology and culture' " (*TWC*, 23). Debray's detailed taxonomy of the social and legal categories of intellectual workers shows, among other things, that the high intellectuals are well paid by government, universities, and the media in contemporary society and that they are very few in number, perhaps no more than four thousand French people responsible, as it were, for hegemony.

By establishing, at least schematically, the existence of the intelligentsia as a social subject, Debray has made theoretical and political advances and prepared the ground for his mediological history. The intelligentsia appears to be more important in producing symbols and cultural hegemony in the present world than in what Althusser calls Ideological State Apparatuses (ISA). Specifically, the relation of the intelligentsia to the state power and to "civil society"—for Debray a code word for mass market, international corporatism—must be theorized. Once the importance of the intelligentsia is recognized, it should put to rest, once and for all, the mystified and fashionable assertions about the heroic marginality of intellectuals in postmodern life. Perhaps in ISAs, marginal oppositional figures within the cadres of the proletarianized intellectuals can practice subversion. Althusser humanely and admiringly—perhaps romantically—characterizes their situation in this way:

I ask the pardon of those teachers who, in dreadful conditions, attempt to turn the few weapons they can find in the history and learning they "teach" against the ideology, the system and the practices in which they are trapped. They are a kind of hero. But they are rare and how many (the majority) do not even begin to suspect the 'work' the system . . . forces them to do, or worse, put all their heart and ingenuity into performing it with the most advanced awareness.[10]

The margins and crevices left to oppositional practice by an absorbent and expansive late capitalism are important as disparate units only insofar as they may associate to form a collective or serious opposition and so lose their marginality; but they should not be valorized for their borderline status in and of itself. Such fragmented and individualistic rhetoric and values are part of the very ideology of the intellectual subject which obscures its social function.

Debray specifies three major illusions obscuring the view of the intelligentsia and obstructing all attempts to theorize and alter it: "The impression of heterogeneity . . . The impression that it is not organic or closed . . . The under-estimation" by critics focusing on the operations of the ISA (*TWC*, 33). In other words, theories of the marginal intellectual belong to the ideological camouflage of the high intellectuals and obscure their relation to power and their service to the state and corporate power as masters of hegemony. The intelligentsia is never marginal because of its essential and defining relation to power. As Alvin Gouldner has also argued, Western intellectuals do not institutionally approve of research into intellectual power and structures.[11] Debray puts the matter simply: "the sociology of real capitalism ignores (or marginalizes) the intelligentsia in order to conceal it as an active political force and to perpetuate the illusion that it does not exist" (*TWC*, 29). The intellectual careerists who argue for the subversive role of the "marginal" intellectual turn out, perhaps not so unexpectedly, to be not radicals at all but lackeys of the hegemony they deceive themselves and others into thinking they are attacking. (We must return to this theme later.)

Power is always the key term in the milieu of the intelligentsia and all of its relations. Even though these vary with the economic and technological environment, the fact of power does not. This fact can be studied in many ways, from many disciplinary perspectives. Debray's mediology systematizes the relations of power existing between the intelligentsia and the media:

The frontier that allows a distinction to be drawn between the high and lower intelligentsia is each member's ability or inability to gain access to the means of mass communication. That ability is not individual: it is socially determined. It is not aleatory: it presupposes the observance of strict rules. It is not a complementary or a side issue: It involves the intellectual activity itself, the realization or non-realization of its concept as the action of man on man through symbolic communication, as a project of influence. (*TWC*, 32)

The history of the intelligentsia is the history of its relations to the changing means for gaining and spreading influence; as such, it is a part of social and technological history and cannot be written separately. But writing such a history, which Debray only begins to do here, would mean following Nietzsche, Marx, and Foucault in writing a history of power.

Debray's history of French intellectuals divides the period from 1880 to the present into three parts: the period of the Third Republic and the dominating influence of the university (1880–1930), the moment of dominance by publishing (1920–1960), and the mass mediatic, begun in 1968 and still in dominance. The third of these is, for Debray, totally regressive.

The university and the publishing house both produced culturally legitimate values that were not subject to the pauperization of the marketplace inflicted on all symbolic communication by the mass media. But both failed to defend their own primacy in the face of increasing massification and commodification because their social awareness was too narrowly moralistic and too dependent upon bourgeois codes of "proper" intellectual behavior to police cultural production. Neither mode of conduct resisted or even understood the political-economic changes surrounding them.

The high intellectuals were attracted to and reproduced by the university during and after the reform period of 1871–1885 because the Third Republic, attempting to stabilize and legitimate itself, made the university the source of its own cultural defense. In opposition to the church, the state recruited liberal, progressive intellectuals into the quite self-conscious cause of defending the Third Republic and its social orders. Mulhern correctly outlines the differences between this explicit creation of the university as the cultural arm of the republic and the entirely different relation in England and America between intellectuals and the state. No simple translation of Debray's history from France to abroad is possible. But what is of interest is Debray's analysis of shifting vectors of power as the university rises and falls in influence.

"What concerns us here," Debray writes, "is less the decline itself than the redistribution of forces it produced within the intellectual order and, more generally, the modification of the basis of hegemony in France" (*TWC*, 44). As is clearly the case also in America now, the university has lost the right to reproduce itself except to further proletarianize itself in its lower ranks. The intellectual aristocracy of the ruling class does not depend for its power upon the medium or base the university provides. Gramsci writes in *The Prison Notebooks* that a history of a society can be written monographically as a history of a party.[12] Debray writes the history of modern France's cultural decay by following the career of the intellectuals and their own regression into a state of betrayal. The dominance of culture by teachers provided society with much of its moral and symbolic resilience. The university preserved whatever memory society had; as "a pocket of memory" it was "a total reservation for the ethics of truth." It valorized "abnegation" precisely as part of the code for success and influence. "Integrity, obscurity, selflessness; the words raise a smile, but the archaism of the vocabulary derives from the downgrading of the practices of the schools, not vice versa" (*TWC*, 49). With the loss of university sanction of intellectual reproduction and reward comes the loss of "deontology" which closes off "the gateway to all moral philosophies." The administrative cohesion the university provided the intelligentsia established the ground for its relative independence from superstructural influence, but now, without it or the publishing house, the intellectual has no form of social cohesion with which to resist even if he or she so desires.

There are two closely related and crucial consequences to the decline of the university: the first, the destruction of the humanities as critique; the second, the reorganization of the intelligentsia under another hegemony. The intelligentsia follows power and so moves toward the mass media, which is part of the "private sector" because, despite government control where it exists, always already "market logic" is "inherent in the workings of the media" (*TWC*, 46). It is axiomatic in the kind of analysis Debray is carrying out that the mass market "homogenizes" the people and dissolves traces of independence so that the humanities must decline. Specifically, capital's direct dominance of the intelligentsia—and, we might add, Reaganomics' dramatic shoving of the university into the "charitable" hands of banks and corporations—will allow the final (dis)-solution of "the hard core of the classic intelligentsia, that irritating stone that formed in the arts subjects . . . over the years" (*TWC*, 47). "Economic factors" and "the job market" are catch phrases within academia today, describing not only the "reasons" why students study "job-related" subjects but also the voluntary and self-destructive measures taken by academics to satisfy the students' "needs." Of course, these academics are doing what is "necessary" to "save" their departments by being realistic, and it is not fair to say they are only saving their jobs. But despite protestations and counterintentions, the general system-wide result is the destruction of the humanities as the location of critical training. This state of affairs is not a matter of simple left–right ideology. As Debray points out, the mediatic society destroys all memory of bourgeois philosophy and so makes it nearly impossible to go beyond it. The Mandarins of the left and the right are at the bottom (*TWC*, 59).[13]

Debray's analysis of the university's decline begins from and extends a basic axiom of mediology that is worth quoting in full:

The breakup of the university corps obviously relates to the organic decadence of French society: it is both symptom and factor, cause and effect. In immediate terms it is equivalent to a transfer of power. The ideological field is magnetic: as one force of attraction weakens, the other grows stronger. But the iron filings still form a pattern; and as the intellectuals must cluster around something, they will go wherever the organicity, and therefore the potential for organization and promotion, is greatest: the more ambitious into the media and private capital, the more scrupulous into the state administration. The disorganization of the university means the historical disorganization of the intelligentsia, or in other words its reorganization under the aegis of rival hegemonic interests. (*TWC*, 46)

The truth of Debray's thesis of attraction is the very aporia of his own critique and his own position vis-à-vis his object.

The period of publishers' dominance ended when it could no longer "polarize the magnetic field of the literary intelligentsia" and was itself subsumed by the laws of the media and distribution. Of course, this had happened in the United States much earlier than in France. The cultural value of the publishers' era lies in the high quality of its product. Whenever production and distribution coincide as they did, for example, in Gallimard and *NRF*, value and productivity increase (*TWC*, 67ff.). Simply put, publishers could sustain a market situation in which many "intensive" works of art sold slowly, keep them in print, and so enrich the "symbolic pool," as it were, of cultural reproduction. The dominance of distribution over production and editing in the postmodern world subjects books to the velocity of turnover, generic homogeneity, and advertising sensationalism. Symbolic production is regulated and reduced, and culture is impoverished—perhaps to the point of social death. The era of publishers' dominance had also shown that "mass intellectual" journals were possible in which communication and exchange between writers, specialists in many fields, and the general public took place. Reviews provided the material conditions for writers to move into politics and for workers' discourse to come to the writers. But today's information apparatus makes intellectual reviews essentially "stage props," irrelevant to symbolic production (TWC, 73–79).

The subservience of publishers and academics to the principles of the marketplace brings about the dominance of the mass media, once itself a dominated element of cultural production but now in a position to legitimate writers' and teachers' careers and productions. Celebrity status is the logical conclusion of a career directed at acquiring the power of influence. Frequently, guests on such "distinguished" shows as *The MacNeil/Lehrer News Hour* are academic authors of successful intellectual books or studies who also write for and/or are reviewed by certain organs of "mass" intellectual influence such as the *New York Times Book Review, The New York Review of Books*, or any number of important "op-ed" pages. Such guests do not legitimate *MacNeil/Lehrer* but gain legitimacy from their appearances. They gain the license to speak publicly on public matters and often acquire greater stature, power, and market value with their publishers and deans because of their increased visibility. Debray analyzes the "logistics of power" (TWC, 105) involved in such intellectual behavior in terms of the media and shows how it is the completion of the internal logic of the intelligentsia's own identity as a "social subject."

Debray's work follows from Hegel's characterization of the "intellectual animal" in the *Phenomenology of Mind* as the point of departure for any theory of the intelligentsia. Hegel's analysis is a myth of origins fully visible only now that this animal has matured into the mediocracy. The scene of instruction, as it were, for the intellectual is that transitory moment between Reason and Spirit, "between abstract theoretical forms and the concrete history in which the Spirit will be made incarnate" (TWC, 5). The intellectual emerges in the history of the Spirit as an individuality which is both *an sich* and *für sich*, in itself and for itself, a necessary but temporary figure of deluded self-consciousness.[14] The intellectual, Hegel argues, loses contact with *die Sache selbst*, is apart from others, and detached from the Idea. Ultimately, as Debray puts it, "The intellectual animal—a figure of absolute individualism—comes face to face with the failure of 'the most individual solution.' " It is this essential vacuity and failure that motivates the entire intellectual project in history and leads to the current situation of betrayal. The significant element in the intellectual's makeup is the drive to constitute an identity as a "personality" to mask or compensate for the real nonidentity "within" the intellectual.[15] Neither Reason nor Spirit, non-self-identity germinates the intellectual and injects this animal into the zoo of power:

> He wants to make his personality his work, attributing essentiality not to his . . . works, but to his subjective ability to create and thus to his talent or personal genius. He claims to make his "operations" serve an objective cause, but really he cares nothing for it and systematically fails it. So the intellectual deceives himself, just as he deceives others. He has no work and "operates" in a void. After this false exit, the unhappy consciousness has to turn back on itself. Again, it is a failed odyssey. The intellectual animal struggles and strives to return to his own being, but his true being is nowhere. For Hegel and Balzac the intellectual is an individual nonentity who begins by thinking he is someone and finally discovers he is nothing. (*TWC*, 8–9)

If Debray's sense of Hegel focuses through Lacan, as seems likely here, then we are dealing with the dynamics of the mirror stage exaggerated into a permanent neurotic social subject. There is no original oneness to return to, for the uniqueness of the intellectual birth is that its "essence" is nonidentity at the origin. Driven compulsively, the intelligentsia pursues power to gain an identity it can never have. Ultimately, this is a version of what Freud calls the death-instinct because the greater the intellectual "contributions" to civilization, the greater the costs in energy, values, and life. The deadly power drives of the intellectuals are "sublimated," as it were, by the fortuitous historical social formations of the university and the publishing house, but they are fulfilled by the social extension that the mass media provides.

The intellectual needs power to achieve identity or, better, to mask its nonexistence. Identity takes the peculiar form of recognition of personality. But this essentially simple fact actually defines the social reality of intellectual life in the postmodern world and helps explain why betrayal has become the one dominant feature of its existence.

Recognition involves literal visibility provided by the mass media and mass distribution, it involves the power of self-presentation to others, and it involves dominating a hierarchy of unequal relations in order to be acknowledged by both enemies and clients. The mass media grants an intellectual authority by making a spectacle of his or her identity and, in so doing, allows the intellectual to make demands on others' attention. The most unequal power relations emerge in these nonreciprocal orders: information and symbols move down the hierarchy from the pinnacle to the plebs. Three major problems emerge from this structure: first, the Draconian restriction of symbols circulating in society; second, the ability of the mediocracy to speak "directly" to the public, bypassing or supervening other intermediary institutions; third, the fragmentation of the intelligentsia into a free-for-all scramble for access to power to achieve recognition.

Given the ever-increasing concentration of the book, news, and other culture industries, the regulation of cultural production by the laws of commodity circulation is not surprising. Debray cites Jerome Lindon's study *La FNAC et les livres* to show the restriction inherent in any such organization: "But thanks to a classic mechanism . . . the monopolization of distribution ultimately and paradoxically leads to the narrowest possible choice at the highest possible price" (*TWC*, 109). Of course, access to this ever more restricted symbolic circulator means pleasing those who control it, not just the "big bourgeoisie" but also the "ranking" intellectuals at each place in the apparatus. Debray's mediology accepts the idea that intellectuals are the ideological servants of the ruling hegemony but adds to it an analysis of the circuitry of intellectual careerism that recalls both Nietzsche and Foucault in its conclusions:

> For the intellectual order, power does not lie where shallow people think it lies: with those whom everyone calls powerful (state, party, unions). It lies with those who control career prospects, increased print runs and greater social visibility: the great mediocrats. This amphibology to the word power lies behind the many impostures that disguise flunkies (in the true professional sense of the word) as insurgents. (*TWC*, 176)

Debray's analysis along these lines shows how the intelligentsia actually operates within society in accordance with the "overall interests" of the ruling class and the inner logic of its own alienated and deluded existence as a social subject. Identity, mastery of one's own fate, and a position from which to rule and manipulate others—these desires driving the intelligentsia in its manic pursuit of recognition make the high intellectuals the perfect embodiment of the individualistic, competitive, and frustrated ruling ideology and the social force most likely to sacrifice or betray all other values for its own needs. The intellectual lives in a state of betrayal because of the effects of the kind of power he or she pursues. In brief, this is the power to absorb, to consume, to use up others' time. The intellectual is born, Debray writes aphoristically, not to speak but to be listened to. Consequently, the intellectual drifts toward the technological and cultural platform that provides the greatest audience, whose attention validates the intellectual's existence.

"Power lies where scarcity is greatest" (*TWC*, 121), and despite the proliferation of media delivering larger quantities of the same restricted number of goods, greater symbolic scarcity defines the mediatic more than previous ages. Above all, what is scarce in cultural production is not the media but time, the consumer's time. The media sift out which cultural products are available for consumption and circulation and, together with the Draconian rules of the market and the dominance of the leading intellectuals in any particular regional hierarchy of power and opinion, impose certain personalities upon the consumer/audience. Media logic imposes what the "anonymous," self-regulating system of the market chooses. Intellectuals competing in this system for their own literal survival, motivated by the vacuity and negativity at the heart of their/our existence as illusory "identities," cannot help but betray the general interest for their own. The postmodern intelligentsia is not an aristocracy but an oligarchy of the acceptably mediocre. Darwinian competition selects leaders in cultural regression.

The media exacerbate the intellectual instinct for betrayal. Since the value of cultural goods can be realized only by consumption in time, intellectual success depends upon marketing the product so that the mediatic logic compels audience recognition. The successful intellectual is powerful enough to receive attention, to gain even the recognition of criticism. Powerful intellectuals are taken seriously but not as a result of what they say, rather because of their "personalities," that is, the image sold by the media as deserving attention. The intellectual succeeds only by mastering this situation, but since such mastery is also a delusion, success depends upon being mediogenic, which also invariably means being ideologically safe. As Debray points out, the density of intellectual production produces savage competition. Barbarism is the constant shadow lurking in the intellectual world. "The intrinsic nature of the media," Debray writes, "which work on personality and therefore exclusivity, on originality and not therefore on the solidarity of a collective . . . turns the eternal struggle for recognition, which is the destiny of the intellectual into a fight to the death for a little piece of the media" (*TWC*, 121).

Effectively this means that a history of power in the form of a history of the intellectuals must be a history of what Debray usefully calls "acoustics." A history of influence would be the history of the means a given social-technical nexus provides for reaching an audience with cultural symbols. Not a history of ideas, it would study the material means for establishing the effectivity of images and values. In a sense, such a history can be told only as a history of intellectuals because intellectuals alone serve the political purposes of seduction and betrayal. Also, as Hegel's comments make clear, the inner logic of the intellectual as a historical and social subject guarantees that the apparatus of hegemony will always be manned: "In order to influence people, one must first be able to make oneself heard (or seen), which means having access to the place and the forms with the best audience, other things being equal. The desire to 'speak' to men is timeless, but public speaking has a history, that of its successive echo chambers. . . . It is through acoustics that the intellectual species comes into its own and gains the right to leave the zoo." (*TWC*, 128).

Yet access to an audience is not enough for the intellectual, nor is such access merely a neutral self-presentation. Since the intellectual, as Hegel argues, always presents his or her personality and not a work to the audience, "success" depends upon the resonances of that personality throughout the audience. The question of identity is, for the intellectual, a question of existence since that is defined as self-identity. Keeping up this illusion alone sustains a sense of existence. Complex textual strategies for gaining recognition or achieving resonance are essentially all ways of insuring the intellectual's existence through the quantity and degree of effect that his or her personality or identity achieves. The intellectual exists, Debray argues, "only in so far as he is recognized by others as worthy to exist." The mediocracy produces the aporia that is the logical conclusion of the intellectual's subjectivity: "Does the echo make the voice, or the image the body? No echo, no voice; no image, no body—hence the strongly reassuring effect of the media in the intellectual world: they provide a convenient scale of hierarchical insignia" (*TWC,* 146). In this way the ruling classes can and do produce and reproduce their organic intellectuals and assure that all of the high intellectuals who produce cultural symbols are theirs. Within the limits of Debray's analysis, the pessimistic conclusion seems justified as much by the nature of the media as that of the intellectual animal. Yet the pessimism must be kept in focus, for it both overestimates the importance of the intellectual group, even in alliance with the media, and underestimates the antihegemonic elements in society. It does suggest one difficult and painful conclusion, though, which Debray is not afraid to draw: the intellectuals are the most dangerous element in society working against the interests of the people (*TWC,* 194). Debray does not draw another conclusion: that the historical role of the leading intellectual is an ideology no longer acceptable to people struggling to change society.[16]

The danger that the intelligentsia in league with the mediocracy poses is not limited just to narcissism and careerism. Since intellectuals are what Nietzsche calls men of resentment—having discovered and been forced back to their non-self-identity, their nonexistence—out of a spirit of demonic revenge they become the "thought company" (*TWC,* 194) of the public. Out of their own needs to see and hear images and echoes of themselves, they become a collective incubus sapping the social and cultural imagination of the public, limiting debate and restricting the people's ability to imagine alternative realities. They/we have the means, as Debray puts it, "to show a whole nation the world turned upside down and inside out, with left and right reversed, since the outside world can no longer be seen directly, but only through the Great Central Mirror" (*TWC,* 194). Debray's analysis coalesces with Gramsci's theory of hegemony, but his Hegelian–Nietzschean tradition gives him a slightly different emphasis. While the intellectuals are always a profitable investment for the bourgeoisie because they "maintain a permanent preventive counter-revolution" (*TWC,* 195), they do so because their very "nature" as a social animal, in alliance with the media, authorizes them/us to "phantasmagorize reality" (*TWC,* 199), to will the world into nothingness, into insubstantiality, because of their/our will to revenge themselves/ourselves on a world and people that will not testify to their/our illusions of being the *an sich* and *für sich*. Debray's attitude toward the role of the intelligentsia is caught forcefully in an image that unsurprisingly recalls not just Marx's own polemics against the bourgeoisie but, even more, Nietzsche's attacks on aesthetics in *On the Genealogy of Morals*: "An establishment of pariahs or a curia of iconoclasts, mingling the cult of impiety with eroticism of execration, has been built up on the basis of a set of coherent discourses and practices" (*TWC*, 200).

The politics of this nihilism is, apparently, fascism. The higher intellectuals manufacture inequality (*TWC*, 203) both in their competitive social existence and in their products. Specifically, they destroy all collective memory and remove all substance from human reality. The university and the professor were, in their day, pockets of memory and incarnations of value and knowledge. The mediatic replaces these with the "extracultural" rules of the marketplace: "It is the pleasure provided by the author's image and speech that determines market value of a text rather than the pleasure provided by the text itself. The visible valorizes the readable" (*TWC*, 213). What this means, of course, is that the economic comes to control all other instances of production. Such a change in the rules of cultural production "is not politically neutral: it expresses political domination and a class position" (*TWC*, 225). Simply put, the intellectual pursuit of success in achieving visibility and resonance and, hence, effectivity puts personality in place of symbol, image in place of concept. Accepting and exploiting the force of irrational pleasure provided by noncritical personality images produced to market "authority," the intelligentsia is always in league with fascist tendencies. The mediocratic intellectual follows, like all men of resentment, an order of illogic. Debray puts the issue in terms that recall and refute and so-called new philosophers' Solzhenitsyn-like exploitation of the Stalinist gulag: "This cultural fascism is all smiles and no barbed wire. . . . Culture with a human face and fascism both make use of the naturalist reduction, which reduces the intellectual to the physical, a person to his contingency, and consciousness to the body" (*TWC*, 214).

As men of resentment, the final aim of intellectuals is "the extended reproduction of his social relations" (*TWC*, 219), not the production of socially liberating cultural values. Access to power means the ability to reduplicate the actual social reality of this particular social subject throughout society in the most successful exercise of influence in history. The intellectuals' delusion of self-identity reaches its highest point when its own absolute non-self-identity, its own negative collectivity, and its own ambitions come to define all social reality; in other words, when the intellectuals' resentful nihilism is imposed on all men and women as the natural state of affairs, its revenge will be complete. Ironically, to return to Debray's opening problem, the social being of the intelligentsia requires that it deny its own social being as a subject in order better to impose the very disorder of its own social life—which it denies itself—upon all others. Debray puts this situation frequently in different partial formulations: "this social being cannot be himself without denying his sociality"; "the lack of cohesion among individuals . . . is a collective mode of existence" (*TWC*, 227).

Debray departs from the French tradition of speculating on the intellectuals by insisting that theirs is not a moral failing but that they constitute a "total social phenomenon" (*TWC*, 232); that is, they are a political entity and a cultural problem. But they are also, in one of Nietzsche's senses, a problem "beyond" morals because they are the agents of cultural, symbolic, and ethical production. The aporia of intellectual critique means taking on the tropes and symbols of the intellectuals in order to describe and understand them—not to escape them or their errors (see *TWC*, 226)—from a point simultaneously inside and outside of them. It does not mean doing a critique of values that suggests or develops alternative, more "correct" morals; it means a presentation made possible by the most powerful weapons of criticism of the ways power operates within the intellectual arena as part of the history of human corruption.

Such an analysis makes it possible to see one of the central contradictions of intellectual life and its results: the intellectual declares himself or herself as an absolute without any necessary relation to others and, at the same time, requires all others as the sounding board or projection screen that alone can bounce back reassuring testimony to that absolute independence—these contradictions generate regressive repetitions that prevent any real community from developing in our society. And, of course, all critiques are also part of this all-absorbing structure. The media allow the intelligentsia to impose its peculiar reality as ordinary: "The odyssey of the intellectual, this endless spiral, is ultimately a dialectic that does never complete itself, it is full of reversals, but it always revolves around itself. Its motor contradictions are in themselves enough to prevent the intellectual both from finding himself as he wishes, as an essence, and from losing himself once and for all, in order to find himself elsewhere" (*TWC*, 237).

Ironically, the very mark of the intellectual's danger to society is that diacritical "we" that so often dominates the key texts of the liberal cultural tradition. The texts of Arnold and Trilling, for example, invoke a society in which "we" can find ourselves, but, Debray argues, the very existence of the organic high intellectuals makes such a society impossible. As soon as a text invokes the "we" of self-identity, the writer and reader enter a dizzying world of repeated aggrandizement and reduction that is easily dispersed throughout a culture already sickened by the hegemony of bourgeois nihilism: "When it discovers its inessentiality, the essential ego refers to a 'we' which, being inessential in its turn, refers it back to itself." The only work left for intellectuals then "is the dissolution of all works, each work being dissolved by all the others" (*TWC*, 239).

What, then, is to be done? Debray is extremely pessimistic, perhaps because he sees no significant contradictions in mass culture as others, like Fredric Jameson, do.[17] Also, he sees little hope in internal subversion of these "circles of misery." "The supreme irony is perhaps that they cannot be described without being reproduced" (*TWC*, 240). He seems to have little hope that "marginal" oppositional groups can succeed in breaking this hegemony. Some intellectuals might appear to step outside of it because they have a general moral vision—ultimately, however, this is not a moral but a political problem. He believes only a publisher or party can impose order and sense and preserve memory in the face of the amnesic powers of the media to produce "events." Yet when we recall his distrust of all intellectual impositions and his feeling—before Mitterrand's victory—that parties have lost their effectiveness and, indeed, his distrust of effectivity, Debray seems to have boxed in himself and us. He believes that "moralism," the "last resort" of intellectuals, is arriving (*TWC*, 245), and if not, then all earlier "resorts" will be tried first to no avail. He ends with a willful optimism that some unspecified form of "direct action" combined with the application of the weapons of criticism to the mediocracy is our last best hope. He refuses an economistic or evolutionary solution. Whether or not he is correct in this refusal can be discussed. More important, he gives in to the worst French habit. He measures cultural-political realities from Paris, and while he correctly analyzes the horrendous implications of the mediocracy, he gives too little attention to what might be going on in the provinces. Ultimately, he may be right to argue that the resentful mediocracy of postmodernity will drive us back to a Dark Ages, but he must show that nihilism has, in fact, snuffed out all life and deluded the living-dead into thinking they/we are admitted agents of the mediocracy he condemns; he is caught in a way he does not understand, as a dispatcher of despair, futility, dystopia, and resentment.

CHAPTER SEVEN

The End of Humanism

⤲ From the beginning of his career, Foucault's works have been in announced competition with the humanities and the ideological formations of humanism. That is, Foucault's projects have struggled against both the various individual humanistic disciplines—philosophy, history, language theory, and literary criticism, to mention but a few—and the conspiratorial repressions of the humanistic ethos. His struggle has taken place on many levels; for example, he has offered polemical demystifications of cultural history and the history of science; he has projected or "restored" the sciences of archaeology and genealogy to a powerful place inside critical activity, and he has shown that these new sciences can compete effectively with and displace the traditional linear, patriarchal disciplines such as history, economics, biology; and, finally, he has perhaps done more than any other non-Marxist Western thinker to expose the conspiracy of silence surrounding and supporting the power-nature of the moral and ethical values of "humanism" and the discourse—institutional and rhetorical—that supports it.

Rather than rehearse the general shape of the Foucauldian project, I would like to discuss Foucault's relation to the humanities by considering two of his more marginal texts—texts only rather recently translated into English: "Intellectuals and Power" (a "conversation" with Gilles Deleuze) and "Revolutionary Action: 'Until Now'" (a discussion with lycée students).[1] I choose these texts not because of their subtlety or novelty but because of their direct discussion of power and of the role of the intellectual within contemporary society. For I assume that the problem of Foucault's relation to the humanities is really the problem of the critical intellectual's relation to the history, power, and authority of his or her own discipline—or to put it another way, it is the problem of his or her relation to the institutional forms that shape one's activity into patterns predetermined by the discursive practice of the discipline.

Paradoxically, the intellectual's activity assumes two apparently opposed forms: first, a continuation of the post-Classical fragmentation of the field of representation into seemingly unrelated academic specialties; and, second, the humanistic and, centrally, literary critical attempt to interdict each and all of the spreading sectors of specialized knowledge by encircling them within a stabilizing curriculum, a hopeful vision of moral or anagogic unity, or a synoptic critical balance. In the recent past of the critical discipline, one need remember only much of the finest work of Lionel Trilling, I. A. Richards, and Northrop Frye: refining and expanding the domain and power of critical knowledge and practice while preserving much of our cultural inheritance from illiberality, proliferating ambiguities, and a forgetful, unsystematic, or New Critical eclecticism. Perhaps misunderstanding the enunciations of Jacques Derrida, Jacques Lacan, Paul de Man, Fredric Jameson, and Harold Bloom, these strong-willed Anglo-Saxon forefathers of ours would see our contemporary critical comedy as merely confirming their worst apocalyptic nightmares. But, nonetheless, despite the delicate differences within and between their texts and concerns (which any equatable examination would only foolishly forget), one should perhaps recognize their common predicament: representing themselves as hopeful yet realistic oppositional figures employing the very weapons, tactics, and values of the "enemy" that educates them in the techniques of specialized knowledge.

Not forgetting the ability of Trilling, Frye, or Richards to alter received ideas, bridge disciplines, and inspire heirs—in other words, to make the most of the power of reason, truth, and language to maintain the Western tradition—one must recall that they do draw their strength from precisely the forces assaulting that tradition, forces organized in such reproductive and self-protecting ways that they not only can withstand "subversion" but require it as a means of producing yet more subtle, more detailed, more powerful knowledge. Simply and reductively put, the fragmenting, specialized, sometimes opaque disciplines authorize the critical humanistic struggle for traditional values, for sensibility, for enlightenment—even the courageous investigations of the darkness of the psyche. The critical humanist, following Matthew Arnold, vowing his disinterest in power and concern for culture, must either dissemble to grasp power and authority or fail. But even in dissemblance, caution is in order. For even grasping for power against the culture, as Richards certainly did and with a success marked by his self-replication in his critical heirs—even grasping for power in such a way offers no assurance that the balance of one's achievement is nevertheless not weighted in favor of the forces one opposes. This is a circumstance no academic intellectual, even the genealogical researcher, can avoid. But, like all unavoidable agonistic situations, different strategies and tactics seem to produce different results or to represent new possibilities of transformation.

Generally, the humanistic strategy represents an observing or forgetting of power, of the dissemination of one's progenitors, while the genealogist's strategy depends upon the recognition of power and the disclosure of its persistent transformations. Genealogy, as Foucault would put it, writes the history of the present operations of knowledge, thereby providing a knowledge potentially liberating and potentially nihilistic—a knowledge of the sound disciplinary basis from which most modern and almost all academic intellectual production begins.[2] It is from precisely such a basis that the humanist elaborates an encircling, totalizing vision to contain proliferation, to arrest eccentric practices, and to mold newly produced knowledge along (modified) traditional lines—usually Christian-Platonic—into smooth, flexible receptacles to be whisked between nations and generations.

Although I could discuss any one of a number of academic humanists as a way of suggesting the differences between Foucault's project and humanism, I have chosen to focus my attention upon Irving Babbitt for historical and rhetorical purposes: his work is situated at the onset of the transformation from bourgeois to consumer capitalism, with all of the cultural crises this generates, and his rhetoric persistently reflects the interests, tactics, and nostalgia of modern humanism.[3] Babbitt's notoriety and influence, the importance of his allies and opponents, mark his centrality in the lineage of modern humanism. Moreover, his texts are transparent repositories for stabilized, authorized versions of figures extending back from Arnold and Emerson to Montaigne and Plato and therefore serve to create and advocate a mosaic of secular Christian values and ideas—in other words, to present the central topoi of modern humanism. If space and time allowed, one could interestingly map Babbitt's tropes upon past interpretations of his central figures and trace their strength to similar figures in the high and popular cultures of his time. One could also trace the persistence of those figures "forward" to I. A. Richards and the reforms in higher education of the late 1940s; the General Education Program at Harvard; and, more recently, the Harvard Core Curriculum's program for stabilization of knowledge within certain privileged, and recognizable, figures, areas, fields, or receptacles for research and instruction.[4] And in literary criticism one may follow the variations on these Babbitt-figures, not only to the subtle, delicate, tactful, and detailed—although incomplete—Natural Supernaturalism of M. H. Abrams and the skeptical, qualified, gracious, and balanced Samuel Johnson of Walter Jackson Bate but also to the somewhat less controlled, miscarried polemical preoccupations of Gerald Graff's Literature Against Itself.[5]

Running like a thread through all of these instances of humanistic concern I have just enumerated is an attention to the needs, claims, and benefits of humanistic education, especially of literary education. Once again, Babbitt's relatively direct presentation of the importance of English education in the colleges is a locus classicus of this concern and, hence, another reason for considering his as in some ways a "typical" representation of modern humanism as an academic's program.[6]

One must recall Babbitt's distaste for the proliferation of electives in colleges, for the advance of German research goals in American universities, and, in fact, for the very transformation of colleges into universities. Babbitt also dislikes the extension of professionalism and repeatedly calls for a reestablishment of the amateur spirit, of a kind of *sprezzatura* in literary study. He is nostalgic for the aristocratic forms and values of humanism at a time when, in America, Germany, and England, consumer capitalism begins to undermine the social authority of the upper bourgeoisie. Babbitt correctly intuits that a defense of his interests against the capitalistic ethos of the production and consumption of intellectual knowledge should be fought on the grounds of powerful humanistic ideology and that it should be fought over the issue of the college or university as a crucial means of societal reproduction. A lengthy analysis of Babbitt would need to confront in detail his class biases, his advocacy of selective group memory, his defense of enduring human essences, his authoritative use of the patriarchal metaphor, and so on. But since I cannot do this here, I want to repeat that I am using Babbitt as a "type" to represent a major dimension of humanistic theory, value, and study in America in this century against which Foucault projects the power of his work.

In *Literature and the American College*, Babbitt writes:

> Both our colleges and preparatory schools need to concentrate on a comparatively small number of standard subjects selected in this democratic way, that is to say, so as to register the verdict and embody the experience of a large number of men extending over a considerable time. Those who are taken up with every new subject and untried fashion are not educational democrats, but educational impressionists. As a result of this impressionism, our colleges and preparatory schools, instead of doing thorough work in a few studies of approved worth, are falling into that encyclopaedic smattering and miscellaneous experiment—which according to Plato are especially harmful in the training of the young. The scientist is interested apparently only in natural selection; the impressionist would make selection purely individual; but what is imperative in the college is humane selection, in other words, a choice of studies that will reflect in some measure the total experience of the race as to the things that have been found to be permanently important to its essential nature. (*L&AC*, 85)

This passage is important because it reveals the actual state of humanistic education at the beginning of this century: a "proliferation" of courses that introduce nonstandard or eccentric subjects of study and disrupt the authentic and central unity of a tradition that contains all experience relevant to those matters of permanent importance to "the race." Babbitt is advocating in this passage an ideological memory that forcibly includes and excludes entire realms of knowledge and experience from the canon of the human tradition. In fact, Babbitt's text acts as a defense of the very notion of a canon because this critical figure is itself capable of extending the authority and power of an aristocratic elite throughout society. By drawing on the power inherent in the metaphysical and social desire for stability, order, and transcendence, the idea of a canon reflecting the eternal values of man effectively silences the claims of marginal or eccentric texts, experiences, and voices. So, curiously enough, Babbitt's ethnocentric exclusion of so-called extraneous or exorbitant experiences and texts from the humanistic canon corresponds to his attempt to subjugate all knowledge to a few manageable disciplines or courses so interrelated and so conservative of the tradition that they can, in fact, be said to constitute not only a unified core for humane education but also the central machine for the reproduction of his hoped-for ruling class. I am trying to suggest, from a Foucauldian perspective, that Babbitt's text is an enactment of power within the circuitry of discourse from the late nineteenth and early twentieth centuries. It is a text made possible by the humanistic need to compete with other knowledge, desires, and interests imposed upon all of us by the structures of late capitalism. Further, it is a text empowered by the decline of its own class interests, for it attempts to reacquire power by reforming and reformulating the grounds upon which its authority continues to rest even as it fades. Like not only Arnold but all of those other powerful reforming humanists after him—I. A. Richards, Northrop Frye, the authors of the Harvard Core Curriculum—Babbitt dislikes power, repression, and imperialism and disavows the affiliation of his own project with power (*L&AC,* 55, 62). Indeed, like other humanists, he justifies his project by assigning priority to some "higher" sovereign than will or power in human activity. For, as Babbitt points out, the humanist is not a propagandist interested "in schemes of the elevation of mankind as a whole" but rather an advocate of the perfection of the individual (*L&AC,* 8). Yet despite his renunciation of social or progressive schemes for the masses, Babbitt, like other humanists, is an ideologue who would impose his position upon others by making it appear necessary and natural. In fact, in the following passage Babbitt compares the necessity of his position to the Law itself:

The humanist is equally on his guard against the excess of sympathy and the excess of selection, against the excess of liberty and the excess of restraint; he would have a restrained liberty and a sympathetic selection. He believes that the man of to-day, if he does not, like the man of the past, take on the yoke of a definite doctrine and discipline, must at least do inner obeisance to something higher than his ordinary self, whether he calls this something God, or, like the man of the Far East, calls it his higher Self, or simply the Law. Without this inner principle of restraint man can only oscillate violently between opposite extremes. . . . With this true restraint, on the other hand, he can harmonize these extremes and occupy the space between them. . . . In the absence of religious restraint, not only individuals but society as a whole will oscillate violently between opposite extremes, moving, as we see it doing at present, from an anarchical individualism to a utopian collectivism. . . . What is already apparent is the inevitable drift toward imperialistic centralization. (L&AC, 60–62)

Babbitt suggests that anarchy or bolshevism are the only alternatives to his doctrinaire form of Protestant liberal humanism and that these alternatives are essentially alike in their common aspiration toward either individual or collective power. Liberal humanism, on the contrary, is the only viable form of culture because it alone represents harmony and restraint—that is, the products of reason and beauty rather than power—as civilization's defenses against encroaching chaos, tyranny, and bureaucratic centralization. What is evident, even from this caricature, is the opposition for the humanist between reason and power; or better, from Foucault's point of view, what is evident is the humanist's obscuring of the workings of power, especially in "culture" and "education," by a mythology of disinterested and "objective" reason.

In "Revolutionary Action: 'Until Now,'" Foucault discusses humanism's involvements with some of the major elements of institutional control in our society, especially education and the university. "Revolutionary Action" is a record of an exchange between Foucault and some lycée students about the interpenetration of knowledge and power and of the institutional devices society has developed to reproduce itself by "disciplining" its members. The discussion takes place in 1971, and Foucault and the others find it necessary to consider the educational "reforms" resulting from the "revolution" of May 1968 and the efficacy of "reformism" and "revolutionary action" as modes for dealing with institutionalized power.

In many ways the discussion in "Revolutionary Action" extends Foucault's previous and persistent presentation of the knowledge-power complex in such works as The History of Madness, in the direction of his studies of disciplining mechanisms in Discipline and Punish and The History of Sexuality, in which an all-pervasive, subtle, and discrete "power" obsesses Foucault. For example, he points out that the minute operations of power are often not perceived in the daily routine of modern life. A student comments that "our classes are not immediately experienced as repressive," to which Foucault responds: "You're right, of course, since the communication of knowledge is always positive. Yet, as the events of May showed convincingly, it functions as a double repression: in terms of those it excludes from the process and in terms of the model and the standard (the bars) it imposes on those receiving this knowledge" (RAUN, 219). Foucault is not merely repeating the cliché that hierarchical power structures dominate the "traditional" learning situation. More than that: Both the presentation of knowledge by those who "have" it and the acquisition of it by those who conform to the artificial mode for "getting" it are political acts that train individuals through the "mastery" of a "discipline" to reproduce the authorized knowledge and forms of research of a neocapitalist enlightenment society: "Knowledge initially implies a certain political conformity in its presentation" (RAUN, 219).

Including oppressed groups by disciplining them rather than excluding them defends the interests of capitalism. In *Discipline and Punish,* Foucault makes clear that modern society bases its knowledge and order on an ever-expanding, ever-refining political technique of leveling and individuation.[7] The panopticon and incarceration are machines, metaphors, and models for societal powers that homogenize populations through knowledge, separation, observation, and experiment but do so only by "individualizing" people in cells and classroom desks, by examination and experimentation. For power-knowledge produces "norms" against which specialists measure "individuals." In fact, the very power of the representations of "normalcy" makes "individuals" conform to and thereby reinforce and replicate those "norms." The disciplining that Foucault finds everywhere in our society is, he points out in *Discipline and Punish,* discreet and indiscreet; for despite the omnipresent surface operations of the mechanisms for enforcing disciplinary "norms"—medicine, education, psychiatry, etc.—the functions of power go largely unseen. They so successfully represent themselves as "natural" and so effectively disseminate themselves that they remain anonymous and unexamined (*D&P,* 177).

Institutions such as prisons, clinics, schools, and universities are the material forms of this disciplinary society. Consequently, they cannot be successfully "reformed" or "taken over." Foucault insists that the property metaphor mystifies the nature of power, for the microtechniques of power have always already coopted even those traditionally said "to have power." For this reason, Foucault points out, "we should not be fooled by the modernized educational program, its openness to the real world: it continues to maintain its traditional grounding in 'humanism' while emphasizing the quick and efficient mastery of a certain number of techniques. . . . Humanism reinforces social organization and these techniques allow society to progress, but along its own lines" (RAUN, 221). Not only is Foucault once again prefiguring his insistent theme in *Discipline and Punish*, that the operations of power are positive, but he is also suggesting another idea he will develop at length: training in the power-knowledge operations of the individual humanistic "disciplines" is a necessary element in the self-sustaining microtechniques of neocapitalist power. To make this point, Foucault insists on the fact that the way in which texts are presented denies or obscures their status as "events," as markers of any "radical break" in society. Foucault's analysis implicates literary criticism, as well as psychoanalysis and Marxism:

> The system is telling you in effect: "If you wish to understand and perceive events in the present, you can do so only through the past, through an understanding—carefully derived from the past—which was specifically developed to clarify the present." We have employed a wide range of categories—truth, man, culture, writing, etc.—to dispel the shock of daily occurrences, to dissolve the event. The obvious extension of those famous historical continuities is to explain. (RAUN, 220)

Hence, in Foucault's own work the attention to surface, rupture, leakage, and transformation; hence also his stylistic obsession with catachretical figures, paradoxes, and apocalypses.[8] Foucault's difference from humanistic reformers is precisely this different scholarly and compositional practice. For scholarly writing is one of the central institutions of disciplinary activity; and if it is to make a difference in a struggle against power, to help the oppressed "take" power, it must be practiced with a difference—indeed, with that stylistic and erudite difference that bothers so many of Foucault's Anglo-American critics. The accepted disciplines of writing and research cannot be turned to "better purposes." For Foucault detects a common failing in all reformers and humanists: "Humanism is based on the desire to change the ideological system without altering institutions; and reformers wish to change the institution without touching the ideological system" (RAUN, 228). Humanism and reformism do not grasp the complexity of the material interpretation of knowledge-power. Humanism's inability to attend to its own involvement, contrary to its expressed desires, in the concrete operations of power—in other words, its naive faith in aesthetic and moral "disinterest" as well as its refusal to recognize the "origins" of reason in power—frustrate its confessed desires for moral or ideological reform. In fact, modern humanism's systematic blindness in just these areas demonstrates that our neocapitalist, disciplining society has deputized it as a legitimating ideology empowered to close off from view precisely those areas of discursive organization that normalize and reproduce accepted configurations of power.

Foucault proposes "revolutionary action" as an alternative to humanism's misleading and dangerous moralizing: "Revolutionary action, on the contrary, is defined as the simultaneous agitation of consciousness and institutions; this implies that we attack the relationships of power through the notions and institutions that function as their instruments, armature, and armor" (RAUN, 228). This is a beginning description of the project Foucault takes up in *Discipline and Punish*. It involves, among other things, subverting and displacing humanism's discursive inhibitions upon the critical-historical or genealogical pinpointing of the effects of power.

Humanism is such a compressed, "naturalized" compilation of figures and received ideas that when Foucault offers his most direct description of, and objection to, "humanism" generally, he seems to be directly invoking Babbitt in *Literature and the American College*. This situation is, in fact, another sign of Babbitt's paradigmatic function in our intellectual heritage:

> By humanism I mean the totality of discourse through which Western man is told: "Even though you don't exercise power, you can still be a ruler. Better yet, the more you deny yourself the exercise of power, the more you submit to those in power, then the more this increases your sovereignty." Humanism invented a whole series of subjected sovereignties: the soul . . . consciousness . . . the individual . . . basic freedom. . . . In short, humanism is everything in Western civilization that restricts the desire for power: it prohibits the desire for power and excludes the possibility of power being seized. The theory of the subject (in the double sense of the word) is at the heart of humanism and this is why our culture has tenaciously rejected anything that could weaken

its hold upon us. But it can be attacked in two ways: either by a "desubjectification" of the will to power (that is, through political struggle in the context of class warfare) or by the destruction of the subject as a pseudosovereign (that is, through an attack on "culture": the suppression of taboos and the limitations and divisions imposed upon the sexes; the setting up of communes; the loosening of inhibitions with regard to drugs; the breaking of all the prohibitions that form and guide the development of a normal individual). I am referring to all those experiences which have been rejected by our civilization or which it accepts only within literature. (RAUN, 221–22)

Humanism is an ideology of mystification and ascesis; it does not enrich or enlarge. In fact, it restricts desire by creating submissive man, by projecting into society through discourse and discipline a taboo upon power. Moreover, one can say that the discourse of humanism injects men and women into master–slave relations by assigning power to a "naturalized" and "transcendent" elite; and as a result, in the name of the highest ethical and cultural values of the West, humanism denies power to the oppressed. Civil rights, religious freedom, the critical intelligence, human nature—all of these and other images help cloak the power of discourse within an illusion of a just and stable society.

I take Foucault's central point to be the disclosure that humanism is merely a substitutive sign for the metaphysical "will to power." But it is, as I have already suggested, a duplicitous sign because it uniquely disguises its associations with the crudities of power as it engagingly denies its own coercive substratum and deflects the desires of the oppressed away from a seizure of power and toward a greater submission to an ideology marked as "natural." It must be pointed out that, for Foucault, humanism always necessarily oppresses by the projection of a sovereign, of a leader, or of the need for leadership—and hence mass submission—into the social and cultural order. The sovereign may be God, the state, the father, the doctor, or the teacher, but it is always a figure that interdicts the oppressed's approach to the object of desire. More: this figure represses the very desire for power and by so doing creates an eternally incompetent class unable to exercise power for itself within society. Humanism's interdictory figures cover over the actual need of the oppressed for concrete mechanisms to oppose the operations of power; they mystify the consciousness of the oppressed and alienate the oppressed from the knowledge of their actual needs. Moreover, this mystification works because it prevents the association of the oppressed both by fragmenting and disciplining their interests and by valorizing the ideology of the discrete, stable, and powerful, one might say "self-sufficient," "subject." But this mystification is not, for Foucault, simply a matter of controlling how people think but rather a matter of how ideological representations take on and extend power concretely in a society.

When Babbitt insists that humanism takes the perfection of the individual as its goal, he is merely announcing the central strategy and defending the central figure of repression. First, this enfigurement of power as the "individual" isolates the subject's will and consciousness as the battleground for cultural reproduction within the humanistic society. And as long as the humanist ideology maintains the image of the subject's "natural" priority in the order of things, the mechanisms of humanistic oppression will paradoxically revolve around the ideal of having the individual subject accept responsibility for its own normalcy, for its own self-regulation in the light of recognizable external needs for order. In other words, as long as the individual subject is represented by the humanists as the privileged location of human values and civilized accomplishment, the fetishization of self-control, self-regulation, and self-discipline will not only assure the standardization of experience and value but also effectively neuter and mute all other rhetorics and practices attempting to locate value elsewhere and in different modes of experiences. It is possible, by virtue of Foucault's critique of humanism, to see that the humanist's rhetoric functions as a representation of society and history (the latter in the form of "tradition"), which, masked as a neutral statement of eternal values and by means of its power as a representation of the nature of man, assures oppression by attempting to stabilize society in an image of harmony, restraint, and law.

It must also be pointed out that Foucault's analysis of the subject as a body and mind caught up within the disciplining apparatus of humanistic society describes not only how the individual subject is the battleground for control over man but also how this apparatus creates and sustains the individual subject as precisely such a battleground to extend the power of humanism, which as a rhetorical, epistemological system must suppress all other representations of human being in a competition for hegemony. For all other potential representations must, by definition of their attack on the individual subject, foreground the possible association of the oppressed in group practice and group knowledge capable of counterpointing pressures from the disciplinary measures of humanism. Hence Foucault's insistence upon an attack on "culture" not as an assault against power considered broadly—not, that is, as a frontal attack against the state or capital—but rather as a series of guerrilla skirmishes in prisons, factories, schools, and universities—wherever the nakedness of power reveals itself beneath the cloak of humanism: "We wish to attack an institution at the point where it culminates and reveals itself in a simple and basic ideology, in the notions of good and evil, innocence and guilt" (RAUN, 228). When Foucault advocates "the breaking of all the prohibitions that form and guide the development of a normal individual," he is directly challenging the authority and assurance of the culturally acceptable figures of "normalcy" projected, sustained, and reproduced by the humanistic disciplines—medicine, jurisprudence, psychology, philosophy, and literary criticism—figures in fact accepted and desired, on some level, by the disciplined themselves.

Foucault's work suggests that the intellectual must engage in the concrete historical research of genealogy to discover and to disclose the systems of relays among figures, ideas, and practices within and among disciplines or discourses. Such research can suggest how it is that the disciplined so desire their discipline that they have come to need their oppression. The modern intellectual can only oppose the extension and reproduction of power if he or she understands the ways in which the detailed history of the figures of each discipline—its filiations and affiliations, its deformations and reformations, its institutionalization and growth or decline—can alone disclose how each act of training within the discipline—whether of a soldier in the army or of a student in a seminar—is an extension of power. Specifically, genealogical analyses of the humanities can reveal how, under the oppressive guise of a neutral humanistic rhetoric, in the name of man and justice, intellectuals "transform [man] into [an] object and instrument in the sphere of 'knowledge,' 'truth,' 'consciousness,' and 'power'" (IIP, 208).

In "Intellectuals and Power," Foucault and Deleuze both represent the positive interaction of power, interest, and desire in forms of oppression as a "total enigma," unstudied and unspecified—although, as Foucault insists, it does often seem possible to identify the "particular direction" in which power operates. They agree that the contemporary intellectual can no longer define "reality" or "politics" simply in terms of the traditional narrow structures that represent the "competition and distribution of power." For, as Deleuze puts it, "Reality is what actually happens in factories, in schools, in barracks, in prisons, in police stations" (IIP, 212). Recognizing the local nature of "reality" leads to the further recognition that the classical concepts for the understanding of power are crude and imprecise. Foucault puts the situation this way:

> The question of power remains a total enigma. Who exercises power? And in what sphere? We now know with reasonable certainty who exploits others, who receives the profits, which people are involved, and we know how these funds are reinvested. But as for power . . . We know that it is not in the hands of those who govern. But, of course, the idea of the "ruling class" has never received an adequate formulation, and neither have other terms, such as "to dominate," "to rule," "to govern," etc. (IIP, 213)

In fact, these key terms have stabilized the representation of power in the discourse of the modern intellectual. Like the authorized figures of humanism, they are ruling metaphors that restrict the perception of the operations of power. They mediate the understanding of power by disguising and sheltering it; they deflect research away from the operations of power per se toward single facets or partial representations of power—such as private property—which are in turn mistaken for the entire "object" of investigation. To deal with this ubiquitous "object," Deleuze, like Foucault, insists that intellectuals must "initiate localized counter-responses, skirmishes, active and occasionally preventive defenses. . . . We must set up lateral affiliations and an entire system of networks and popular bases" (IIP, 212). To cast light on power, to indicate how and where power oppresses, the intellectual must "match" the complex circuitry of power with an equally complex series of relays in his own rhetoric and practice, relays among different disciplines, different interests, and different desires.

But a peculiarly Foucauldian point must be made here. In genealogical research the intellectual must not become the representative of the oppressed; the intellectual's proper role is not to "enlighten" the oppressed. To assume the role of "representative" is itself hegemonic;

it provides "leadership" and hence merely extends power and revalues the subject. Moreover, Foucault writes with reference to May 1968, "the intellectual discovered that the masses no longer need him to gain knowledge." Genealogical research reveals that "intellectuals are themselves agents of this system of power—the idea of their responsibility for 'consciousness' and discourse forms part of the system" (IIP, 207). I take this statement to be a partial reconfirmation of Foucault's project in *Madness and Civilization*: to let the silent voice of madness be heard against the discourse of reason and enlightenment that otherwise mutes its silent cry. But I take it also to be a realignment of the project away from granting the intellectual the right to function as a maieutic Hermes, bringing to voice the obscured message of the oppressed in his own text. Rather, he must first tend to his own garden. For the intellectual's project is to engage in a struggle against the mechanisms of power as they extend and reproduce themselves through his or her disciplinary critical, teaching, and scholarly activity. Even the literary intellectual must engage, above all, in a regional confrontation with power and thus indirectly join forces with others—workers, women, gays—who are struggling in their own areas.

The intellectual's weapon in the battle against power is theory, not abstraction or obfuscation but theory as a practice, as a struggle against power. "This is a struggle against power," Foucault writes, "a struggle aimed at revealing and undermining power where it is most invisible and insidious. It is not to 'awaken consciousness' that we struggle (the masses have been aware for some time that consciousness is a form of knowledge; and consciousness as the basis of subjectivity is a prerogative of the bourgeoisie), but to sap power, to take power" (IIP, 208).

The power of the intellectual disciplines to reproduce society in the image of the dominant ideology consists, as Gramsci might put it, in the willed assent of the intellectuals to the values and social codes produced by that ideology. The intellectual shares this potential assent to the figures of power with all other oppressed groups, but the Foucauldian intellectual's painstaking genealogical research can produce texts that not only expose the origins of this assent in the disciplines but also compete with the canonical codes and values and displace them by forcing intellectual institutions to attend to what they perpetuate, to the interplay of desire, power, and interest structuring a given humanistic discipline. In fact, the genealogist's theoretical competition should not accrete power to a private, highly subjective enunciation. This is not the purpose of the often odd-seeming erudition of a Foucault. Rather, the intellectual's activity should be impersonal counterstatement, a disclosure of the secrets of power and an attempt to subvert power itself:

> And if pointing out these sources—denouncing and speaking out—is to be a part of the struggle, it is not because they were previously unknown. Rather, it is because to speak on this subject, to force the institutionalized networks of information to listen, to produce names, to point the finger of accusation, to find targets, is the first step in the reversal of power and the initiation of new struggles against the existing forms of power. . . . The discourse of struggle is not opposed to the unconscious, but to the secretive. (IIP, 214)

This statement makes an unavoidable claim upon the literary intellectual to examine the history, affiliations, and functions of his discipline within society. This is a demand to name the interchange of power, interest, and desire inherent in judging the value of poetry and criticism, in valorizing select critical terms—form, balance, irony, paradox, *différance, supplément,* competence—and in acquiring and teaching certain methods of reading and writing as well as defending those methods on the grounds that more subtly refined and detailed readings are cultural necessities. This passage demands that critics radicalize criticism as a subversive action opposing the local expression of the dominant ideological manifestations of power within our discipline.

A genealogical study of the discursive formation of literary criticism in the academy suggests that from I. A. Richards's practical criticism to the deconstructionism of American graduate schools and avant-garde journals, certain institutional, pedagogical, and ideological strains in our most subtle and powerful criticism have extended and obscured the operations of power. Not surprisingly, genealogical research into the institutions of advanced criticism and advanced literary education reveals their intersection with many of the more overtly disciplinary formations Foucault identifies in neocapitalism: behaviorism, progressive education, psychoanalysis, and bureaucratized specialization. (Precisely those things against which Babbitt reacted.) Let me caution that in saying this I am not attempting to indict modern criticism and literary pedagogy in an absolute way, for only their participation in the (uneven) applications of power enabled their finest achievements. I do, however, want to make two points. First, genealogical research does reveal something about literary critical institutions that humanism does not recognize: criticism is a "relay" in modernity's disciplining of its culture and population to fulfill and defend a capitalist organization of society. Second, the paradox of the oppositional critics I described at the beginning of this essay operates here and enmeshes the genealogist: Deleuze points out in his discussion of Foucault's genealogies that they inevitably expand into other disciplines, exposing previously unsuspected connections between institutions and rhetorics (IIP, 206). This process of disclosure Foucault and Deleuze valorize as a counterpractice to the operations of power, a skirmish to overcome power by denying it its secrecy. Such scholarly activities are nonreformist because the knowledge of power they provide helps the oppressed to "refuse any attempt at arriving at a new disposition of the same power with, at best, a change of masters" (IIP, 216). Put in another, more reductive way, such genealogical illuminations of the forces that produce the intellectual and the discipline and carry his or her assent to its furthest extension can undeniably make a difference. Literally, genealogical tracings of the power formations of the intellectual's practice and ideology result in different texts, different knowledge, different configurations of power. For example, Foucault's work is a conduit for the discourse of prisoners and patients against the dominant penal and clinical discourse. In other words, such genealogies, which let the oppressed be heard and which enact an opposition, fragment the totalizing discourse of the disciplinary society, for in and through its knowledge-producing apparatus, the society totalizes its deployment of power and its distribution of individuals under the guise of "truth." Genealogy points out the series of changes in the "truth-producing" discourse sustaining the disciplines, not only to reveal that "truth" is a product of certain power-knowledge configurations but also, paradoxically and necessarily, to produce more knowledge. Deleuze and Foucault consistently employ the classical metaphor of illumination. They share this metaphor with all post-Enlightenment humanistic disciplines. This is a sign of the paradoxical situation I described confronting all oppositional intellectuals: their subversions and displacements can be effective only because they are in various ways extensions or, at best, transformations of the powerful disciplines already in place, disciplines in which they have been trained and upon which they draw. Again, I am not trying to minimize the differences between Foucault and the humanistic totalizers; certainly, the content and method of their works are substantially different, and, I believe, Foucault's are far less mystified and potentially more liberating. Yet one cannot ignore the degree to which the disciplinary society seems able to produce and sustain its own apparent antagonists. In *Discipline and Punish,* Foucault seems at times to approach despair over this dilemma—for example, when he suggests that the disciplining society has not reached its limits of expansion or subtlety (*D&P,* 162).

I take such an observation to be an extension of a central Nietzschean insight into a persistent question: of what value is knowledge and the will to knowledge? Are the skills and disciplines of genealogical research merely producing more knowledge—admittedly more self-aware "power-knowledge"—and more training to extend the range of science so that greater areas of human life and social action may fall under the (secret) control of knowledge? I am suggesting, in other words, that despite the absolute need for the humanities, and especially literary criticism, to examine their genealogies to understand their operations, limits, and controls, there may be a double bind at work transforming the research for liberation into an extension of the dominance of a society resting on a discourse of power. History of interpretation, history of scholarship, history of graduate and college English education—these are necessary beginnings for the intellectual who hopes to oppose power. The real danger I see is not, as Foucault suggests is historically the case, that the intellectual who speaks "the truth" (IIP, 207) will be outcast but that the "truth" will be taken up as part of the disciplinary apparatus, as my research has begun to suggest happened to I. A. Richards's practical criticism and as others have suggested has happened to the discourse and practice of deconstruction. Although genealogical studies of modern knowledge offer some hope for liberating the intellectual from the discourse of power, one fundamental uncertainty remains: is it true that genealogy has not been and cannot be coopted as a discipline for reproducing this discourse of power? If so, how can we know this? If we cannot know, then can we continue to accept it as a locally useful weapon in the skirmishing of the oppressed against power? Or perhaps to put the dilemma more boldly, should we even inquire into the efficacy of genealogy in these terms, or should we avoid such speculations and engage in the practice of describing genealogical affiliations and permutations as part of our new interest in the worldliness and materiality of discourse?

The threat to genealogical research lies in the academic industry of scholarship. Foucault's texts are themselves different from the work of the disciplines for two reasons. First, they probe into sometimes hidden fields of research, but more often they delicately expose the surface, the function of what we all "see," by aligning surface phenomena in new forms that disclose how power sustains and utilizes them. Second, to a large degree, Foucault's texts are themselves revolutionary acts: in their practice, in their research and writing, in their speculations and catachreses, they are the concrete, material, habitual extensions of power through pedagogy and scholarship. But if the academy makes of the "results" of such action and research merely a reserve of knowledge to be tapped for information, metaphors, or authority, then genealogy will have become only the latest extension of the disciplinary power. Hope resides in genealogy's having addressed itself directly to the processes by which such neuterings of difference and revolt occur. Put reductively, the question is this: Is genealogy powerful enough to control its own reading, or will the plethora of interpretations and heirs it produces overwhelm its revolutionary practice and comfortably inscribe it back within science and the academy—from which home it wishes to depart—*as merely another fold of self-consciousness?*

CHAPTER EIGHT

Power and Freedom

On the critical side—I mean critical in a very broad sense—philosophy is precisely the challenging of all phenomena of domination at whatever level or under whatever form they present themselves.
—Michel Foucault, "the ethic of care for the self as a practice of freedom" (1984)

‌‌‌ With the publication of *Discipline and Punish* and the first volume of *The History of Sexuality,* Foucault's critics begin to assert that his thinking about power, discipline, and the panopticon leaves no room for freedom or resistance to power. This line of criticism derives from the earlier charge that his "archaeological" method could not account for change. In "Criticism Between System and Culture," for example, Edward Said argues that Foucault's work has been haunted by an "asymmetry in his work between the blindly anonymous and the intentional." Foucault has been concerned "with . . . the subjugation of individuals in society to some suprapersonal disciplines or authority." In effect, Said insists, what Foucault has done is provide "a prodigiously detailed set of possible descriptions whose main aim is . . . to overwhelm the individual subject or will and replace it instead with minutely responsive rules of discursive formation, rules that no one individual can either alter or circumvent."[1]

Of course, number of key Foucauldian texts ground just such an interpretation. In a lecture of 14 January 1976, for example, Foucault speaks of the disciplines as displacing the order of sovereignty and producing a new code, a new "norm": "The code they come to define," Foucault writes, "is not that of law but of normalisation." Foucault's lecture describes the relative displacement of juridical and sovereign organizations of power and right by a newer, modern form of social organization based on the disciplines' powers to normalize life. In the process, he makes several remarks that help open up the discussion of the human sciences as a technology for forming a normalized or disciplinary society:

> I believe that the process which has rendered the discourse of the human sciences possible is the juxtaposition, the encounter between two lines of approach, two mechanisms, two absolutely heterogeneous types of discourse: on the one hand there is the reorganisation of right that invests sovereignty, and on the other, the mechanics of the coercive forces whose exercise takes a disciplinary form. . . . the procedures of normalisation come to be ever more constantly engaged in the colonisation of those of law. I believe that all this can explain the global functioning of what I would call a *society of normalisation*.[2]

Foucault's comments have helped critics understand the importance of hegemonic elements of societal organization and have guided many oppositional critics' examinations of the determining roles played by the institutionalized practices and discourses of the human sciences in the constitution of relations of knowledge and power between individuals and institutions and among individuals. Also, they have helped make possible a number of genealogical investigations into how these seemingly determinant relations have come about, into just what their histories have been. By their emphasis on norms, they have also helped make us aware of the importance of difference; by their emphasis on truth and power, they have helped us see how the "regimes of truth" need to be changed. In addition, they have helped us understand the continuing if unsatisfactory importance of the older discourse of "rights" in the face of newer and older forms of power; women and minorities in particular have made much good use of this line of argument in order to defend the remaining value of a juridical code of "rights."

In the humanities, Foucault's ideas of the late 1970s helped make possible what Jonathan Arac nicely calls "critical genealogies," that is, narratives of the various disciplines' histories as they need to be told if we are both to understand how the present has come to be and how it might be different. In this way, Foucault's work has been relevant to the humanities' disciplinary self-examination, to the professionalism debate, and to the end of theory movement. In a different way, as certain recent developments at Berkeley suggest, Foucault's work has been made one element underlying what has come to be called the New Historicism, a movement whose actual political function in the United States needs to be considered at greater length elsewhere.

Foucault's writings after the publication of volume 1 of *The History of Sexuality* seemingly raise a number of questions different from those we find before. A very large number of critics and commentators note that the late Foucault turns in the direction of ethics, of the self, of style, of agency and away from matters of power, knowledge, discipline, and normalization. Foucault himself constantly responds to questions about a turn in his work, often trying to assert a continuity from his earliest writings on psychiatry to his last work on "governmentality." It is not unusual to hear critics wonder at the facility and power of Foucault's own apparent self-revisions; indeed, an interesting essay could be made to trace Foucault's changing self-representations.

But on one matter that importantly concerns the "Humanities as a Social Technology," one must decide if there has been a change, an evolution, or self-correction in Foucault's thought, and that has to do with the persistent question of the individual will's relation to the collective order no matter whether the latter is conceived as discourse or discipline. Two points are at stake: first, Said's typical charge that Foucault is "Borgesian," that is, politically quietistic; second, the question of whether or not Foucault offers some way of conceiving the human sciences as technologies for freedom.

Critics have often noted that Said needed continually to differentiate himself from Foucault throughout the 1970s. His immediate political work—to name and encourage the Palestinian resistance while exposing the workings of "orientalism"—required a critical, political discourse that made more of both the intellectual's engagement on the side of the oppressed and the nature and availability of resistance than did Foucault's. Closely related to this project was Said's insistence that academic intellectuals not be caught up within the networks of "textuality" to the detriment of their political, critical responsibility to take up more worldly matters in a materialist way.

In a justly famous essay, "Traveling Theory," Said puts the case against Foucault in a powerful theorized political conclusion:

The disturbing circularity of Foucault's theory of power is a form of theoretical overtotalization superficially more difficult to resist because . . . it is formulated, reformulated, and borrowed for use in what seem to be historically documented situations. But note that Foucault's history is ultimately textual, or rather textualized; its line is one for which Borges would have an affinity. Gramsci, on the other hand, would find it uncongenial. He would certainly appreciate the fineness of Foucault's archeologies, but would find it odd that they make not even a nominal allowance for emergent movements, and none for revolutions, counterhegemony, or historical blocks. In human history there is always something beyond the reach of dominating systems, no matter how deeply they saturate society, and this is obviously what makes change possible, limits power in Foucault's sense, and hobbles that theory of power.[3]

Much could be said about Said's own critical practice and genealogy in this passage, but it must stand as a powerful instance of a charge against Foucault that, if true, not only devalues Foucault's work but makes suspect projects that come after it.

There are times when Foucault seems to be responding directly to Said's charges as when in "the ethic of the care for the self as a practice for freedom"—from which I've taken my epigraph—he says: "One cannot impute to me the idea that power is a system of domination which controls everything and which leaves no room for freedom."[4] Readers find it hard to believe this comment from 1984 when they recall some others from 1976; Foucault seems to be practicing the art of self-revision. In articulating his notion of "bio-power," which puts "life" and its management at the center of political control and social organization, Foucault makes some comments about power that tellingly raise the issue of the state and suggest that he has forgotten some of his earlier comments on power:

If the development of the great institutions of the state, as *institutions* of power, ensured the maintenance of production relations, the rudiments of anatamo- and bio-politics, created in the eighteenth century as *techniques* of power present at every level of the social body and utilized by very diverse institutions . . . operated in the sphere of economic processes. . . . They also acted as factors of segregation and social hierarchization, exerting their influence on the respective forces of both these movements, guaranteeing relations of domination and effects of hegemony.[5]

Gramsci—perhaps through Althusser—is more present in this passage than at most other moments in Foucault's speculations on power, but nonetheless Foucault revises Gramsci here by defining state institutions as institutions of power and by getting at—even though not fully clarifying—the existence of a network of relations between the state and population, between domination and hegemony—that in fact underlie them both—that anticipates his own later concerns with governmentality.

Before developing this connection, though, one should note that, as long ago as 1976, in the same lecture quoted above, Foucault himself saw the political and intellectual inadequacy of any theory of power that left individuals the victims of anonymous will. Having argued that disciplinary formations largely replaced the sovereign will and its juridical legal apparatus in modernity, Foucault cautioned that the disciplines' opponents should not invoke theories of "right" of the sort that "invest sovereignty." Precisely because the disciplinary and sovereignty "are two absolutely integral constituents of the general mechanism of power in our society" (p. 108), invoking the later against the former is a "dead end" in a struggle for freedom.

Foucault's comments on people's desire to "object" to the operations of disciplinary power can be found throughout his work of the 1970s. It is not only the case, as I have argued elsewhere, that he clearly thought of his own genealogies as acts of "opposition" to the established order; it is also the case that he often thematized the felt need to stand "against" the operations of discipline—even though he often formulated the question so that there seemed no way effectively to be "against" the disciplines. As we read Foucault's descriptions of the workings of the panopticon and other forms of disciplinary or bio-power, we often wonder about the concrete possibilities of resistance work represents: we know his own work is a form of resistance, but other than the critical and stylistic power of his writing, what forms might "resistance" take in Foucault? What might it mean to "be against" in his work? For example, in volume 1 of *The History of Sexuality*, having developed the notion of bio-power, he points out that historically all resistance to its regime circulates through it: "against this power that was still new in the nineteenth century, the forces that resisted relied for support on the very thing it invested, that is, on life and man as a living being."[6]

Nonetheless, Foucault often tried to articulate the need to find such a way of "being against." In the lecture of 14 January 1976, for example, having told us an appeal to "right" cannot be meaningful as a mode of opposition in modern disciplinary society, he writes the following:

> If one wants to look for a non-disciplinary form of power, or rather, to struggle against disciplines and disciplinary power, it is not towards the ancient right of sovereignty that one should turn but towards the possibility of a new form of right, one which must indeed be anti-disciplinarian, but at the same time liberated from the principle of sovereignty.[7]

Juxtaposing these two quotations suggests two directions for thought. First, that Foucault was dissatisfied with the easily available means of "being against" that disciplinary society offered, precisely because they recycled the effects of power in that order. Second, that Foucault's genealogy of power specified the limited historical possibilities for resistance precisely in order to point out the need to find new ways to resist and, indeed, the existence of the possibility of those new ways. Of course, these two lines of thought converge on one point: "being against." That the lines of resistance to bio-power took the form of defending life against that very power did not, in itself and in advance, as it were, make meaningless the struggle waged in that form, through that set of relays: "life as a political object," writes Foucault, "was in a sense taken at face value and turned back against the system that was bent on controlling it."[8] Were power capable of the all-absorbing control that eliminates struggle—as Said and others have claimed—then Foucault's very problematic would have ceased to exist. The issue for Foucault was different: given that the relations of struggle are as much implicated by and in the operations of power as these constitute relations between and among agents—whether conceived as institutions or individuals—and given that, as Said might say, something "irreducible" appears in the very act of struggle within, against, and by means of the dominant, how then can one avoid drawing the conclusion that, for Foucault, agents—who might be individuals or collectives—are capable of struggling for themselves, for "freedom" to limit the dominating effects of power systems, no matter what the dominant structure might be at a given time?

This line of thought suggests that the so-called "turn" in Foucault's late work results from his taking certain issues up in a finer resolution. Perhaps tracing some of the connections between two of these more finely seen issues will usefully lead to the question of "The Humanities as a Social Technology."

Foucault's concern with opponents of disciplinary power—expressed as early as January 1976—deepens with his continuing work on "governmentality" and his emerging work on "ethics." In January 1984, for example, he explicitly returns to the problem of how to be against disciplines, but now he casts the discussion in terms of "freedom." By this time, Foucault has come to see "relationships of power as strategic games between liberties."[9] If you will, this is a form of power that defines relationships between and among individuals and is, as it were, at the other end of the spectrum from "states of domination" that involve the largest institutions and the greatest forms of power and force. These "games between liberties" occupy the space that concerns itself with "ethics" and the "aesthetics of the self"— that is, the topics of his last two books.

Foucault's new emphasis upon "freedom" and "liberty" makes clear that he now intends to study less the order of disciplines that regulates the range of choice and action delimiting agency and to examine more explicitly the possibilities of self-definition in relation to the dual operations of power as, first, strategic games of liberty and, second, governmentality conceived as a "political technology of individuals." This set of concerns may come as a surprise to some, but it should not. One should see these concerns as consistent with his suspicion of all discourses of liberty: they neither depend upon nor enforce any narrative of liberation; they avoid any idealist notion of a "free" subject, taken as a class or individual self, conceived as a metaphysical unity and substance. In "The Subject and Power," we recall, Foucault theorized power as relationship and the relationships of power as actions upon actions: "What defines a relationship of power is that it is a mode of action which does not act directly and immediately on others. Instead it acts upon their actions: an action upon an action, on existing actions or on those which may arise in the present or the future."[10] Foucault now comes to stress the idea of possibility in such phrases as "those which may arise." Even in formulating the two essential components of power relationships, he emphasizes that they always induce—even in the one over whom power is exercised—effects of openness: "a power relationship," he writes, "can only be articulated on the basis of two elements which are indispensable if it is really to be a power relationship: that 'the other' . . . be thoroughly recognized and maintained to the very end as a person who acts; and that, faced with a relationship of power, a whole field of responses, reactions, results, and possible inventions may open up."[11] Power does not, in other words, preclude resistance; rather it depends upon "freedom." Were there no range of possible responses within power relations, there would be slavery or violence but not power. In Foucault's writings, there is no narrative of repressed freedom that needs to be released or liberated; there is not even a Gramscian vision of hegemonic institutions inducing consent. Or better, there is hegemony but only because relations of power open up fields of response that can eventuate in consensus and agreement. Since Foucault sees power as "a structure of actions brought to bear upon possible actions," it cannot be adequately described in any subject-centered narrative of liberation. In this, it reminds us of Nietzsche, whose critique of the metaphysical subject in *On the Genealogy of Morals* insists that language deludes us into positing the necessary existence of a substantial subject as the only adequate cause of actions taken to be effects (p. 45). But what is most important in Nietzsche's critique—namely the persistence of the will, of willing, despite the lack of a metaphysical subject—gets taken up and transmuted in Foucault's theory so it reappears as "freedom," the capacity to act within an open field of induced effects, itself the "effect," as it were, of a structure of actions upon a range of possible actions in the present and future. Only "violence," as in slavery, can eliminate this capacity.

"Violence" acts upon the body: "It forces, it bends, it breaks on the wheel, it destroys, or it closes the door on all possibilities. Its opposite pole can only be passivity."[12] And, we should add, its political aim is to eliminate all possible action or reaction, all possible choice, precisely by closing down any field of possibilities. Freedom, for individuals or collectivities, exists only when they "are faced with a field of possibilities in which several ways of behaving, several reactions and diverse comportments may be realized" (SP, 221). In tyranny, in totalitarianism, in occupied territories, indeed, in strongly empowered hegemonies, the political aim of the ruler is to foreclose relations of power because these always and only exist as a result of complex interrelations with freedom and choice. The oppressor's aim is best understood as an effort to preclude power relations opening fields of choice, not as an effort to repress the freedom given man by nature or to bring about some form of social "order" by regulating the supposedly bestial and sinful animal, man, in some constitution.

Having abandoned the grand narratives of liberation and having given theoretical reasons for doing so, Foucault offers that we think power and freedom so that each is the condition for the possibility of the other's existence. We have something like a theory for the possibility of freedom offered in something like a structural paradigm of necessary interrelations. No theory that thinks one as prior to the other, no theory that thinks one alone can begin to understand social existence. Echoing Nietzsche once more, Foucault suggests that we should think the relationship of power as a permanent agon that denies neither the free attempt to act on others' actions nor the desire to remain free of those actions—while acting oneself. "At the very heart of the power relationship," writes Foucault, "and constantly provoking it, are the recalcitrance of the will and the intransigence of freedom. Rather than speaking of an essential freedom, it would be better to speak of an 'agonism,' of a relationship which is at the same time reciprocal incitation and struggle" (SP, 221–22).

But this struggle exists socially and individually, or, in terms central to Foucault's last work, it exists as a problem of "government"— which is a problem of ethics—and as a problem of aesthetics—which is also a problem of ethics. In "The Subject and Power," Foucault saw "government" as an issue pertaining to the collective, concerning primarily "the way in which the conduct of individuals or of groups might be directed" (SP, 221). By 1984, however, following his research into the ancients, he had come to conceive the notion more broadly: "I say that governmentality implies the relationship of self to self, which means exactly that, in the idea of governmentality, I am aiming at the totality of practices, by which one can constitute, define, organize, instrumentalize the strategies which individuals in their liberty can have in regard to each other."[13] Foucault's research led him to conclude that this "totality of practices" involved power structures existing on at least three levels: "states of domination," that is, the largest forms of power, such as the state and its affiliated institutions;

"games of power," struggles among people to control others' actions; and "governmental technologies," which extend from control of the self, to forms of domestic control, to control of the economy: "It did not only cover the legitimately constituted forms of political or economic subjection, but also modes of action, more or less considered and calculated, which were destined to act upon the possibilities of action of others" (SP, 221). "Governmentality," in other words, extends as a concept from the operation of the "police," in the extended sense Foucault recovers and Donzelot employs, to the relations among family members, to the individual's struggle for self-mastery in aesthetic style.

Foucault's theory of power has not only been misread by those who have wanted to condemn him for failing to take "resistance" seriously, but also by others who have tried to adapt it for their own research into and arguments against the professionalization of the humanities within the institutions of the university. Some harm has been done by the second group—among whom it is no doubt only fair to put myself, but I hope only in part. Too many facile calls for trans- or interdisciplinary work, for "cultural studies," for "new" kinds of "historicism"—too many rapid dismissals of the institutionalized forms of humanistic study have followed on the reading that would have Foucault saying that disciplines and the human sciences are "repressive"—a category which, as we know, Foucault spent much of his time trying to overthrow as too closely linked to the dominant forms of rationality.

Foucault's thoughts on "freedom/power"—I put that as we used to put "power/knowledge"—lead to ways to reconsider the social operations of the institutionalized human sciences in terms of an all-important question: do they promote domination? Since Nietzsche we have been unable to say simply and moralistically that relations of power are somehow, in themselves, "bad" or "immoral." The question regarding relations of power—which are technologies—becomes how to practice them without destroying them. Foucault's objections to Habermas no doubt have to do with the latter's hope for an undistorted form of communication, absent power and force—a possibility Foucault thinks of as Utopian. Indeed, Habermas's line—we cannot treat it at length here—cannot produce a theory of the intersection of power, freedom, ethics, politics, rationality, and style. In criticizing Habermas, Foucault gives a general sense of his project's aim:

> I don't believe there can be a society without relations of power, if you understand them as means by which individuals try to conduct, to determine the behavior of others. The problem is not of trying to dissolve them in the utopia of a perfectly transparent communication, but to give one's self the rules of law, the techniques of management, and also the ethics, the *ethos,* the practice of self, which would allow these games of power to be played with a minimum of domination.[14]

Foucault's critics should immediately object to this as a liberal formulation that puts too much authority in and value on the individual as an autonomous figure and extends the notion of "micro-physics" to the point where it seems to dissolve all collectivities into something uncomfortably like a "million points of light," as some U.S. politician might have it. Foucault has stressed the individual's responsibility to acquire—"to give one's self," as he says—the means to minimize domination in the strategic games of liberty. Of course, this is typical of Foucault's revisions of Althusser.[15] Rather than theorize the individual's relation to the symbolic in terms of an interpellation into ideology, Foucault imagines individuals minimizing domination in the games of freedom by asceticism, self-knowledge, and self-mastery— all of which, presumably, allow for a maximized use of the field of possibilities presented by power but without dire effects upon the other in the relationship. The objections to Foucault on this level might ramify through the examples he gives: "We know very well that power is not an evil. Take for example, sexual relationship or love relationships. To exercise power over another, in a sort of open strategic game, where things could be reversed, that is not evil. That is part of love, passion, of sexual pleasure."[16] The objections, presumably, would have to do with the private nature of this example and, to many, with its apparently naive formulation of reversibility in sex. Indeed, we might argue, the Foucault of the 1960s and 1970s would have helped us understand why this reversibility would itself be restricted by the discourses, disciplines, and institutions that constituted the sexuality of the partners: the relations would not allow for complete and free reversal.

But the late Foucault is not, I think, trying to displace the early Foucault, whose work has, in part, been misread as either a theory of repression or, more cleverly, a theory of restricted production. Rather, Foucault tried to offer a sort of general field theory of power relations extending from the self in conflict with itself and others in relatively private spaces, where liberty was least restricted by larger social forces and forms, through the very broad space where the games of liberty and the technologies of government intersect and identify, and come to underlie, to underpin the levels of domination within the state and economy. The vast intent of this incomplete project is fairly clear in Foucault's late works—quite precisely despite their focus on the ancients. Perhaps their most powerful effect is to show that other relations of power have been possible—the current ones are not "natural" despite their status as "self-evident"—and, despite the imagined objections that this is mere liberalism, to show that "care for the self" in the form of self-mastery in style, not code or norm, has been possible before and can be seen as an open possibility even in today's order of political rationality.

The question, of course, is how can one imagine the significance of these games of liberty as political? Foucault's example of reversibility in sex and love seems weak on this point, although one could draw attention to the fact that even the "private" games of love, as a game, is still not entirely outside the realm of sexuality—*The Use of Pleasure* makes this fairly clear. But perhaps Foucault's second example will help us answer this question:

> Let us also take something that has been the object of criticism, often justified: the pedagogical institution. I don't see where evil is in the practice of someone who, in a given game of truth, knowing more than another, tells him what he must do, teaches him, transmits knowledge to him, communicates skills to him. The problem is rather to know how you are to avoid in these practices—where power cannot not play and where it is not evil in itself—the effects of domination which will make a child subject to the arbitrary and useless authority of a teacher, or put a student under the power of an abusively authoritarian professor, and so forth. I think these problems should be posed in terms of rules of law, of relational techniques of government and *ethos*, of practice of self and of freedom.[17]

Most important in this passage is Foucault's assertion that what at first seem to be matters between individuals—teacher and student, for example—matters that have to do with the "strategic games of liberty"—must be treated as matters of governmentality and ethics. "Governmentality" is a crucial concept in Foucault's oeuvre because it links the domains of the individual and large, powerful institutions, such as those of the state, and because it opens a theoretical space in which Foucault can combine his critique of discursive and institutional forms of domination and hegemony with his concern to show that these often establish and maintain themselves through governmental techniques.[18] Critics have always known that Foucault was interested in objecting to the abuses of power as these appear in clinical medicine, psychiatric practices, prisons, and humanistic disciplines in general throughout the social security state. Foucault's problem has always been how to theorize the possibility of "being against" forms of domination—however and wherever they appear—without simply reintroducing the worst effects of the empowering practices, often themselves necessary to "object" to the forms of domination. The issue is put in his thoughts on how individuals and collectives have objected to governmental practices and the affiliated disciplinary apparatuses that developed to regulate "life," as population, precisely by intensely insisting on the value of "life" and the knowledge about "life" generated by those regulative disciplines. As we have seen, being "inscribed," as we like to say now, within the system does not create a hopeless double bind; objecting to the governmental and disciplinary attempts at regulation and domination has indeed gone on; the problem is how to understand the possibility of these objections and how to theorize it as the ground for a politics that will force us to alter the order of political, social rationality that currently exists but is being challenged.

Foucault surely was committed to what we might call the "materiality of thought," even though some others might call it "mere idealism." In "Practicing Criticism," an interview given in 1981 and collected in Lawrence Kritzman's distinguished edition of Foucault's work *Politics, Philosophy, Culture*, Foucault, discussing the value of critique, says: "We must free ourselves from the sacrilization of the social as the only reality and stop regarding as superfluous something so essential in human life and in human relations as thought. Thought exists independently of systems and structures of discourse. It is something that is often hidden, but which always animates everyday behavior. There is always a little thought even in the most stupid institutions."[19] Heidegger's influence on Foucault encouraged this formulation. "Thought" comes up in this context because it is Foucault's contention that critique must try to "unearth" and influence this thought "by showing that things are not as self-evident as one believed." Foucault gives the intellectual a high place in the task of maintaining a state of "permanent criticism" that agitates and so changes thought, that denies the self-evident and keeps open fields of possibility. But the intellectual's role is neither privileged nor unique in a theory of freedom's agon with itself and power, with its own liberties and its desires to impose its will. If we keep in mind that Foucault accepts and broadens Gramsci's definition of the intellectual as anyone with special expert competences, then we understand that, in the following lines, he is denying leadership authority not only to the state but to its intellectuals and to all intellectuals aspiring to regulate the games of freedom: "the answers will not come from those who administer [state institutional] authority: answers ought rather to come from those who are trying to counter-balance the prerogative of the state and who constitute counter-powers. What comes . . . may possibly . . . open up a space for intervention."[20] This is a familiar note in Foucault, especially in light of his ritual refusal to assume the magisterial intellectuals' role of "proposing" futures for others. What perhaps strikes some as important is his once more singling out the state and its opponents as the site for exemplary struggle: in passages like these, the issue seems to be the very existence of the state itself as a form of domination that attempts to preclude possibility precisely by inducing dependency and thereby, predictably, opening up the limited opportunity for individuals to learn to play in the field of actions its own governing field of actions helps bring into play.

Although Foucault's concerns with the state's ability to effect actions appears throughout his writings on psychiatry, sexuality, and social security, it is in his attempt to retrieve earlier understanding of "police" that he most extensively lays out his concerns by theorizing the relation between the state and governmentality.

The "police" function of the state—which leads it to develop its technologies of government—itself results from the modern political order of rationality caught in the slogan "reason of state," which, as Foucault writes, "refers to the state, to its nature, and to its own rationality."[21] With "reason of state," a new relation emerges between politics and knowledge; politics comes to be practiced on the basis of a new sort of positive knowledge generated precisely to help the state maintain and extend itself and help politicians acquire the specific technical and intellectual practical competences to bring this about. The problem becomes how to govern populations in the interest of the state:

> Since the state is its own finality and since the government must have for an exclusive aim not only the conservation but also the permanent reinforcement and development of the state's strengths, it is clear that the governments don't have to worry about individuals; or government has to worry about them only insofar as they are somehow relevant for the reinforcement of the state's strength. . . . From the state's point of view, the individual exists insofar as what he does is able to introduce even a minimal change in the direction of the state, either in a positive or negative direction.[22]

When the state's intellectuals begin to theorize how individuals and populations can be best disposed, they develop the notion of "police" from the emerging practices of administrators and politicians. Foucault's genealogy of the category recovers its breadth. In sum, there was nothing that was not in the realm of the police: "In short," he writes, "life is the object of the police." Or, as Turquet puts it, " 'The police's true object is man.' " When the techniques of governmentality become theorized and academicized in the university as "police," as schooling in the administration of individuals and populations; when administration itself is systematized, the new political problem becomes: how do we stand in relation to the state and its administrators, which is to say, how do we stand in relation to the technologies of governmentality. In Foucault's late theory, domination—not violence—rests on these governmental technologies; they extend "freedom/power" 's desire to act upon the actions of others, and do so, perhaps, to the point of denying others' freedom and thereby turning power into tyranny.

Foucault would have it—given the failures of actually existing socialism and his analysis of the political disasters that follow on leading intellectuals' ambitions—that revolution is not clearly desirable in relation to the state or any of its orders of governmentality. Perhaps one needs to add that in relation to tyranny—as in the case of the shah of Iran—Foucault allows that revolution, even though it will settle down into its own order of governmentality, is necessary as a way of reestablishing power relationships, that is, freedom and possibility of action, where none or very little can be said or is felt to exist.

But in the so-called advanced societies that have developed as "social security states," revolution is not self-evidently the desirable political aim of struggle. Insofar as governmentality is linked to and embodied in the "police," in technologies, "maximizing freedom" must always mean struggling to assure that the range of possible actions and reactions is always as large as possible: that clearly is the aim as many groups and individuals struggle toward self-determination in a new set of relations to the state and its institutions. In his disagreements with Habermas and certain liberal political theorists, Foucault insists that posing the state in opposition to some notion of "civil society" not only routinely demonizes the state but forgets that, as a polemical concept, "civil society" originated with liberal economists trying to maintain a sphere of economic action free of state intervention. In other words, in this view, "civil society" must be recalled as a place where some capitalists worked hard to "maximize their own freedom" in order to "minimize the freedom" of most others. Furthermore, as the opposition appears in Habermasian kinds of discourse, "civil society," like the ideal of "undistorted communication," does not allow one to theorize the existence of power throughout society and so cannot take into account what Foucault calls the "danger," presumably to freedom, that exists in every relationship, practice, or technology of government. The "danger" to freedom is of its essence and therefore must be seen as in any and all power. Its omnipresence means that eliminating the state (in the name of "civil society" or some other utopian alternative) would not preclude either the emergence of relations of power nor the problems of controlling their effects: in itself, such a line of thought is a "danger." To put it simply, eliminating the state—were that possible—still would leave open a fundamental problem: "whatever scenario one takes," writes Foucault, "a power relation would be established . . . this relation being . . . dangerous . . . one would have to reflect, at every level, on the way it should channel its efficacity in the best way."[23]

Foucault's late work leaves us with the obligation not only to understand the relations of power and freedom in the humanities, but also to maximize the freedom that exists in the human and collective relations that make up their institutions and disciplines. We can see now that Foucault is neither a quietist nor a theoretician of political defeat. He rather offers us a different set of problems that we must try to deal with carefully. We must hope that we can find means to build ethics, aesthetics, and politics that will minimize domination and maximize freedom—and teach us respect for others' freedom to act and to act on us.

Notes

Chapter 1. Introduction: In the Wake of Theory (pp. 1–24)

1. I am thinking especially of the essay "Reflections on Recent American 'Left' Literary Criticism" (*boundary 2* 8, no. 1 [Fall 1979]: 11–30) in which Said—and here I grossly simplify—objects that academic "critical radicals" accept a profound isolation from the major issues of the day. Said's serious critique, developed from the oppositional politics of Palestinian involvements, converged with the "anti-theory" ravings of the ersatz philosopher who headed NEH and the Department of Education when he, acting as the agent of the Reagan cultural revolution, attacked "theory" as itself an assault on Americanism, the university, and Western values. No one could possibly confuse Said and Bennett; I want only to note the fact that their differently motivated statements both effectively weakened—for good and ill—the practice of literary theory. Said's efforts often led younger critics toward a more historical and theoretical criticism than the more rarefied forms of deconstruction and, in so doing, helped reform the academy toward the critical multiculturalism that Bennett and his allies so dislike. I hope that the essays that follow, on Said and Alan Bloom, help sharpen this argument.

2. Yet on the potential ways in which discourses of justice themselves reinscribe oppositional figures, see my comparative discussion of Foucault and Chomsky in *Intellectuals in Power* (New York: Columbia University Press, 1986).

3. Stuart Hall, *The Hard Road to Renewal* (London: Verso Books, 1988).

4. I say this despite being the editor of two volumes of that title. See Bové, "Revising the Anglo-American Tradition" *boundary 2* 7, nos. 1 & 2 (1979). I wrote in the introduction to those volumes that "the need for an issue revising our perception of the Anglo-American tradition seems acute at a moment when the well-known rhetorics and procedures of the academic critical institutions are being pressed to re-align themselves in light of 'Postmodern' developments" (p. 2).

5. We are all familiar with the former, and we can see the relatively mainstream politics of the second in Elaine Showalter's limited feminist agenda in "Feminist Criticism in the Wilderness," *Critical Inquiry* 8 (1981): 243–70.

6. See his Introduction to *Out There*, ed. Cornel West et al. (Cambridge, MA: MIT Press, 1990).

7. Trans. John Macquarrie and Edward Robinson (New York: Harper and Row, 1962); hereafter referred to parenthetically in my text as *BT*.

8. See my earlier book, *Destructive Poetics* (New York: Columbia University Press, 1980), for my first published work on Heidegger, wherein I indeed attempted, mistakenly, to develop a sort of unrestricted critical theory.

9. See Patrick Brantlinger's *Crusoe's Footprints: Cultural Studies in Britain and America* (New York and London: Routledge, 1990) for a story of "theory"'s transformation into "cultural studies."

10. "Freud and Lacan," in *Lenin and Philosophy and Other Essays*, 2nd ed., trans. Ben Brewster (London: New Left Books, 1977), 178–79.

11. See, as a point of contrast, Edward W. Said's insistence upon and adaptation of Gramsci's requirement that intellectuals must make and compile an inventory of the traces history has deposited on and in them (*Orientalism* [New York: Pantheon Books, 1978], 24).

12. See my analysis of Charles Taylor on this point in "The Foucault Phenomenon: The Problematics of Style," the Foreword to Gilles Deleuze, *Foucault*, trans. Sean Hand (Minneapolis: University of Minnesota Press, 1988), esp. pp. ix-xix; reprinted in Bové, *Mastering Discourse* (Durham, N.C.: Duke University Press, 1991).

13. Of course, one can without much difficulty imagine the KBM's response. Such speech is seemingly endlessly empowered in our society, and critics should not engage with it on its own terms. If they "keep on going on"—as Beckett puts it when voicing the speaking egg-shaped head in *The Unnameable*—then others are not obliged to pay attention.

14. This is a fact about Heidegger's work that has been noted in English at least since 1970. See Michael Gelven's elementary but useful gloss, *A Commentary on Being and Time* (New York: Harper and Row, 1970), 60–61.

15. "The kind of dealing which is closest to us is as we have shown, not a bare conceptual cognition, but rather that kind of concern which manipulates things and puts them to use; and this has its own kind of 'knowledge'" (*BT, 95*).

16. The KBM position would be, of course, to object around the use of the word *understanding* here. That objection can be argued away by recalling the complex sense of "understanding" in Heidegger that will not support the binaries that the KBM objections would rest on. "Pragmatism and Literary Theory, III, A Reply to Richard Rorty: What is Pragmatism?" *Critical Inquiry* 11 (March 1985): 466.

17. KBM:

Our point is that no one, in practice, can ever be more or less pragmatist than we are. Our arguments from the start have taken the form of showing that whatever positions people think they hold on language, interpretation, and belief, in practice they are all pragmatists. They all think language is intentional, and they all think their beliefs are true. In theory, they may distinguish between speech acts and language, between having beliefs and claiming to know, between having true beliefs and really knowing. To think the distinction between these things matters or even to think that it doesn't matter—just to think there is a distinction—is to be a theorist. In practice, there are no such distinctions and, in practice, there are no theorists. ("A Reply to Richard Rorty," 472)

18. "Dasein's Being is care"; "The most primordial and basic existential truth, for which the problematic of fundamental ontology strives in preparing for the question of Being in general is the *disclosedness* of the meaning of the Being of care" (*BT,* 329, 364).
19. Stephen Greenblatt, "Towards a Poetics of Culture," in *The New Historicism,* ed. H. Aram Veeser (New York: Routledge, 1989), 5; hereafter cited parenthetically in my text as PC. For the definitive demonstration that Greenblatt's work, despite its claims, does not advance the enterprise of decolonization, see Donald Pease, "Toward a Sociology of Literary Knowledge: Greenblatt, Colonialism, and the New Historicism," in *The Consequences of Theory, Selected Papers from the English Institute, 1987–88,* n.s., 14, ed. Jonathan Arac and Barbara Johnson (Baltimore: The Johns Hopkins University Press, 1991), 108–153.
20. See Paul A. Bové, "Madness, Medicine, and the State," in *Rethinking the History of Madness,* ed. Irving Velody et al. (London: Routledge, 1992).
21. In "Towards a Poetics of Culture," Greenblatt does explicitly identify Foucault's presence on the Berkeley campus as one influence on his sense of "historicism." This is not the place to do it, but someone should write a critical essay on the California appropriation of Foucault's writings.
22. It is acknowledged that Greenblatt's move against theory, especially against deconstruction, has been successful and that this makes Greenblatt "king of the hill." See an article to this effect, written by Richard Bernstein, in *The New York Times,* 19 Feb. 1991, pp. 11, 16. For further evidence of the truth of the matter, as it were, take note of the fact that Dominick LaCapra, setting forth from Cornell University, still the home of *Diacritics,* once the premier journal of French theory, attacks Greenblatt and the "new historicism." The old paradigm, as it were, jousts with the new for authority. See Dominick LaCapra's "History and Critical Theory." While Stanley Fish in no way concedes that the "young and the restless" have taken the "high ground," in his comment on the "new historicists," from his own liberal position, he severely indicts Greenblatt et alia for passing over difficult problems by the use of a "familiar formula." See Fish, "Commentary: The Young and the Restless," in H. A. Veeser, ed., *The New Historicism* (New York: Routledge, 1989), 306.
23. This is a project already begun with great rigor by Terry Cochran in an as yet unpublished conference paper, "The Resistance to History." In what might be Cochran's most important contribution, which I cannot follow up in this context, he concludes by writing that "without reconceiving the mo-

dalities of agency, there is no way to move from an ontical history that operates exclusively within what is disclosed, to an ontical history that operates ontologically in accounting for its disclosures" (MS, p. 20).

24. Brook Thomas, "The New Historicism and other Old-fashioned Topics," in H. A. Veeser, ed., *The New Historiciam* (New York: Routledge, 1989), 182–203, is the best and earliest of these critiques, but even Thomas mistakes poststructuralism for a form of perspectivism or relativism. See his comments on Beard, etc., p. 195. What's missing, in a sense, is an understanding of poststructuralism's turn away from Hegel.

25. Of course, in this regard one should see William V. Spanos, *Heidegger and Criticism: Retrieving the Cultural Politics of Destruction* (Minneapolis: University of Minnesota Press, 1992), especially for its discussion of "repetition."

26. See once more Brook Thomas, "The New Historicism," on this point (esp. pp. 191ff). Of course, Jacques Derrida also proposed this idea of multiple histories to legitimate "deconstruction." See his *Positions,* trans. Alan Bass (Chicago: University of Chicago Press, 1981; previously published in Paris by Éditions de Minuit, 1972).

27. See Brook Thomas, "The New Historicism"—again, the best analyst in this group.

28. One should again see Cochran ("Resistance to History") on Heidegger for his insistence that Heidegger's theory of histories requires a new notion of agency.

29. See Bové, "Madness, Medicine, and the State," for some effort to describe this project.

30. The sort of anxiety about historicism that René Wellek and some of the U.S. New Critics had is not an issue for Heidegger.

Chapter 2. The Function of the Literary Critic
in the Postmodern World (pp. 25–47)

1. See Charles Altieri, *Act and Quality* (Amherst: University of Massachusetts Press, 1983).

2. For some of the problems with this term, see "An Interview with Paul de Man," *Critical Inquiry,* 12 (Summer 1986): 793.

3. See Jean-Francois Lyotard, *The Postmodern Condition,* trans. Geoff Bennington and Brian Massumi (Minneapolis: University of Minnesota Press, 1984), 60–67; and Frank Webster, "The Saatchi Society," *New Socialist,* 1985, no. 27:3–4.

4. See the intense and unembarrassed competition among institutions, eventually won by Carnegie-Mellon University, to house the Defense Department's software development institute.

5. See "The Barbarians Within: Xerxes' Hordes Are at the Gate," *infra.*

6. Louis Althusser, "Ideology and Ideological State Apparatuses," in *Le-*

nin and Philosophy and Other Essays, 2nd ed., trans. Ben Brewster (London: New Left Books, 1977), 148.

7. Richard Ohmann, *English in America* (New York: Oxford University Press, 1976); Gerald Graff, *Literature Against Itself* (Chicago: University of Chicago Press, 1979); Edward W. Said, *Orientalism* (New York: Pantheon Books, 1976), *The World, the Text, and the Critic* (Cambridge, Mass.: Harvard University Press, 1983); Geoffrey Hartman, *Criticism in the Wilderness* (New Haven, Conn.: Yale University Press, 1980); Frank Lentricchia, *After the New Criticism* (Chicago: University of Chicago Press, 1980), *Criticism and Social Change* (Chicago: University of Chicago Press, 1983).

8. Of course, some critics try to be "men of letters" in the service of the status quo. See, for example, the ubiquitous reviews and middlebrow collections by Denis Donoghue.

9. See Antonio Gramsci, "The Modern Prince," in *Selections from the Prison Notebooks*, ed. and trans. Quintin Hoare and Geoffrey Nowell Smith (New York: International Publishers, 1971), 150f; hereafter cited in my text as *PN*.

10. One must, of course, acknowledge the valuable exceptions: individuals like Edward W. Said and journals like *Jump Cut* and *New German Critique*, which are at least in part concerned with such issues. Yet even in such publications one looks in vain for treatment of such matters of immediate political concern as Central America and South Africa or of such institutional importance as the history and function of media popular culture studies in North America. The excellent essay by John Beverley, "El Salvador" (*Social Text*, no. 5 [Spring 1982]: 55–72) is, in part, remarkable for being unusual. Beverley has combined history and political analysis with an understanding of the cultural role of poetry in the revolutions of Central America.

11. See Paul A. Bové, *Intellectuals in Power: A Genealogy of Critical Humanism* (New York: Columbia University Press, 1986), esp. chap. 2, "A Free, Varied and Unwasteful Life: I. A. Richards' Speculative Instruments."

12. Consider, for example, Richard Lanham, whose career began with traditional "lit. crit." and moved to the more lucrative areas of composition theory and "pedagogy," explaining the complexities of "theory," and mapping curricular reform. A full analysis of the ideological function of figures like Lanham would be mildly interesting since he so purely represents the "English Studies professional" in America. See "Composition, Literature, and the Lower-Division Gyroscope," in *Profession 84* (New York: Modern Language Association, 1984), 10–15; *Analyzing Prose* (New York: Scribner's, 1983); and *The Motives of Eloquence* (New Haven, Conn.: Yale University Press, 1976). As of 1984, Lanham was also "Executive Director of the Writing Program" at UCLA.

13. Some small indication of the direction research should go in treating this question is provided by John Fekete, *The Critical Twilight* (London: Routledge & Kegan Paul, 1977), 35–36; and Alvin Gouldner, *The Coming Crisis of Western Sociology* (New York: Basic Books, 1970), 333–37.

14. For an important comment on the failures of critical intelligence in the axioms of modern social scientific method and practice, see Theodor W. Adorno, "The Sociology of Knowledge and Its Consciousness," trans. Samuel Weber, in *The Essential Frankfurt Reader*, ed. Andrew Arato and Eike Gebhardt (New York: Continuum, 1982), 452–65.

15. Of course, this point is not original with me. See Frank Lentricchia, *After the New Criticism*; and Edward W. Said, "Traveling Theory," in *The World, the Text, and the Critic*, 226–47.

16. See Daniel O'Hara, *The Romance of Interpretation* (New York: Columbia University Press, 1985).

17. "The Barbarians Within," *infra*.

18. For some sense of my suspicion of this choice of terms, see my critique of the masterful intellectual, *Intellectuals in Power*, passim.

19. For another example of how like an incestuous carousel the pluralism debate can be, see *Pluralism and Its Discontents* (Special Issue), *Critical Inquiry* 12 (Spring 1986).

20. For recent testimony to the empirical accuracy of Gramsci's comment, see Jurgen Habermas, "A Philosophico-Political Profile," *New Left Review*, no. 151 (May/June 1985): 76.

21. See Cornel West, "The Politics of American Neo-Pragmatism," in *Post-Analytic Philosophy*, ed. John Rajchman and Cornel West (New York: Columbia University Press, 1985), 259–75.

22. See Bové, *Intellectuals in Power*, chap. 1, "Mendacious Innocents."

23. See Charles Altieri, "An Idea and Ideal of a Literary Canon," *Critical Inquiry*, 10 (September 1983): 51–52.

24. Lest it seem that the sociology of knowledge might be the key exception to what I am arguing, see Theodor Adorno, "The Sociology of Knowledge and Its Consciousness." See also Fritz Ringer, *The German Mandarins* (Cambridge, Mass.: Harvard University Press, 1969), 434, for a fine critique of Mannheim's project.

25. See Thomas McCarthy's discussion of this issue in Habermas, *The Critical Theory of Jurgen Habermas* (Cambridge, Mass.: MIT Press, 1981), 300f.

26. See Pierre Bourdieu and Jean-Claude Passeron, *La Reproduction: Éléments pour une théorie du système d'enseignement* (Paris: Les Éditions de minuit, 1970), esp. pp. 131–67.

27. For a concise sense of why liberal functionaries are essential to this operation keep in mind Cornel West's succinct explanation of liberal expectations:

The liberal response is to accept the commodification of culture and attempt to find some kind of authentic human existence within it. This response is naive and self-defeating. It is naive because it refuses to see this cultural process as a modern structure of domination and hence wrongly equates it with 'progress.' It is self-defeating in that it manages only to tease out of this culture some semblance of authenticity within a process that parades each new 'style' of authenticity for each succeeding market-season. ("Harrington's Socialist Vision," *Christianity and Crisis*, 43 [12 December 1983], 485)

28. See Alvin Gouldner, *The Future of the Intellectuals and the Rise of the New Class* (New York: The Seabury Press, 1979).
29. As far as I know, no one has discussed the growing interest among some younger American humanists, especially literary critics, in radical politics and the status of the profession in terms of the drying-up of the job market.
30. See Sacvan Bercovitch, "The Problem of Ideology in American Literary History," *Critical Inquiry*, 12 (Summer 1986), 631–53.
31. For one attempt to work out this question, see Edward W. Said, "Secular Criticism," in *The World, the Text, and the Critic*, 1–30.
32. It is also more than the professional self-celebration of those who joyously denigrate the value of critical self-consciousness as well.
33. That it is often consciously intended to be such see Frank Kermode's address to the Lionel Trilling Seminar at Columbia University, 19 February 1981, in which Kermode wrote: "Yet it must be obvious that the formation of rival canons, however transient, is very dangerous; that in allowing it to happen we risk the death of the institution. Its continuance depends wholly upon our ability to maintain the canon and replace ourselves, to induce sufficient numbers of younger people to think as we do." See also Paul A. Bové, "Variations on Authority: Some Deconstructive Transformations of the American New Criticism," in *The Yale Critics*, ed. Jonathan Arac et al. (Minneapolis: University of Minnesota Press, 1983), 6f.
34. See Said, "Secular Criticism," and Bové, "Criticism and Negation," in *Intellectuals in Power*.
35. On the unifying possibilities of bloc politics, see Paul A. Bové, "The Ineluctability of Difference: Scientific Pluralism and the Critical Intelligence," *Postmodernism and Politics*, ed. Jonathan Arac (Minneapolis: University of Minnesota Press, 1986), 3–25.
36. By inserting the female pronoun into Gramsci's text I do not mean to suggest that in Gramsci's revolutionary model men and women will occupy the same position in relation to discourse, nature, or power. One should see, generally, the work of Gayatri Chakravorty Spivak to understand the complexity of this problem.
37. I stress this because it is left largely untouched in the work of Said, who, along with Lentricchia and Joseph Buttigieg, has produced the finest theoretical elaboration of Gramsci in the literary academy.
38. For a discussion of some of the best work already done in this area, see Bové, "Introduction," *Intellectuals in Power*.
39. On this last, see Daniel T. O'Hara, *Lionel Trilling: The Work of Liberation* (Madison: University of Wisconsin Press, 1988).
40. See Bové, "A Free, Varied and Unwasteful Life: I. A. Richards' Speculative Instruments," *Intellectuals in Power*, chap. 2.
41. Fekete, *The Critical Twilight*, 35f.

42. Alvin Gouldner, *The Coming Crisis in Western Sociology*, 354–61.

43. The New Critics argued that their insistence on irony's formal characteristics was in opposition to the dominant modes of "linear" expression typical of the social sciences and the "declarative sentence." Nonetheless, despite this oppositional effort, it can be shown that the New Criticism was, at the same time, idealist, destabilizing of communal values, and a form of cultural subjugation that reinforced the dominant structure. The relation of Modern Anglo-American criticism to international forms of functionalism needs to be researched further to make all of this clear. See Paul A. Bové, "Cleanth Brooks and Modern Irony," in *Destructive Poetics* (New York: Columbia University Press, 1980), 93–130. On the persistence of some of these values and functions around the concept of irony in contemporary criticism, see Bové, "Variations on Authority."

44. For a critique of the contradictory function of this term, see Paul A. Bové, "The Penitentiary of Reflection: Soren Kierkegaard and Critical Activity," *boundary 2*, 9 (Fall 1980): 233–58.

45. The vanguard party has been seriously critiqued by many who see it in fact or potential as an agency of domination threatening the possibility of the dialectical self-criticism that is the basis of all Gramscian theory and practice. Foucault and Habermas have also been persistent critics of the vanguard party. See also Rudolph Bahro, *The Alternative in Eastern Europe*, trans. David Fernbach (London: Verso Books, 1978), 307–14; and George Konrad and Ivan Szelenyi, *The Intellectuals on the Road to Class Power: A Sociological Study of the Role of the Intelligentsia in Socialism*, trans. Andrew Arato and Richard E. Allen (New York: Harcourt Brace Jovanovich, 1979), 156–83.

46. See Michel Foucault, *The History of Sexuality*, vol. 1, *An Introduction*, trans. Robert Hurley (New York: Pantheon Books, 1978), 53–54.

47. Despite Foucault's fundamental differences with Louis Althusser it hardly seems possible to think that he was not influenced on this matter of "speaking for" by Althusser's theory of ideology; see "Ideology and Ideological State Apparatuses," 123–73.

48. See *Intellectuals in Power*, "Introduction," and chaps. 1, 5, 6.

49. I am aware that intellectuals of different gender are positioned differently within the structure of power and subjectivity. I thank Gayatri Spivak for drawing my attention to the need for such disclaimers in a discipline not yet aware of their obvious truth.

50. See Stanley Aronowitz, *The Crisis in Historical Materialism: Class, Politics and Culture in Marxist Theory* (New York: Praeger, 1981) for an extended treatment of this formation. Michel Foucault makes his argument in *Language, Counter-Memory, Practice*, ed. Donald F. Bouchard (Ithaca, N.Y.: Cornell University Press, 1977); hereafter cited in my text as *LCMP*.

51. Frank Lentricchia, "On Behalf of Theory," in *Criticism in the University*, ed. G. Graff and R. Gibbons, Triquarterly Series on Criticism and Culture, no. 1 (1985): 105–10.

52. See Jacques Derrida, "Cogito and the History of Madness," in *Writing and Difference*, trans. Alan Bass (Chicago: University of Chicago Press, 1978), 31–63. Derrida originally presented this paper on 4 March 1963 at the *Collège philosophique*.

53. See Gayatri Spivak, "Can the Subaltern Speak?" forthcoming in *Marxism and the Interpretation of Culture*, ed. Cary Nelson and Larry Grossberg (Urbana: University of Illinois Press).

54. I say this not despite but because of Stuart Hall's insistence on the historically specific, moderately abstract nature of Gramsci's concepts. See, e.g., Stuart Hall, "Authoritarian Populism," *New Left Review*, 151 (May/June 1985), esp. pp. 118–20.

55. Edward W. Said, "The Essential Terrorist," *The Nation*, 14 June 1986, pp. 828–33.

56. *Teachers, Writers, Celebrities: The Intellectuals of Modern France*, trans. David Macey (London: New Left Books, 1981), esp. pp. 114ff.

57. See Aronowitz, *The Crisis in Historical Materialism*, and Anthony Giddens, *A Contemporary Critique of Historical Materialism* (Berkeley: University of California Press), 157ff.

58. See Altieri, esp. *Act and Quality* and "A Report to the Provinces," in *Profession 82* (New York: The Modern Language Association, 1982), 27f.

59. For some small elaboration of this problem, see Bové, *Intellectuals in Power*, 290ff. See also Gayatri Spivak's forthcoming *Master Discourse, Native Informant* (Cambridge, Mass.: Harvard University Press).

60. This claim would require a much longer analysis to be demonstrative.

61. Jurgen Habermas, "Toward a Reconstruction of Historical Materialism," *Communication and the Evolution of Society*, trans. Thomas McCarthy (Boston: Beacon Press, 1979), 167; hereafter cited in my text as HM.

62. See Habermas, "A Philosophico-Political Profile," esp. pp. 82, 104.

63. Habermas, "A Philosophico-Political Profile," 103.

64. On this possibility, Habermas converges momentarily with his strenuous opponent, Jean-François Lyotard, *The Postmodern Condition*.

65. For a brilliant analysis of this failure in modern and postmodern literary theory, see O'Hara, *The Romance of Interpretation*, esp. pp. 234–35.

66. See Bové, *Intellectuals in Power*, 239–310.

67. Habermas, "Modernity versus Postmodernity," trans. Seyla Ben-Habib, *New German Critique*, 22 (Winter 1981): 3–14; see also Habermas, "The French Path to Postmodernity," trans. Frederick Lawrence, *New German Critique*, 33 (Fall 1984): 79–102.

68. I realize this is a sweepingly unjustified gesture here. For a thoughtful working out of the problem see Jonathan Arac's "Introduction" to *Postmodernism and Politics*, ed. Jonathan Arac (Minneapolis: University of Minnesota Press, 1986), ix–xliii.

Chapter 3. Notes Toward a Politics of "American" Criticism
(pp. 48–66)

1. See Paul A. Bové, *Intellectuals in Power* (New York: Columbia University Press, 1986).

2. See, for example, Burke's "progressive" 1937 article, "Literature as Equipment for Living," reprinted in *Contemporary Literary Criticism,* 2nd ed., ed. Robert Con Davis and Ronald Schleiffer (New York: Longman, 1989), pp. 76–81; see also Wayne Booth's *The Company We Keep: An Ethics of Fiction* (Berkeley: University of California Press, 1988).

3. A detailed and extended study of Bercovitch's work taken as a "career" is beyond the scope of this essay. It would, however, allow one to see his writings as interventions within politically contested, culturally cathected structures of "truth-production."

4. "Afterword," *Ideology and Classic American Literature,* eds. Sacvan Bercovitch and Myra Jehlen (Cambridge: Cambridge University Press, 1986), 428; hereafter cited in my text as A. I am not treating Myra Jehlen's work in this essay but not because it is unimportant, quite to contrary. It embodies powerful feminist revisionist criticism and scholarship, the relation of which to the image I am trying to summon from Bercovitch's work cannot be adequately dealt with here—since it is the dominant discourse I am trying to discuss. The already classical revision of Bercovitch's position can be found in "New Americanists," ed. Donald E. Pease, *boundary 2,* 17 (Spring 1990).

5. See Frederick Crews, "Whose American Renaissance?" *The New York Review of Books,* 35 (27 October 1988): 68–69. See Donald E. Pease's irrefutable explanation of Crews's position, "New Americanists," *boundary 2,* 17 (Spring 1990): 1–37.

6. For a listing of many of the most important works, see the notes to Bercovitch and Jehlen, *Ideology,* 439–42.

7. Perhaps one can distinguish certain sorts of "American" feminism from some of the more theoretically inspired European versions by noting the difference between "andro-" and "phallocentric." The latter term depends upon the Lacanian rereading of Freud in the light of semiotics; the former seems more empirically motivated, associated with anthropology. The difference is not universal, but see, in the context of Emily Dickinson and Adrienne Rich, Patrocinio Schweikart's prizewinning essay, "Reading Ourselves: Toward a Feminist Theory of Reading," *Gender and Reading* (Baltimore: Johns Hopkins University Press, 1986), 31–62.

8. F. O. Matthiessen, *The American Renaissance* (New York: Oxford University Press, 1941).

9. Edward W. Said, "American 'Left' Literary Criticism," in *The World, the Text, and the Critic* (Cambridge, Mass.: Harvard University Press, 1983), 175.

10. Arac offered this direct formulation in conversation; see also his *Critical Genealogies* (New York: Columbia University Press, 1987), 32, 169f.

11. For some discussion of the dangers of "pluralism" to criticism in the United States, see Bercovitch and Jehlen, *Ideology*, 438f.

12. For a powerful critique and alternative view to Bercovitch's, one that is as extensive and eloquent, see Pease, *Visionary Compacts* (Madison: University of Wisconsin Press, 1987).

13. See Gilles Deleuze, *Foucault*, trans. Sean Hand (Minneapolis: University of Minnesota Press, 1988).

14. See Michel Foucault, "The Political Technology of Individuals," in *Technologies of the Self*, ed. Luther H. Martin et al. (Amherst: University of Massachusetts Press, 1988), 145–62.

15. That this is quite ordinary in national traditions can be seen from the work of Benedict Anderson, *Imagined Communities* (London: Verso, 1983).

16. Harvard English Studies 13 (Cambridge: Harvard University Press, 1986).

17. For some analysis of this figure of the masterful intellectual, see Bové, *Intellectuals in Power*.

18. Arac, *Commissioned Spirits: The Shaping of Social Motion in Dickens, Carlyle, Melville, and Hawthorne* (New Brunswick, N.J.: Rutgers University Press, 1979); *Critical Genealogies: Historical Situations for Postmodern Literary Studies* (New York: Columbia University Press, 1987); " 'A Romantic Book': *Moby Dick* and Novel Agency," *boundary 2*, 17 (Winter 1990): 40–59.

19. "American Manscapes," *The London Review of Books*, 12 October 1989, p. 18.

20. One should again see Arac's essay on Melville, which, in part, is a study of the possibility of agency, as an instance of this project.

21. See Daniel T. O'Hara, "The Poetics of Critical Reading," *Poetics Today*, forthcoming: "the productive power of critical reading must be balanced by an appreciation for the achievement being read" (MS, p. 20).

22. For the beginnings of critique of the value and function of "reflection," recall Kierkegaard's critique of reflection in Hegel. For a discussion of this issue, cf. Paul A. Bové, "The Penitentiary of Reflection: Søren Kierkegaard's Critical Activity," *boundary 2*, 9 (1980): 233–58; reprinted in *Kierkegaard and Literature*, ed. Ronald Schleifer (Norman: University of Oklahoma Press, 1984), 3–35.

23. Said, "Secular Criticism," in *The World, the Text, and the Critic*, 8ff. See also Bové, *Intellectuals in Power*, 271–75.

24. Said, "Secular Criticism," 8–9.

25. Think, for example, of how complex the differentiation must be when the term "exile" describes or points to enabling conditions in intellectuals as different as Auerbach and C. L. R. James. See James, *The Black Jacobins: Toussaint L'Ouverture and the San Domingo Revolution*, 2nd ed, rev. (New York: Random House, 1963; originally published in 1939). See also Said, "Nationalism, Colonialism, and Literature," *A Field Day Pamphlet* No. 15 (Derry, Ireland: Field Day Theatre Company Limited, 1988), esp. p. 6ff.

26. See Michel Foucault, "the ethic of care for the self as a practice of

freedom," trans. J. D. Gauthier, S.J., in *The Final Foucault*, ed. James Bernauer and David Rasmussen (Cambridge, Mass.: MIT Press, 1988), 13; the interview was conducted on 20 January 1984.

27. Spivak rightly catches the oppositional edge in laying out this sort of criticism in "Explanation and Culture," in *In Other Worlds* (New York: Methuen, 1987), 103–17; see esp. p. 109, where Spivak discusses the relation of critics to the culture as mediated through the university:

. . . individuals in the chosen profession of humanists can only be tolerated if they behave in a specific way. . . . (1) to reproduce explanations and models of explanation that will take so little notice of the politico-economico-technological determinant that the latter can continue to present itself as nothing but a support system for the propagation of civilization (itself a species of cultural explanation) . . . (2) to proliferate scientific analogies in so-called humanistic explanations . . . (3) at the abject extreme, the open capitulation at the universities by the humanities as agents of the minimization of their own expense of production."

28. Habermas, "A Kind of Settlement of Damages," trans. Jeremy Leaman, *NGC* 44 (Spring/Summer 1988): 25–39, esp p. 29; see also in the same issue of *NGC*, Habermas, "Concerning the Public Use of History," 40–50. To put these essays in context, see Charles S. Maier, *The Unmasterable Past: History, Holocaust, and German National Identity* (Cambridge, Mass.: Harvard University Press, 1988), esp. pp. 9–33.

29. Habermas, "Settlement of Damages," 28.

30. It was precisely Gramsci's intent to theorize this state of affairs in regard to the 19th century that led him to formulate the still crucial notion of the "passive revolution." See Gramsci, *Selections from the Prison Notebooks*, ed. and trans. Quintin Hoare and Geoffrey Nowell Smith (New York: International Publishers, 1971), 106–08.

31. Gramsci, *Selections from the Prison Notebooks*, 59. See also Partha Chatterjee's comments on "passive revolution" in *Nationalist Thought and the Colonial World* (London: Zed Books, 1983), esp. pp. 50–52.

32. On some of the dangers in certain historicist projects see Donald E. Pease, "Greenblatt, Colonialism, and New Historicism," in *Some Consequences of Theory*, ed. Jonathan Arac and Barbara Johnson, English Institute Papers (Baltimore: Johns Hopkins University Press, 1990), 343.

33. Gramsci, in Notebook 8, n. 150, writes of the "demiurge" in its "original sense" as "one who works for the people, for the community (artisan)" and points out that this precedes and underlies the modern sense of the demiurge as the "creator." Here I translate from the French edition of the *Quaderni, Cahiers de Prison*, books 6–9, trans. from the Italian by M. Aymard and P. Fulchignoni; ed., annotated, and introduced by Robert Paris (Paris: Éditions Gallimard, 1983), 343. My thanks to Joseph Buttigieg, who is preparing the English edition of the *Notebooks*, for pointing out this note.

34. *Discipline and Punish: The Birth of the Prison*, trans. Alan Sheridan (New York: Pantheon Books, 1977), esp. pp. 8off.

35. See, among many recent books, Wayne C. Booth, *The Company We*

Keep: An Ethics of Fiction, p. x, where Booth tells us it is his aim "to restore the full intellectual legitimacy of our common-sense inclination to talk about stories in ethical terms." We need not note at any length that throughout this commonsensical book, intended for specialist and "general reader" alike, the former president of the MLA thinks he carries out this restoration without even bothering to mention the most rigorous and important critic of the notion of "common-sense" in current discourse, Gramsci. Perhaps this is simply another example of the grace all "moderate pluralists" possess not to be complete in their scholarship. On this, Gramsci has a good point: "Scholastic activities of a liberal or liberalising character have great significance for grasping the mechanism of the Moderates' hegemony over the intellectuals." It is one of the few avenues "open to the initiative of the petite bourgeoisie" *(Prison Notebooks,* p. 103).

Chapter 4. Intellectual Arrogance and Scholarly Carelessness, Or, Why One Cannot Read Alan Bloom (pp. 67–79)

1. R. P. Blackmur, *Language as Gesture* (New York: Columbia University Press, Morningside Editions, 1981), 372.
2. *The American Jeremiad* (Madison: University of Wisconsin Press, 1978), xiv; hereafter cited as AJ.
3. "Dante," in *Selected Essays,* new ed. (New York: Harcourt, Brace & World, 1964), 204.
4. "The House of Fame," in *Chaucer's Poetry,* ed. T. Talbot Donaldson (New York: The Ronald Press, 1958), 466.
5. Ibid., 955.
6. Ibid., 484–85.
7. Ibid., 485.
8. Ibid., 488.

Chapter 5. Closing Up the Ranks: Xerxes' Hordes Are at the Gate (pp. 80–97)

1. Cambridge, Mass.: Harvard University Press, 1983.

Chapter 6. Celebrity and Betrayal: The High Intellectuals of Postmodern Culture (pp. 98–121)

1. *Teachers, Writers, Celebrities: The Intellectuals of Modern France,* trans. David Maccy (London: New Left Books, 1981). All further references to this work will be given parenthetically as TWC.
2. Antonio Gramsci, "The Intellectuals," in *Selections from the Prison Notebooks,* ed. and trans. Quintin Hoare and Geoffrey Nowell Smith (London: Lawrence and Wishart, 1971), 3–23.

3. See Joseph Buttigieg, "The Exemplary Worldiness of Antonio Gramsci's Criticism," *boundary 2*, 11 (1983), forthcoming; and "The Responsibility of the Critic: A Gramscian Approach to the Politics of Criticism," unpublished manuscript.

4. See Alvin Gouldner, *The Dialectic of Ideology and Technology* (New York: Seabury Press, 1976).

5. Althusser, "Ideology and Ideological State Apparatuses," *Lenin and Philosophy and Other Essays*, trans. Ben Brewster (London: New Left Books, 1971), 162.

6. In France, some of Debray's predecessors are Julien Benda, *La Trahison des clercs* (1927); Paul Nizan, *Les Chiens de garde* (1932); Jean-Paul Sartre, *Qu'est-ce que la litterature* (1948); and Raymond Aron, *L'Opium des intellectuels* (1955).

7. London: New Left Books, 1979.

8. "A Modest Contribution to the Rites and Ceremonies of the Tenth Anniversary," *NLR*, May–June 1979, pp. 45–65.

9. Althusser, "Ideology and Ideological State Apparatuses," 41.

10. Ibid., 148.

11. *The Coming Crisis in Western Sociology* (New York: Basic, 1970).

12. "The Modern Prince," in *Prison Notebooks*, 151.

13. See Edward W. Said, "Reflections on Recent American 'Left' Literary Criticism," *boundary 2*, 8 (1979): 11–30, reprinted in *The Media of Testing*, eds. W. V. Spanos, Paul A. Bové, and Daniel O'Hara (Bloomington: Indiana University Press, 1981), 11–31. Said too easily limits the term "Mandarin" to the "right" represented by Paul de Man and the deconstructors and fails to consider either the esoteric nature of much "left" theorizing or the conservative institutional and social position of many of those who announce themselves as "radical critics."

14. *The Phenomenology of Mind*, trans. J. B. Baillie (New York: Oxford University Press, 1967), 414 ff.

15. The theoretician of this process as it is worked out in literary texts is not Harold Bloom but Daniel O'Hara; see *Tragic Knowledge: Yeats' Autobiography and Hermeneutics* (New York: Columbia University Press, 1981); "The Romance of Interpretation," *boundary 2*, 8 (1980): 259–84; and "The Prophet of Our Laughter: Or Nietzsche As—Educator?" *boundary 2*, 9–10 (1981): 1–19.

16. For two powerful critiques of the role of the "leading intellectual" in postmodern society, see Michel Foucault, "Intellectuals and Power," in *Language, Counter-Memory, Practice*, trans. Donald F. Bouchard and Sherry Simon, ed. Donald F. Bouchard (Ithaca, N.Y.: Cornell University Press, 1977), 207; and Stanley Aronowitz, *The Crisis in Historical Materialism* (New York: Praeger, 1981). For further discussion of this issue and some of its political implications, see Paul Bové, "The End of Humanism: Michel Foucault and the Power of Disciplines," *Humanities in Society*, 3 (1980): 23–40; and

"The Ineluctability of Difference: Scientific Pluralism and the Critical Intelligence," *boundary 2*, 11 (1983), forthcoming.
17. "Reification and Utopia in Mass Culture," *Social Text*, no. 1 (Winter 1979): 130–48.

Chapter 7. The End of Humanism (pp. 122–140)

1. In *Language, Counter-Memory, Practice: Selected Essays and Interviews*, ed. Donald F. Bouchard, trans. Donald F. Bouchard and Sherry Simon (Ithaca, N.Y.: Cornell University Press, 1977), 205–17, 218–33; these articles hereafter referred to as RAUN and IIP.
2. Foucault is, of course, himself indebted to and has explored brilliantly the works of several eccentric or marginal writers from de Sade to Nietzsche—and, in the process, made them a bit more "central" to scholarship and writing.
3. See Stanley Aronowitz, *False Promises: The Shaping of American Working Class Consciousness* (New York: McGraw-Hill, 1973), 279:

In the twentieth century the colleges and universities served several narrowly defined functions. The most important task of schools such as Harvard and Yale was, and remains to a lesser degree today, the preparation of political and economic elites for social rule. Higher education consisted in assisting the student to become aware of the broad dimensions of historical knowledge. Among those of inherited wealth and power, technical and professional training for such occupations as the law or medicine was an option reserved for a minority who possessed either intellectual curiosity or a sense of personal and social mission. But the chief object of the schools of higher learning was to provide a means for members of the emerging ruling class to make contact with one another and to internalize the values and needs of their own class as personal goals. It was common knowledge that the university was a kind of finishing school that made the student a "cultured man" or served to give him social graces appropriate to his class.

4. For a genealogical reading of modern humanistic higher education as it "culminates" in the Harvard Core Curriculum, see William V. Spanos, *The End of Education: Interpreting the Harvard Core Curriculum* (Minneapolis: University of Minnesota Press, 1991).
5. *Natural Supernaturalism* (New York: W. W. Norton, 1971); *Samuel Johnson* (New York: Harcourt Brace Jovanovich, 1977); *Literature Against Itself* (Chicago: University of Chicago Press, 1979). See also my review of Graff, *Criticism* 22 (1980): 77–81.
6. Irving Babbitt, *Literature and the American College: Essays in Defense of the Humanities* (Boston: Houghton Mifflin, 1908). Hereafter referred to as *L&AC*. For a sign of the renewed interest in Babbitt, see Douglas Bush, "Irving Babbitt: Crusader," in *Reappraisals, The American Scholar* 48 (1979): 515–22. I want to thank Jonathan Arac for pointing out this essay to me.

7. Michel Foucault, *Discipline and Punish,* trans. Alan Sheridan (New York: Pantheon, 1977), 139; hereafter *D&P.*
8. See Hayden White, "Michel Foucault," in *Structuralism and Since: From Lévi-Strauss to Derrida,* ed. John Sturrock (New York: Oxford University Press, 1979), 81–115.

Chapter 8. Power and Freedom (pp. 141–157)

1. Edward Said, *The World, the Text, and the Critic* (Cambridge, Mass.: Harvard University Press, 1983), 186.
2. Michel Foucault, "Two Lectures," trans. Alessandro Fontana and Pasquale Pasquino, *Power/Knowledge,* ed. Colin Gordon (New York: Pantheon, 1980), 107.
3. Edward Said, "Traveling Theory," in *The World, the Text, and the Critic,* 246–47.
4. Trans. J. D. Gauthier, S.J., in *The Final Foucault,* ed. James Bernauer and David Rasmussen (Cambridge: MIT Press, 1988), 13; the interview was conducted on 20 January 1984.
5. Michel Foucault, *The History of Sexuality,* vol. 1, *An Introduction,* trans. Robert Hurley (New York: Pantheon Books, 1978), 141.
6. Ibid., 144.
7. Foucault, "Two Lectures," 108.
8. Foucault, *The History of Sexuality,* 145.
9. Foucault, "the ethic of the care for the self as a practice for freedom," in *The Final Foucault,* ed. James Bernauer and David Rasmussen (Cambridge: MIT Press, 1988), 19. One might want to make a distinction between Foucault and Lyotard on this point. Just let it be said that, in Foucault, there is none of the utopian facility that one sometimes associates with Lyotard.
10. "Afterword by Michel Foucault," in Hubert L. Dreyfus and Paul Rabinow, *Michel Foucault: Beyond Structuralism and Hermeneutics,* 2nd ed. (Chicago: University of Chicago Press, 1982), 220.
11. "The Subject and Power," *Michel Foucault,* 220; hereafter cited as SP.
12. Ibid.
13. Foucault, "the ethic of care for the self," 19.
14. Ibid., p. 18.
15. We might say simply that Foucault's work on the microphysics of power as a mode of subject formation is a direct challenge to Althusser's overemphasis on the importance of ideology. One should read both *Discipline and Punish* and the first volume of *The History of Sexuality* in this light.
16. Foucault, "the ethic of care for the self," 18.
17. Ibid., 18–19.
18. Ibid., 19.
19. Michel Foucault, "Practicing Criticism," trans. Alan Sheridan, in *Politics, Philosophy, Culture,* ed. Lawrence Kritzman (New York: Routledge, 1989), 155.

20. Michel Foucault, "Social Security," trans. Alan Sheridan, in *Politics, Philosophy, Culture,* ed. Lawrence Kritzman (New York: Routledge, 1989), 167; originally published in 1983.

21. Michel Foucault, "The Political Technology of Individuals," in *Technologies of the Self,* ed. Luther H. Martin et al. (Amherst: University of Massachusetts Press, 1988), 150.

22. Ibid., 152.

23. Foucault, "Social Security," 168.

Index

UNIVERSITY PRESS OF NEW ENGLAND publishes under its own imprint and is the publisher for Brandeis University Press, Brown University Press, Clark University Press, University of Connecticut, Dartmouth College, Middlebury College Press, University of New Hampshire, University of Rhode Island, Tufts University, University of Vermont, and Wesleyan University Press.

ABOUT THE AUTHOR

Paul A. Bové has taught at Columbia University and is now Professor of English and Cultural Studies at the University of Pittsburgh. He is the author of *Destructive Poetics: Heidegger and Modern American Poetry* (1980); *Intellectuals in Power: A Genealogy of Critical Humanism* (1986); and *Mastering Discourse* (1991). He has edited *Revising the Canon* (1977) and is coeditor of *Questions of Textuality: Strategies of Reading in Contemporary American Criticism* (1982). He has been the editor of *boundary 2* since 1989.

Library of Congress Cataloging-in-Publication Data

Bové, Paul A., 1949–
    In the wake of theory / Paul A. Bové.
    p. cm.
    Includes bibliographical references and index.
    ISBN 0–8195–5244–5. — ISBN 0–8195–6254–8 (pbk.)
    1. Literature—History and criticism—Theory, etc. 2. Criticism—
United States—History—20th century. I. Title.
PN45.B58 1991
801'.95'097309045—dc20   91–50366